CIVIL WAR VETERANS

OF TUSTIN CALIFORNIA

TIMOTHY P. ZIERER

Published 2026 by the Tustin Area Historical Society,
(in co-operation with Wilson/Barnett Publishing)
395 El Camino Real, Tustin, CA 92780. (714) 731-5701.
www.TustinHistory.com

Library of Congress Control Number: 2023943105
ISBN: 978-0-9797619-3-5 (Paperback)
ISBN: 978-0-9797619-2-8 (EPUB)
r-2

Contents

Acknowledgements

This booklet rests on the foundation provided by ***Soldiers in Blue and Gray, Civil War Veterans in Orange County***, by the late Gordon Bricken, and the work of the Orange County, California Genealogical Society Civil War Veterans Project. Most of the veterans profiled in this book are listed in Bricken's book and on the OCCGS website. The book and the website are the gold standard for Orange County Civil War research, and anyone interested in a county Civil War veteran would do well to start with them.

I would also like to thank Charles Beal for steering me in the right direction on GAR research. Charles was also instrumental in creating the OCCGS website that I used extensively in my research.

Fellow members of the Tustin Area Historical Society were a great help. When Vicki Gray and I realized we were working on similar projects, we began to share research, and she also became my unofficial fact checker and proofreader, saving me from several errors. When I hit a research roadblock, I went to Donna Marsh Peery, and she more often than not was able to find what I could not. Donna also generously agreed to proofread the manuscript for me, as did my son Harrison. TAHS Former-President Steve Sauers was supportive of this project and allowed me to research while I was volunteering at the museum and could have, and probably should have, been performing more docent-like duties.

Thanks also go out to Jaime Cornejo and his excellent staff at the History Room of the Santa Ana Public Library. They were most helpful and patient with my fumbling use of the microfilm reader. Also, Tara Fansler, the Director of the Drum Barracks Civil War Museum in Wilmington, California, went above and beyond shed light on the William Jerome/Charles H. Ward story. Thanks to Beverly Lane, curator of the Museum of the San Ramon Valley in Danville, California, for making the family files of Joseph A. Wilkes available to me.

I also need to thank my friend and fellow history buff, Paul Loya. Paul spent many hours with me tramping through cemeteries, and he took many of the photographs of headstones in this book. I also appreciate that he refrained from ridiculing me over my continual inability to use the GPS app on my phone.

Special thanks also go to Guy Ball for spending countless hours formatting the book for publication and lending his expertise to the project. I don't know that I could have completed this book without his help. Thanks also to T.M. Cromer, whose professional publishing expertise helped us get this book into your hands.

And finally, I have to thank my wife, Catherine, for putting up with my obsession with these long-gone Tustin pioneers as I commandeered our dining room table for my research for the better part of a year.

Timothy Zierer
Tustin, CA
December 2025

Introduction

In the early morning hours of April 12, 1861, Southern forces fired on Fort Sumter in Charleston Harbor, signaling the beginning of the American Civil War. By the time the guns fell silent four years later, over 650,000 Americans were dead, large areas of the South were in ruins, over 4 million formerly enslaved human beings were free, and the country had been changed forever.

This book contains biographical sketches of thirty-three men, thirty Union and three Confederate, who served in the war and eventually made the small southern California town of Tustin their home.

These thirty-three men were born in fifteen different states and two foreign countries. At the time of their enlistments, they were young men; in fact, fourteen were teenagers, the youngest just fifteen years old. Most were single, but six were married, and one was a widower. Not surprisingly, most were farm laborers, but two were blacksmiths, and there was even a doctor among the group.

They served in the infantry, cavalry, and artillery; two served on ships in the US Navy, and another was in the Marine Corps. Most of these men served in the Western Theater of Operations and some saw action at major battles such as Shiloh, Vicksburg, Chickamauga, and Atlanta as well as numerous less-heralded engagements. A number of them participated in Sherman's March to the Sea. A few served in the Eastern Theater and were on the battlefields at Fredericksburg, Gettysburg, The Wilderness, and Spotsylvania.

Several of these men were wounded, and one lost an arm. Two were awarded a controversial Medal of Honor, and another sat out the last few months of the war in a notorious southern prisoner of war camp. The majority of these soldiers were enlisted men, though a few were officers, including one who served in an all-Black regiment. The highest rank achieved among these veterans was that of Major.

All these men had their own individual stories, unique to them, but all shared one thing in common: after the war, they were all part of a great westward migration that ended for each of them in Tustin, California.

NOTE: *Although footnotes have been omitted, I have included an extensive source list for each veteran at the end of the book.*

Tustin

Not one of the thirty-three veterans profiled in this book shouldered his musket and left hearth and home in Tustin to fight in the war, for the simple reason that the town of Tustin did not yet exist. The war ended in 1865, and in 1868, Columbus Tustin, with his business partner, Nelson O. Stafford, traveled down from Petaluma to southern California and purchased the acreage that would become the town of Tustin. Columbus Tustin was a native of Pennsylvania who came to California during the Gold Rush and prospered not as a miner but as a merchant, farmer, developer, and carriage maker.

The city today recognizes 1868 as its anniversary date, while most historians believe that 1870, when Tustin moved down with his family and filed the first town plat map, is the more appropriate date to celebrate.

Around the same time, Columbus Tustin was laying out his town site, William Spurgeon was founding the nearby town of Santa Ana, and the two would become rivals for the southern terminus of the Southern Pacific Railroad. Santa Ana won the railroad battle in 1877 and went on to become the county seat, while Tustin remained a small agricultural village for many years.

After the war, the westward movement of settlers accelerated. The completion of the transcontinental railroad made travel easier and opened up huge tracts of land for sale. Despite the advances of the Industrial Revolution, the country remained primarily agrarian, and large numbers of veterans moved west in search of cheaper, more fertile land to farm.

The earliest Civil War veterans came to Tustin in the mid-1870s. They continued to arrive over the next twenty-five years, some possibly hoping to make a new start, driven by the economic depressions of the 1870s and 1890s. Some of the veterans may have been enticed by the Southern California land boom of the mid-1880s. Realtors, land speculators, local boosters, and the railroads printed books and pamphlets extolling the ideal climate, fine soils, and affordability of land in southern California. This promotional literature was sent east, often with land agents, to lure pioneers westward. At one point, railroad rate wars dropped the fare from St. Louis to Los Angeles to one dollar per person, and between 1880 and 1890, over 340,000 people moved to California. New towns popped up overnight, and many disappeared just as quickly during this boom-and-bust period.

Many of the veterans who made it to California moved westward incrementally, stopping in several midwestern states before finally reaching Tustin. Those veterans who came to Tustin in the mid-1880s found a town with a business district consisting of two stores, a blacksmith shop, an insurance office, a post office, a school, and three churches. Most of these buildings were clustered around the town center at the intersection of Main and D streets. These businesses and churches served the farmers and orchardists living on the farms and ranches surrounding the town. The roads were all unpaved, and street signs would not appear until early in the next century (with fundraising help from a civil war veteran).

While their new home was definitely no metropolis (population 350 in 1895), the veterans who settled in Tustin were, for the most part, civic-minded and were soon involved in the schools, churches, business organizations, and local government, and their efforts in these pioneering days were instrumental in the development and growth of their adopted town.

Columbus Tustin, founder of the town that bears his name

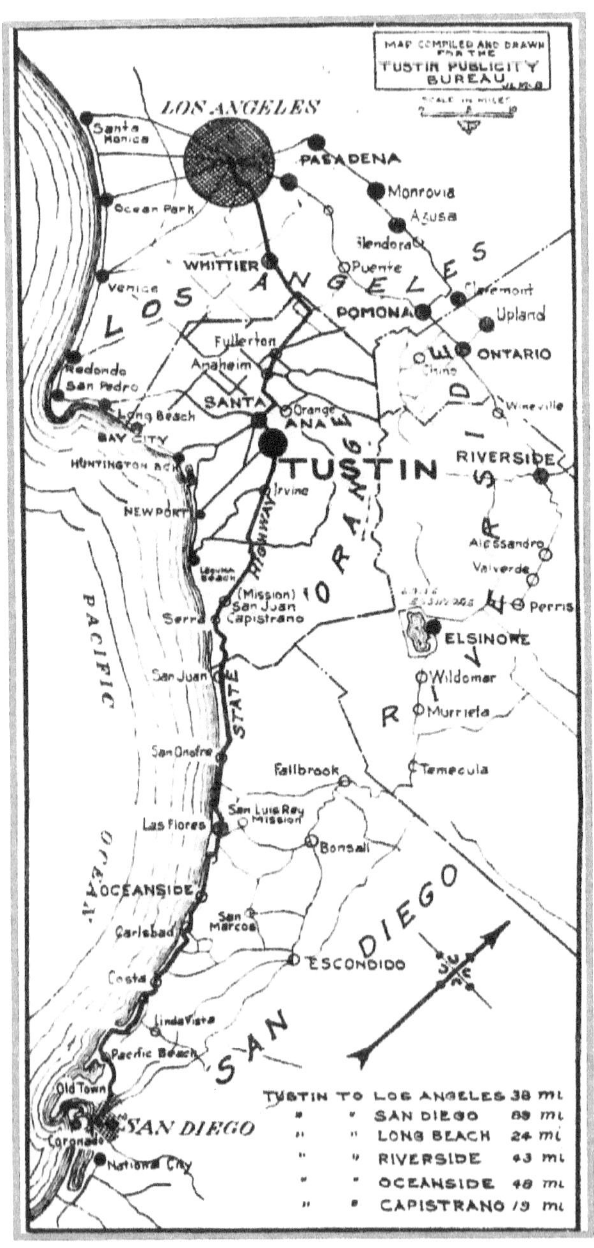

This map showing the location of Tustin was placed in a local newspaper by the Tustin Publicity Bureau in June, 1915.

The map below is from a 1940s city directory and shows that central Tustin had not changed much since the Civil War veterans lived there. Note that Highway 101 on the lower right was also known as Laguna Road and is now part of El Camino Real, as is D Street.

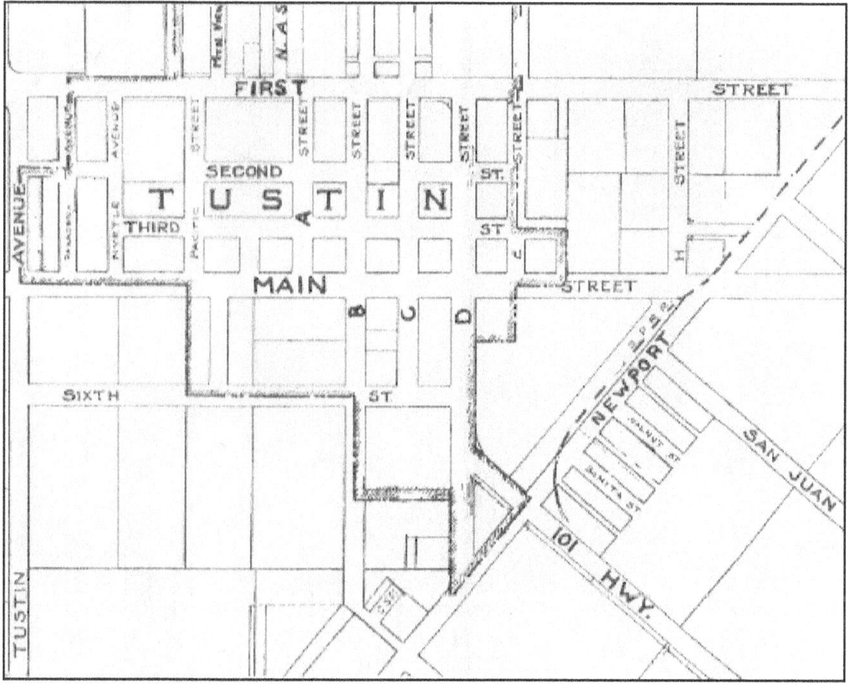

Peter T. Adams

Lt., Co. B, McCord's Frontier Regiment

46th Texas Cavalry

P.T. Adams was raised on a cattle ranch in West Texas. As a young Texas Ranger, he fought the Kiowas and Comanches, and also as an officer in a Confederate cavalry regiment during the Civil War. A dozen years after the war, he sold his large ranch and moved to Tustin, where he became one of the most successful and prominent of the veterans to settle in that small community.

Peter Taylor Adams was born on November 22, 1834, in Collierville, Shelby County, Tennessee. He was the ninth and final child of Peter and Sarah (Walton) Adams, both natives of North Carolina. Two years after the birth of their last child, the couple moved the family to what would become Harrison County, Texas. In the same year they moved, 1836, the Alamo fell, and later Texas won its independence from Mexico when Sam Houston led the American revolutionaries to victory at the Battle of San Jacinto.

In 1849, when Peter was fourteen, the family moved to Bexar County, near San Antonio, and began a cattle-ranching empire. The senior Peter Adams died in 1854, leaving the ranch to Sarah and the Adams boys. Most of Peter's older brothers were named after famous American statesmen: John Quincy Adams, Daniel Webster Adams, William Carroll Adams, Henry Clay Adams, David Green Adams, James Monroe Adams, and Martin Van Buren Adams. (Perhaps his parents had run out of historic names by the time of Peter's arrival.)

West Texas before (and after) the Civil War was wild frontier country, and Peter Adams and his brothers were members of the Texas Rangers, guarding the scattered settlements against raids from Comanches and Kiowas and chasing down cattle rustlers. His brother Henry Clay Adams was a Lieutenant commanding a Ranger unit when he was killed in a skirmish with Indians along the Nueces River in Ulvalde County on February 22, 1861. Another brother, Martin Van Buren Adams, was shot and severely wounded in a clash with Indians but recovered.

The Adams brothers opposed secession and voted against it, but when Texas joined the Confederacy, they, like many southerners, chose loyalty to their state over their country. All seven remaining Adams brothers served as officers in the Confederate army.

Peter Adams was a Texas Ranger at the outbreak of the war when he joined an outfit known as McCord's Frontier Regiment. Commanded by Colonel James McCord, the regiment was tasked with guarding the western settlements against Native American raids, much the same duty Adams had performed as a Ranger. With so many Texans away fighting in the east, the local Native American tribes, especially the fierce Comanches and Kiowas, were emboldened by the absence of these men to strike at the outlying settlements and ranches.

A private in the Rangers, Adams must have shown leadership qualities, for he was commissioned a second lieutenant in the Frontier Regiment. When the regiment was transferred to regular Confederate service in March 1864, it was redesignated the 46th Texas Cavalry Regiment. The regiment served in the Trans-Mississippi Department, encompassing Louisiana, Mississippi, and Texas. While in Texas, the regiment continued to serve as a buffer against Native American incursions.

It was while serving with the 46th Texas Calvary that Adams was put in command of Company B and was addressed as Captain. Although it is not clear if he was ever officially promoted, it was a designation he would answer to for the rest of his life. In city directories forty years later, he would be listed as Capt. P.T. Adams.

At its high-water mark, the regiment contained over a thousand men, but by the end of the war in April 1865, it totaled only 102 men. With the loss of Vicksburg in July 1863, the Confederacy had been cut in half, and the western portion (including Texas) had been left to die on the vine. Perhaps the hopelessness of the cause in the last year of the war had moved many men to drift away from the army and back to their homes and families. Years later, Adams would be honored for his Civil War service, receiving the Southern Cross from the Emma Sansom Chapter 449 of the United Daughters of the Confederacy, a group based in Santa Ana, California.

Captain Adams returned to ranching after the war. On October 25, 1865, he married Henrietta Downs, a native of Iowa. Over the next ten years, the couple built their family and their ranch. Their first four children were born in Texas: Henry (1866), Anna (1869), Frank "Cood" (1871), and Edward (1876).

The cattle ranch grew and prospered. At one point, in partnership with his brother Martin, their herd numbered between 100,000 and 125,000 head of cattle. The herds were driven from the ranch north to the cow towns and railheads in Kansas. In 1875, the year before Peter Adams left Texas, another brother, David Green Adams, a well-known and respected frontier scout, was killed in a clash with Native Americans at Pena, Texas, on November 29, 1875.

It is unclear why Adams would leave a seemingly prosperous cattle ranch to move west. Perhaps beef prices dropped or a drought cut down the size of the herd. Whatever the reason, in 1876, P.T. Adams sold out and moved his family to California. He spent a year searching for the right location and, in November 1877, settled in Tustin. It is probable that his in-laws influenced his decision. The Downs were among the first settlers in Tustin and are credited with building the town's first house.

In 1878, Adams had a house built in Tustin that he and Henrietta lived in for the rest of their lives. The house was off Main Street, west of Tustin Avenue on what is now Williams Street, and sat well back from the street. When Adams bought the property, there was a small one-room house on the lot. Samuel Tustin, son of town founder Columbus Tustin, claimed it was the house his father built and lived in when he first moved to the area.

Peter and Henrietta had two more children after moving to Tustin. The first died in infancy in 1879, and the second, Frances Ideala Adams, was born on June 16, 1888.

Adams initially grew oranges and limes on his property but soon became one of the first walnut growers in the area. Eventually, eighteen of his twenty-four acres were planted to walnuts, and he was consistently able to harvest over forty-thousand pounds of walnuts each year. One of the most successful growers in the area, he served for several years as president of the Santa Ana Walnut Growers Association.

The Adams House in Tustin. It was razed in 1964 to make way for a condominium complex.

It was not all work for Adams. There is an account of a two-week camping trip in the nearby Santa Ana Mountains in December 1890. His companions on the trip were fellow Tustin rancher T.C. Matheny and Dan Baker, editor of the Santa Ana Standard newspaper. The trio traveled through Silverado Canyon, checked out local mining operations, camping out each night, and eventually ended their trip in San Juan, soaking in the hot springs.

Peter Adams became a widower when Henrietta passed away on May 5, 1892, at the age of forty-four. Adams never remarried and continued to live at the ranch house. At various times, his grown children or other relatives lived there with him.

Captain Adams, being a Confederate veteran, was a strong Democrat in a largely Republican County. Although never a candidate, his obituary referred to him as a "wheelhorse" of the local Democratic Party. He always served as a delegate to the conventions, and his advice was often sought on political matters. He was also an active member of the Santa Ana Elks Lodge and at the time of his death was its oldest member.

Peter T. Adams passed away at his home in Tustin on December 3, 1924, at the age of ninety. He was buried at Fairhaven Memorial Park beside Henrietta, who had preceded him there by thirty-two years. His nine decades had taken Adams from the hills of Tennessee to the plains of Texas to the orchards of Tustin. He had raised cattle and grown walnuts and was successful in both endeavors, and at the end of his life was a respected and honored member of his community.

Henry M. Adams, the oldest son of Peter and Henrietta, married Katherine Blanche Fall. They had two daughters, Kathryn and Martha. Henry founded the Tustin Water Works with Hiram Willard but eventually sold out his interest and, for many years, owned a lumber company in Anaheim. Henry passed away on March 29, 1946, at the age of seventy-nine. Katherine died in 1958 at the age of eighty-one.

Anna Darling Adams married John Gowen. They had two children, Frank and Henrietta Ideala Gowen. John Gowen was a partner with Charles F. Willard in Gowen & Willard Fruit Packers. Anna died in a tragic accident on January 12, 1911, when a gasoline iron she was using exploded. She passed away in the hospital shortly after the accident at the age of forty-two. John Gowen died in 1938.

Frank Cood Adams married Elizabeth Fall, the sister of his brother Henry's wife. (Cood was the Native American name for "Little Chief" which was given to his father, being the youngest of the eight Adams brothers.) Cood carried on the family farming operations, first in Tustin and then in Santa Ana. He became a successful and prominent grower in the area. The couple had one son, Charles Henry Adams. Cood died on May 16, 1950, in Santa Ana, and Elizabeth passed away on August 30, 1967.

Edward L. Adams never married and passed away on July 24, 1902, at the age of twenty-six.

Frances Ideala Adams married Hugh Plumb. Hugh was the Orange County Tax Assessor for many years until his retirement in 1965. The couple lived in the old Adams home in Tustin, where Frances was born. They had three sons: Donald, Ralph, and Hugh, Jr. Hugh, Sr. passed away in 1967, and Frances died on October 31, 1979, at the age of ninety-one. Their son Ralph was the first Tustin man to die in World War II when Japanese bombers struck his ship during the Battle of the Coral Sea, May 7, 1942. He was an ensign in the Navy and survived the attack on Pearl Harbor only to be lost in the first great carrier battle of the war.

The P.T. Adams Family c. 1915
Front Row: Charles Adams, Martha Adams, Donald Plumb
Second Row: Cood Adams, Bess Adams, unidentified, Frances Plumb, Katherine Adams, P.T. Adams, Henry Adams
Third Row: Pearl Adams, Don Adams, Edna Gowen, Frank Gowen, Hugh Plumb, unidentified

P.T.'s older brother, Martin Van Buren Adams, followed him to California and lived in Tustin for a short time, but by 1880 had moved to Orange, where he owned a citrus ranch on north Main Street. Martin had served as a 2nd Lieutenant in the 2nd Texas Cavalry during the war. He was married to Elizabeth Burton Haw. They had no children but raised three of their sister's orphaned children. Martin died on March 27, 1908, in Orange and was buried at Santa Ana Cemetery.

Albert N. Alderman

Private, Company K

29th Ohio Infantry

Albert Alderman was already thirty-six years old and married with children when he enlisted to serve in the Civil War. Wounded in an early battle, he served out his enlistment as a clerk, a non-combat position. Alderman became part of the great post-war westward migration, coming to Tustin in the mid-1870s.

Albert N. Alderman was born in Windsor, Ashtabula County, Ohio, on June 4, 1825. His parents, Jesse M. Alderman and Elura Cook, were New Englanders, both natives of Connecticut. The Aldermans were a large family, Albert being one of twelve children.

Albert grew up working on the family farm, apprenticed to a carpenter as a boy, and then studied bookkeeping in Cleveland, which eventually landed him jobs as a clerk, first on a lake boat and then with a shipping firm. He started his own coal supply business and then sold real estate. In 1854, at the age of twenty-nine, he married nineteen-year-old Irish immigrant Elizabeth Brennan and worked in Windsor as a shoemaker.

Alderman was a thirty-six-year-old married man with three small children when he enlisted in the 29th Ohio Infantry regiment on September 28, 1861. (His sons Charles and Frank died while he was away in the army.) The 29th Ohio was organized at Camp Giddings, Jefferson, Ohio, and comprised of recruits primarily from counties in northeast Ohio. Its first commander was Col. Louis P. Buckley.

Alderman served as a private in Company K and participated in the battles of Winchester and Port Republic before he was wounded at the Battle of Cedar Mountain on August 9,

1862. The Battle of Cedar Mountain, sometimes called Slaughter Mountain, was a one-day battle in Culpepper County, Virginia. The battle was a Confederate victory in which the rebel forces under Stonewall Jackson outnumbered the Union troops led by General Nathanial Banks almost two to one. The battle produced an estimated 2,381 Union casualties (314 killed, 1,445 wounded, and 622 missing). Both of Albert Alderman's tent mates were killed in the battle. The heat index on the day of the battle was 109, making the day even more miserable. Clara Barton, founder of the American Red Cross, arrived on the scene four days later to help care for the wounded in her first official duties of the war.

Apparently, Alderman recovered from his wound quickly because he was soon back in action with his regiment at the battles of Chancellorsville and Antietam. The 29th Ohio was then shifted from the Eastern Theater to the Western Theater (primarily in Tennessee and Georgia), where Alderman participated in the battles of Lookout Mountain, Chattanooga, and then fought in the campaign leading up to the surrender of Atlanta.

The Civil War armies were awash in paperwork; daily and monthly muster rolls, medical reports, payrolls, and requisitions for arms, ammunition, and food were just a few of the responsibilities of each unit. The army was always looking for literate men who could handle the onslaught of paperwork, and apparently, Albert Alderman's bookkeeping experience qualified him for the job.

For two years, Alderman served as the chief clerk of the Provost Department of the Second Division of the Twelfth Corps. One of his most treasured souvenirs from this job was a requisition order for a quart of whiskey signed by General Ulysses S. Grant.

Atlanta fell to Sherman's troops on September 2, 1864, and on September 28, exactly three years from the day he enlisted, Albert Alderman was mustered out of Federal service. By the end of the war the 29th Ohio had suffered 540 casualties (killed, wounded, missing) out of the 1,529 men who had served in the regiment over the course of the conflict.

The regimental flag of the 29th Ohio is on display at the Henderson Memorial Library in Jefferson, Ohio.

The Aldermans were a martial family. Their father, Jesse, had served as a sergeant in the Ohio Militia during the War of 1812, and five of Albert's brothers served in Ohio regiments during the Civil War. One brother did not return from the war and lies in an unmarked grave.

After his discharge from the army, Albert Alderman returned to Ohio to Elizabeth and their daughter Lillian. Alderman spent two years working as a carpenter in Missouri and another two working in Florida, leaving his wife and children with his parents in Windsor, before moving the family to California in 1876. By the time they arrived in Tustin in 1877, Albert and Elizabeth were the parents of three more children: Heber, Alton, and Arlington Ray.

The family settled on a farm in the foothills of north Tustin then known as the Fair Haven Colony. It was founded by Rev. Henry H. Messenger and intended to be an Episcopalian temperance colony. Albert planted twenty acres to oranges and walnuts and supplemented his farm income with carpentry work. In 1881, he was elected the first warden (vestryman) of St. Paul's Episcopal Church in Tustin.

On September 29, 1887, Elizabeth Alderman passed away at the age of fifty-one. By the time of her death, three of her four children were adults. Three years earlier, Lillian had married Clarence Sheats, a member of another pioneer Tustin family. With her husband a vestryman, it is not hard to imagine that Elizabeth was also an active member in the Episcopalian Church. The engraving on her headstone at Santa Ana Cemetery shows she was a member of the Relief Corps, the Women's Auxiliary of the GAR.

In 1906, just two years before his own death, Albert suffered another loss when his thirty-nine-year-old son Heber died from a self-inflicted gunshot in the family walnut grove. A coroner's inquest subsequently ruled the death accidental.

Albert N. Alderman passed away on August 17, 1908, in Hemet, Riverside County, California, at the age of eighty-three. After an Episcopal funeral service at the home of his daughter in Santa Ana, Alderman was laid to rest with military honors provided by his fellow members of the Sedgwick Post 17 of the GAR. His obituary in the local newspaper described him as a life-long Episcopalian, chronicled his wartime experiences, and closed with, "He was a life-long Republican, and believed in the expansion of our territory and the gold standard."

All the children of Albert and Elizabeth Alderman were born in Ashtabula County, Ohio.

Charles A. Alderman was born in 1854. He was six years old on the 1860 census, but then he disappears from the records. It appears that he died while his father was away in the army in 1862.

Elizabeth Lillian Alderman was born on March 8, 1859. She came to Tustin at the age of seventeen with her parents. In 1885, she married Clarence Sheats (1857-1930). They lived in Santa Ana and had one daughter. Lillian passed away on July 6, 1941, at the age of eighty-two.

Frank Alderman was born in 1861 and died in 1862.

Heber B. Alderman was born on August 2, 1865. He was never married and worked as a citrus rancher in Tustin. He died of a self-inflicted gunshot on January 8, 1906, which was ruled accidental by the county coroner.

Alton L. Alderman was born in August 1867. He was married to Bertha Candice Scanlon on February 9, 1907, in San Jacinto, California. They lived in Hemet, had no children, and eventually divorced. Before his death, Alton served for a time as a Deputy City Marshal. He died in San Bernardino at the age of fifty-five and is buried at Grandview Memorial Park in Glendale, California.

Arlington Ray Alderman was born on January 22, 1873. He came to Tustin with his parents at the age of three. He married Rebecca C. Robbins on December 1, 1901, in Los Angeles. They had two children. Rose died in 1935, and Arlington was living with a widowed daughter when he died in San Diego on September 4, 1944, at the age of seventy-one. He is buried in Oceanside.

Albert Alderman's military headstone

It is interesting to note that Albert Alderman has two stones at Santa Ana Cemetery. One is a military headstone and the other shows his membership in the Masons. Elizabeth's stone shows the Relief Corps medal from the GAR Women's Auxiliary.

Albert Alderman's Masonic headstone

Elizabeth Alderman's headstone

Edwin F. Ambrose

Private, Company B

7th Rhode Island Cavalry Squadron

Edwin Ambrose went off to war with his college classmates. Their enlistment was very brief, but it proved to be one of the most unique experiences of any group of young men during the Civil War. A lifelong educator in New England, it was a serious health issue that drove Ambrose west, eventually landing him in Tustin in the early 1890s.

Edwin Freeman Ambrose was born January 12, 1837, in Ossipee, New Hampshire, the son of Nathaniel and Hannah (Roberts) Ambrose. Nathaniel Ambrose died in the spring of 1841 when Edwin was just four years old. Hannah then married a widower, John Smith, and in 1850, thirteen-year-old Edwin was living with his blended family on a farm outside Ossipee.

Ten years later, twenty-three-year-old Edwin was one of sixteen students living and studying at the New Hampton Institute. Located in New Hampton, New Hampshire, the institute was run by fifty-eight-year-old clergyman Benjamin Manson and his wife, Eliza, with their twenty-three-year-old daughter Mary as the music teacher. The school was a private college preparatory school founded by Baptists in 1821 and is still in existence. It must have served its purpose with Edwin, for the following year, he enrolled at Dartmouth College.

Dartmouth, a small liberal arts college chartered in 1769 and a member of the Ivy League, is located in Hanover, New Hampshire, along the Connecticut River that borders Vermont. Its most famous alumnus was Daniel Webster, Class of 1801, who went on to become one of the great orators of the antebellum US Senate. The school was also known as one of the few institutions of higher learning to accept African Americans. In fact, by the end of the Civil War, twenty black men had attended the college or its medical school.

It was while a student at Dartmouth that Edwin Ambrose entered the Union Army. As the 1862 school term neared an end, Confederate General Robert E. Lee threatened an invasion of the North, and President Lincoln called for 40,000 volunteers to enlist for three months' service. Many of the young men at Dartmouth, already anxious to enter the fight, volunteered. Edwin Ambrose was among them. Enough men from Dartmouth (around 100), joined by students from nearby Bowdoin, Union, and Norwich colleges, comprised enough men to form two companies. The governor of New Hampshire refused to muster them into service, so they turned to Rhode Island, where they were accepted by Governor William Sprague and mustered into federal service on June 24, 1862, in Providence. They were designated the 7th Rhode Island Cavalry Squadron, with Ambrose serving as a private in Company B, which became known as the "College Company."

The squadron immediately headed south to Washington, D.C., where they trained daily until mid-July, when they crossed over the Potomac River into Virginia. In late July, during a cavalry raid near Port Royal, the squadron captured Belle Boyd, the infamous southern spy. (She was sent to the Old Capitol Prison in Washington, held for a month, and then released. This was one of the six times she would be arrested and released during the war.)

The squadron was then sent to Harper's Ferry, Virginia, near the Maryland border, where it narrowly escaped capture. When the squadron arrived, it found that Harper's Ferry had been cut off and surrounded by Confederate forces under Stonewall Jackson. This was part of General Lee's strategy that would culminate several days later in the bloody battle of Antietam. The 7th Rhode Island made a perilous night ride and just avoided capture, arriving in Greencastle, Pennsylvania, on the morning of September 15, 1862. On that same morning, the entire Union garrison at Harper's Ferry, over 12,000 men, surrendered to Jackson. The day following their escape from the enemy lines the squadron was able to redeem itself, participating in the capture of over 100 wagons from the supply train of General James Longstreet.

Ten days later, Ambrose returned with his squadron to Providence, Rhode Island, and was mustered out of service on September 26. They had not lost any men in battle, but one student had died from disease. The experience of these college boys was unique in the annals of the Civil War; they had spent their summer break fighting for their country and were able to return to school in time for the fall semester, and in their narrow escape from capture at Harper's Ferry, they avoided turning a three-month enlistment into a long stay in a southern prisoner of war camp.

Unfortunately, the war was not over for the Ambrose family. About the time Edwin was mustered out, his older brother, Thomas Lyford Ambrose, enlisted. Thomas, a minister, served as the chaplain for the 12th New Hampshire Infantry regiment. He was captured on May 3, 1863, at the Battle of Chancellorsville but was eventually paroled. He returned to his regiment and was wounded in the right leg at Petersburg on June 24, 1864. The leg had to be amputated, but infection must have set in, for he died on August 19, 1864, at Fort Monroe, Virginia, and his body was returned to Ossipee for burial.

Edwin Ambrose graduated from Dartmouth in 1864 and immediately took a job as principal of an educational academy in Fryeburg, Maine. After just a year, he moved to Chicago, where he enrolled in a business college and worked in a bookstore. This set a pattern he would follow for much of his life: alternating work as an educator with stints as a businessman.

He returned to Maine in 1867 and taught at the Liberal Institute in the town of Norway. He stayed there two years, the final year as principal of the institute. It was in Norway that he met and married Emily Jane Goodwin; the wedding took place on

November 11, 1869. Emily, a native of Ireland, came to America with her parents in 1856 at the age of 13. The couple would have only one child, Thomas, born in 1872.

Shortly after the wedding, Edwin and Emily moved to Dexter, Maine, a small village about 42 miles northwest of Bangor. For the next eight years, Edwin served as the principal of the high school in Dexter, but by 1880, the family was living in Malden, Massachusetts, where he was again teaching school. Edwin then spent the next five years working in the mercantile business, first in Boston, then in Revere, Massachusetts.

A Dartmouth alumnus sketch of Ambrose states he spent some time around this period recovering his health. It is probable that at this time he was diagnosed with tuberculosis, the disease that would eventually take his life. Commonly referred to then as consumption, one of the recommended cures was for the patient to reside in a hot, dry climate. This would explain Ambrose's move to Santa Fe, New Mexico, in August 1885, after a lifetime spent in New England.

Ambrose spent a year in Santa Fe as the superintendent of an Indian boarding school. These schools were part of a government-sponsored program to "civilize" Native American tribes in the Southwest. The students had their hair cut, their native clothing taken away, and replaced with current fashions, and they were prohibited from conversing in their native languages. It was part of an effort known as "killing the savage to save the man." Ambrose spent only one year in this oppressive system before resigning and moving his family to Newport Beach, California.

Edwin Ambrose spent the next seven years in Newport Beach, where he engaged in farming, probably for the first time since he was a boy. From an 1892 California voter register, we get a physical description of Ambrose: 55 years old, 5'9" tall, with a light complexion, brown eyes, and white hair.

In December 1892, Ambrose attended a conference of the Christian Alliance in Santa Ana. The alliance was an ecumenical organization of like-minded congregations in the area that supported missionary work, and Ambrose, though not a minister, was elected president of the local chapter. (His wife was elected secretary.)

The month following the convention, Edwin and Emily moved from Newport to Tustin. Unfortunately, Edwin's stay in Tustin was short-lived, for on February 22, 1894, he succumbed to the consumption that had plagued him for so many years. He died at his home in Tustin at the age of fifty-seven and was laid to rest two days later at Santa Ana Cemetery.

Following the death of her husband, Emily Ambrose lived with her son in Los Angeles, and it was there that she died on May 10, 1922, at the age of seventy-seven. She was buried at Forest Lawn Memorial Park in Glendale, California.

Thomas Lyford Ambrose, the only child of Edwin and Emily, was born September 28, 1872, in Dexter, Maine, and was the namesake of his uncle, who was killed in the Civil War. Thomas was a teenager when the family moved to Southern California. After the death of his father, Thomas moved to Los Angeles, where on October 18, 1905, he married Sara I. Tuthill. The couple would have two children, Edwin Freeman and Thomas Jr. Thomas owned a grocery store in Los Angeles for over a decade before becoming an attorney.

Thomas Ambrose was appointed Justice of the Peace for Los Angeles Township in 1923 and in 1926 was appointed one the first municipal judges of the city. He sat on the municipal court bench until 1934 when he was elected to the Superior Court. He served as a Superior Court judge until defeated for re-election by Evelle Younger in 1958. (Younger would later serve for eight years as California Attorney General.)

Sara Tuthill Ambrose died of a heart attack at their Westwood home on April 6, 1957, at the age of eighty-one. Thomas Ambrose died eight years later, passing away on April 11, 1965, at the age of ninety-two. He was buried beside Sara at Forest Lawn Memorial Park in Glendale.

Charles F. Bennett

1st Sergeant, Company G

55th Illinois Infantry

Charles Bennett descended from a prominent New England family and was raised in the abolitionist tradition. As a young man, he assisted runaway slaves on the Underground Railroad and served

throughout the Civil War, participating in numerous battles. After a number of post-war years spent in Nebraska, he was lured to Tustin during the Southern California land boom of the mid-1880s. He quickly established himself in his new community, served a term in the state legislature, and became a widely acknowledged expert on orchard irrigation.

Charles Franklin Bennett was born on April 23, 1842, in Kent, Connecticut, the fourth of William and Sarah (Bronson) Bennett's seven children. The Bennetts were a very old New

England family, their arrival in America dating back to the time of the pilgrims. Charles' great-grandfather, Isaac Bennett, was one of the principal contractors who built the Erie Canal. Sarah Bronson was a Quaker, descended from a man who accompanied William Penn to Philadelphia.

Charles was educated in the East and, at an early age, indoctrinated in abolitionist principles through contact with William Lloyd Garrison and Wendell Phillips. When the family moved to Illinois, Charles helped runaway slaves escape to freedom along the Underground Railroad. His father had moved the family to La Salle, Illinois, where, in addition to farming, he ran a sawmill.

Charles began teaching school at the age of sixteen and was preparing to enter the University of Chicago when the war broke out. Bennett set aside his Quaker pacifist principles, believing the eradication of slavery more important, and at the age of nineteen, he dropped his educational plans and, on August 23, 1861, enlisted in the 55th Illinois Infantry Regiment. A good friend in the regiment throughout the entire war was Johnny Beach, who would later become his brother-in-law.

The 55th Illinois was organized at Camp Douglas, Chicago, and mustered into Federal service on October 31, 1861. Training continued after the regiment moved to Benton Barracks, Missouri. The regiment participated in most of the major engagements of the Western Theater, including the Battle of Shiloh, the siege of Corinth, the Vicksburg Campaign, the battles of Holly Springs, Lookout Mountain, Atlanta, Jonesboro, and Sherman's March to the Sea.

Bennett, who achieved the rank of First Sergeant, participated in all these campaigns, thirty-two engagements in all, and was slightly wounded several times with numerous near misses. It was reported that his hair was clipped, his coat shredded, and his hat band cut by enemy bullets.

Bennett was with the regiment the entire war, with the exception of a furlough from April 16 to June 19, 1864. He returned in time to participate in the fall of Atlanta and Sherman's March to the Sea. He was in charge of a guard detail at Sherman's headquarters and witnessed a conference between Generals Sherman, Grant, and Logan. It was an event he would always remember.

He also witnessed Lee's surrender at Appomattox Courthouse and participated in the Grand Review of the Armies in Washington, D.C. He was then sent to Little Rock, Arkansas, where he was discharged on August 14, 1865. He had been promoted to First Lieutenant on July 21, 1865, but declined the commission and was mustered out with the rank of First Sergeant.

In four years of fighting, the 55th Illinois suffered the loss of 9 officers and 149 enlisted men killed in action. In addition, 2 officers and 127 enlisted men died of disease for a total of 286 fatalities.

Although never seriously wounded, four years of heavy campaigning had taken a toll on Charles Bennett's health. Following his discharge, he returned home to the family farm near La Salle to recuperate. In the fall of 1866, he moved to Chicago and worked in the real estate business. Two years later, he returned home following his father's death and ran the family farm and taught school.

On September 25, 1872, he married Helen M. Beach at St. Andrew's church in La Salle. The groom was thirty and his bride twenty-one. Helen was born in Bridgewater, Connecticut, a small town just eighteen miles from her husband's birthplace. Their first child, a son, was born shortly before they left Illinois.

In late 1877 or early 1878, the couple left Illinois with their infant son, Frederick, and settled in Arapahoe, Nebraska, a small town in Furnas County near the Oklahoma border. Shortly after the move, their second child, Pearl Edna Bennett, was born on Christmas Day, 1878.

The Bennetts lived in Arapahoe for about seven years, where they raised cattle and sheep and ran a small hotel. Charles also owned a hardware and mercantile business and a lumber yard, possibly in partnership with Helen's brother, Johnny Beach. Charles was active in local politics, serving on the town council and a term as mayor. He also helped found GAR Post 104 and was post commander for several terms.

Charles Bennett's Business Card while living in Nebraska.

Perhaps lured by the land boom of the '80s, the Bennetts moved in 1885 from San Diego, California, to Oceanside. A year later, Helen visited friends from Nebraska who had relocated to Tustin. Helen liked the area so much more than Oceanside that she persuaded Charles to sell their property and move. The family arrived in Tustin in 1887, purchased a ten-acre parcel on Tustin Avenue, built a fine house back from the road, and planted a citrus orchard. Charles and Helen would live there for the rest of their lives. (The house was on the east side of Tustin Avenue, opposite Fruit Street, near the present-day hospital.)

The Bennett Home on Tustin Avenue

Two sons were born in Tustin: Charles Arthur Bennett (1888) and Harvey Franklin Bennett (1890). A month after the birth of Harvey, tragedy struck the family when Pearl was killed when she fell from a horse, which she was riding in their Tustin orchard. She died on November 17, 1890, a month and a half shy of her twelfth birthday.

Perhaps to relieve his grief, Charles threw himself into local politics. He had already actively supported the formation of Orange County when it broke away from Los Angeles in 1889, and in 1892, he ran for a seat in the state legislature. Bennett was something of a rarity: the former abolitionist and Union army veteran from Illinois, who in his youth had met Abraham Lincoln, was not a Republican. He was a staunch Democrat but won election to the state assembly as a Populist on the Fusion ticket, relying on votes from both Democrats and Republicans for his victory. He was an Assemblyman representing the 77th District from January 1, 1893, to January 1, 1895.

In his one term in the Assembly, he introduced a bill exempting fruit trees from taxation until they were four years old.

This bill was probably appreciated by the citrus farmers of his district. He also fought to retain school libraries and free textbooks, believing the state school system should be free in every way.

After his term in Sacramento, Bennett turned his attention to expanding his ranching operation. He purchased ten acres in El Toro but would eventually expand his holdings there to over fifty acres, plus five town lots. In addition to oranges, he planted the El Toro property to prunes and apricots. (In 1909, the local newspaper would publish a full-page article on apricot raising and picking written by Helen Bennett.)

Charles commuted from Tustin to manage his El Toro orchards, but after contracting pneumonia in 1910, he found it increasingly difficult, so he turned the responsibility over to his son, Harvey. Harvey left school before graduating and lived in a small house on the ranch property built in 1909. (The house is now part of Heritage Hill Historic Park in El Toro.)

Ten of the El Toro acres had been planted with apricots, and during the summer months, high school girls from Tustin and Santa Ana came to work pitting them. One of the Santa Ana high school girls was Frances L. McDonnell, who in October 1913 became Mrs. Harvey F. Bennett.

Charles Bennett remained an active member of Orange County's agricultural community. In addition to the initial ten acres on Tustin Avenue, he added twenty-two more acres across Tustin and Santa Ana, as well as his El Toro property. He came to be recognized as an expert on irrigation. He was sent as a delegate from Orange County to the national irrigation conventions in Omaha in 1892, St. Louis in 1896, and the International Irrigation Convention in Los Angeles in 1893. He also later owned several mining claims with his son, Frederick, near Oatman, Arizona.

When he died on January 7, 1921, at the age of seventy-eight, Charles Bennett was one of the most prominent and respected citrus growers in the region. He was buried at Santa Ana

Cemetery with members of Sedgwick Post 17 of the GAR as pallbearers. Even though he had left Nebraska some thirty-six years earlier, several weeks after his death, the Arapahoe Mirror published a laudatory obituary of Bennett on its front page.

Helen Bennett continued to live on the Tustin Avenue ranch. She eventually transferred ownership of some of the Tustin property to her son Charles Arthur. In 1928, she transferred most of the El Toro ranch to her son, Harvey Franklin, who had been managing the property for years.

Helen, known as "Mother Bennett" to family and friends, was described as possessing an active mind with many interests. She left the Bennett family many of her writings, one of which included this quote:

"I live in the midst of a ten-acre orange orchard, and I supervise the care of it myself. It entertains me, and I enjoy trying to see what I can do with raising oranges. My orange trees are like friends, always doing something different. Now they have yellow, golden fruit on them, and green fruit for next year. They are also covered with Fall growth of new green twigs and new, fresh, bright green leaves, preparing themselves for next Spring's beautiful white blossoms. An orange tree is always a thing of beauty. I love them."

Helen Bennett passed away on February 13, 1948, at the ripe old age of ninety-six and was buried next to her husband in Santa Ana Cemetery.

The following is a brief summary of the lives of Charles and Helen's four children.

Frederick Wilford Bennett was born June 18, 1877, in Vermillion, Illinois, and was just an infant when his parents moved to Nebraska. He attended school in Tustin and, for a time, attended the University of California at Berkeley, but did not graduate. Around the turn of the century, he took out several mining claims near Oatman, Arizona. He returned to Southern California and died in Norwalk, California, on May 30, 1932, at the age of fifty-four.

Pearl Edna Bennett was born on Christmas Day, 1878, in Arapahoe, Nebraska. She was killed in a fall from a horse on November 17, 1890, at the age of eleven.

Charles Arthur Bennett was born on December 24, 1888, in Tustin. He worked for a time as an automobile dealer but lived for most of his life on the family citrus ranch in Tustin, where he raised and sold nursery stock. He was never married and died on July 5, 1967, at the age of seventy-eight.

Harvey Franklin Bennett was born on October 31, 1890, in Tustin. He married Frances McDonnell on October 29, 1913, in Santa Ana. For many years, Harvey ran the family ranching operations in El Toro and became one of that city's most prominent citizens. He served for thirty-two years on the Tustin Hills Citrus Association Board and for twenty-five years on the Villa Park Lemon Association Board. He was a member of the Orange County Farm Bureau for 50 years and of the El Toro Water District. Harvey died on June 27, 1971, at the age of eighty. Frances passed away on September 21, 1985, at the age of ninety.

James H. Brown

Private, Co. I 27th Maine Infantry

Private, Co. L 2nd Maine Cavalry

Gunner's Mate USS Manhattan

James Brown enlisted in the Civil War as a teenager in Maine. He went on to serve in the infantry, cavalry, and the navy and was awarded a controversial Medal of Honor. He lived in Tustin for over 40 years and, at the time of his death, was one of the last Civil War veterans in the city.

James Henry Brown was born February 28, 1845, in Boston, Massachusetts, to Charles and Mary Brown. It has been written that he was from a seafaring family, but little is known about his father other than that he was a native of Massachusetts. On one federal census record, James' mother is listed as being French-Canadian.

Like his ancestry, little is known about James Brown's childhood. The summer of 1860 found the fifteen-year-old boy living and working on the farm of an older couple near Alfred, Maine. Alfred is a small town in York, the southernmost county in Maine, bordered by New Hampshire to the west.

Brown was only seventeen when he enlisted in the 27th Maine Infantry regiment on September 30, 1862. The 27th was recruited from York County and mustered into service at Portland, Maine, for nine months' service. After less than a month of training, the regiment departed Portland by train and arrived in Washington, D.C. on October 22, 1862. The regiment remained in Washington for the rest of 1862 and the first part of 1863, guarding the capital and the supply lines of the Army of the Potomac. The regiment fought no battles or skirmishes and suffered no casualties.

In late March 1863, the regiment was posted at Chantilly, Virginia, some twenty-five miles west of Washington. On June 24, it was ordered back to Arlington Heights, Virginia, just outside of Washington, to prepare for discharge on June 30, the expiration of their nine-month enlistment.

Meanwhile, Robert E. Lee and his Army of Northern Virginia had moved north into Pennsylvania and were squared off against the Union Army of the Potomac near the little town of Gettysburg. Fearing that a victory by Lee's army would put the capital in danger, President Lincoln and Secretary of War Stanton sent a written request asking the men of the 27th Maine to extend their enlistments until the outcome of the battle in Pennsylvania was known.

On June 30, the letter was read to the men of the regiment, and after much discussion and debate (in true New England tradition), about 309 men agreed to stay, while another 550 left for Washington and the return trip to Maine.

It has been written that the men of the 27th Maine who extended their enlistments were induced to do so by the offer of the Medal of Honor as a reward. This was simply not the case. The regimental commander, Colonel Frank Wentworth, went to the war department *after* the regimental debate to report that 309 men had decided to stay. It was only then that Stanton declared they would receive the medal. There is no evidence that the medal was offered before as an inducement for the men to stay and guard Washington. In fact, the Medal of Honor was so new (authorized by Congress in July 1862) that it was not viewed at that time with the same respect and awe it currently inspires. It would have meant little to the soldiers of 1863.

The Army of the Potomac won the Battle of Gettysburg (fought July 1-3, 1863), and on July 4, Robert E. Lee began to withdraw his army back into Virginia. On that same day, with the capital safe, the 309 men of the 27th Maine left Washington by train for their home state. They had extended their enlistments by four days, for which they received the Congressional Medal of Honor. After arriving at Portland, Maine, James Brown was mustered out of service on July 17, 1863, with the rest of the men of his regiment.

No record was made of the 309 men who had stayed to guard the capital or the 550 who didn't, so in 1864, when Stanton ordered the medals, all 864 men and officers of the 27th Maine were awarded the Medal of Honor. The medals were shipped to the governor of Maine, who forwarded them to Colonel Wentworth. Although he had no list to work from, Wentworth passed out the medals to the 309 men he believed had extended their enlistments to guard the capital, and stored the 550 remaining medals in a box in his stable. We can presume that James Brown was one of those who stayed because he received one of the medals from Wentworth. The awarding of these medals began a controversy that would take over fifty years to resolve.

For years, there were complaints from veterans' groups about what they perceived as the unjustified medals awarded to the men of the 27th Maine. By 1916, the Medal of Honor had come to be recognized as an award for gallantry in action above and beyond the call of duty. That year, a board of retired army officers was created to review the validity of all Medal of Honor recipients. The board concluded that 911 medals were not justified, including all 864 awarded to men of the 27th Maine, and ordered them purged from the rolls. (Also losing their medals were a civilian scout named Buffalo Bill Cody and Dr. Mary Walker, the only female recipient of the award.)

The Judge Advocate General's office then sent a letter to the 183 surviving members of the regiment explaining the decision, asking them to return the medals, and warning them that wearing or displaying them in public was a misdemeanor. Brown's picture wearing the medal implies he either did not receive the letter or chose to ignore it. Following his death in 1935, his wife donated the medal to their church, the Advent Christian Church in Tustin. For about eight decades, the church unwittingly broke the law by displaying Brown's medal in the chapel.

After mustering out, the war was not over for James Brown. In December 1863, he re-enlisted as a private in Company L of the 2nd Maine Cavalry. The 2nd Maine was organized at Augusta from November 30, 1863, to January 2, 1864. The regiment left Maine in April 1864 and was stationed in New Orleans until May 26, when it was moved to Thibodeaux, Louisiana. It did picket duty and scouting around Thibodeaux until July 27, when the regiment was reposted to Pensacola, Florida.

Around the time the regiment moved to Florida, Brown transferred to the Navy and served as a gunner's mate on the *USS*

Manhattan. A new gunship, the Manhattan, was a single-turreted ironclad monitor, commissioned in 1864. Brown fought at the Battle of Mobile Bay under Admiral David Farragut of "Damn the torpedoes, full speed ahead!" fame. During the battle, the Manhattan took the CSS Tennessee, a famed Confederate ironclad, under surrender, and later bombarded Fort Morgan.

The Battle of Mobile Bay, fought on August 5, 1864, was one of the fiercest naval battles of the war, as was the following siege of Fort Morgan. So, it is safe to say that James Brown saw more action on the water than he did on land. The Manhattan later blockaded the mouth of the Red River until the end of the war. Despite a total of three years of service with the infantry, the cavalry, and the navy, James Brown was only twenty years old when the war ended in 1865.

The USS Manhattan

After the war, Brown remained at sea serving on the sailing ship "Flying Cloud" from 1865 to 1868. Perhaps that is how he arrived in Northern California in 1868. In 1870, the twenty-five-year-old Brown was in Bodega, Sonoma County, California, working in a saw mill and living in a lumber camp bunkhouse with twenty-six other men. For about the next twenty years, he remained in Bodega, working as a lumberman, with possible periods spent at sea.

It is not known why, after almost two decades in Sonoma County, Brown moved to Southern California, but by 1892, he was a registered voter in Tustin. Three years later, on March 6, 1895, he married Sarah M. Goodwin. Their wedding took place at the home of a neighbor, W.L. Shatto. The groom had just turned fifty, and his bride was thirty-six. (The newspaper account of the wedding shaved ten years off her age.) The couple never had children.

Sarah Goodwin was born February 6, 1859, in Rushford, Wisconsin, to John and Mary (Daggett) Goodwin. She had an older brother and three sisters. By 1880, the widowed Mary had moved the family to San Francisco, where twenty-one-year-old Sarah worked as a shoe fitter. In 1882, the Goodwins were still in San Francisco, but the following year, both of Sarah's younger sisters were married in Tustin. So, it is highly probable that the family relocated to Tustin in 1883. Sadly, in 1889, Sarah's sister Effie was involved in a murder-suicide that shocked the Southland.

Mary Goodwin passed away in the fall of 1892, and Sarah inherited her house on Pacific and Third streets in Tustin. James and Sarah would make it their home for the rest of their lives. Despite a line in his obituary claiming he helped develop the citrus industry in the area, there is very little evidence that he was ever involved in horticulture or owned an orchard until his later years. In fact, census records and early city directories consistently identified his occupation as a laborer, one specifically denoting "laborer-odd jobs."

James H. Brown & Sarah (Goodwin) Brown
This was possibly their wedding picture.

Regardless of his profession, James Brown was popular in his community. To the younger set, he was "Old Sailor Brown" and was well known for spinning yarns about his time at sea. On his ninetieth birthday, a large party was thrown at his house, attended by dozens of friends. When he passed away at his home on November 8, 1935, at the age of ninety, he had been commander of the Sedgwick Post 17 of the GAR for the past eight years. The local newspaper published two funeral notices, an obituary, and an article describing the funeral service with a picture of the 21-gun salute. The obituary, with a photograph, graced the front page and ran an entire column. His funeral was moved to Shannon Chapel in Orange to accommodate the large crowd of mourners expected to attend. His passing left only five Civil War veterans in the Sedgwick Post, and his graveside service was officiated by the Sons of Union Veterans of the Civil War.

James H. Brown was laid to rest at Santa Ana Cemetery on November 12, 1935, seventy-three years after he had answered his country's call to arms. His death left only one Civil War veteran remaining in Tustin.

Sarah Brown lived in the house on Pacific and Third. She and James had been married for forty years, and, like her husband, she had been community-spirited and involved in veterans' affairs. She served at least one term as president of the Daughters of Union Veterans and sat on the executive board of the California-Nevada Division of the Women's Relief Corps of the GAR. She also served at least one term as president of the Tustin Women's Christian Temperance Union. Sarah passed away on April 7, 1945, at the age of eighty-six and was buried next to her husband at Santa Ana Cemetery.

Levi J. Colby

Private, Company E

24th Wisconsin Infantry

Levi Colby was a New Englander who traveled west to Wisconsin with his parents as a child. After a very brief service in the war, he traveled west again and was probably the first Civil War veteran to settle in Tustin.

Levi Jackson Colby was born May 24, 1831, in Thornton, New Hampshire to James and Betsey (Anderson) Colby. Levi grew up working on the family farm, first in New Hampshire and later in Wisconsin when his family moved near Franklin, just south of Milwaukee.

It was in Milwaukee on August 21, 1862, that thirty-one-year-old Levi enlisted as a private in Company E, 24th Wisconsin Infantry Regiment. The regiment was mustered into Federal service on the day of Levi's enlistment. The regimental adjutant was Arthur MacArthur, who by the end of the war was a Colonel and second in command of the regiment, although only nineteen years old. MacArthur was awarded the Medal of Honor for leading a charge up Missionary Ridge in Tennessee, and later would become the father of future general Douglas MacArthur. Another officer in the 24th was Lt. John Mitchell, whose son, Billy, would also go on to become a general and a controversial proponent of American military air power in the years between the two world wars.

The 24th Wisconsin first saw action at the Battle of Perryville, Kentucky on October 8, 1862. While the battle was a tactical win for the Confederates, it was considered a strategic Union victory because Southern forces withdrew to Tennessee, allowing Union forces to retain control of Kentucky for the remainder of the war. The battle cost the Union forces 4,241 casualties in killed, wounded, missing, and captured.

Perryville would have been the only battle Levi Colby was involved in, for on December 11, 1862, less than four months into his enlistment, he was discharged due to disability. He was undoubtedly suffering from one of the many diseases that were so prevalent in the unsanitary conditions of camp life in both armies.

Colby returned to Wisconsin, regained his health, and sometime around 1866 married Lucretia Douglas. Lucretia, a native of nearby Lake, Wisconsin, was born in 1842, making her eleven years younger than her new husband. In 1870, Levi was working as a merchant in Lake, and he and Lucretia were living with her parents, but within a few years, the couple had relocated to southern California.

Colby was in Los Angeles in 1873, San Bernardino in 1874, and in February 1875, he purchased 27 acres from Columbus Tustin for $1,409. If the Colby's moved to their new property around the time of the purchase, it would make Levi the first Civil War veteran to settle in Tustin.

Levi and Lucretia remained in Tustin for almost ten years where they appear to have prospered. In addition to growing oranges, Levi also dabbled in real estate; the local papers of the period are filled with property transactions of Levi buying and selling acreage around Tustin and Santa Ana.

Colby was also involved in the community. For several years, he served as the Tustin City delegate to the Republican Party County convention, and he was also an active member of Sedgwick Post 17 of the GAR. Levi was also prominent among the local Masons.

In April 1883, Colby sold his 28-acre ranch in Tustin, and he and Lucretia moved to Santa Ana. They owned a home on West Sixth street and Levi continued his citrus ranching operations at the various orchards he still owned in the area. An 1892 Orange County voter registration record describes the then 61-year-old veteran as 6 feet 2 inches tall, with gray eyes and gray hair.

Levi Colby died at the age of 72 at his home at 616 West Sixth Street on July 14, 1903. In various obituaries, he was described as a "pioneer capitalist" and "retired capitalist" of the county. The funeral was held at the home under the supervision of the Masons, and he was buried in the Masonic Garden section at Santa Ana Cemetery.

Lucretia Colby survived her husband by just four years. In November 1906, she moved into a new house on North Broadway in Santa Ana, but soon after, she fell ill and never recovered. She suffered greatly near the end before passing away on August 12, 1907, at the age of 64. After a funeral service at the Episcopal church, she was buried beside her husband at Santa Ana Cemetery.

Lucretia had made out a will the day before she died. When the will was probated, it was discovered that she and Levi had accumulated an estate estimated at $100,000 (3.2 million in 2023 dollars). Because the couple had no children, the estate was parceled out to relatives in Wisconsin, local charitable organizations, and a few friends. One friend, Sarah Eddy, who received $1,000, was the widow of Tustin blacksmith and Civil War veteran Samuel L. Eddy.

Samuel L. Eddy

Corporal

1st US (Michigan) Lancers

Samuel Eddy probably served the shortest enlistment of any Tustin Civil War veteran. He was mustered out of the army after slightly less than three months of service, having never left the state of Michigan. An early pioneer of Tustin, he was one of the town's first and, for a time, only blacksmith before dying suddenly at the age of fifty-eight.

Samuel Lafayette Eddy was born on November 11, 1829, in Providence, Rhode Island, the first of Joseph and Susan (Salisbury) Eddy's seven children. By 1850, the family had relocated to the town of Palmyra, in upstate New York, near Lake Ontario, and Samuel was living with the family of a carriage maker just down the road from his parents' home. His father had a wife, six children, and a mother-in-law to support, so perhaps Samuel struck out on his own to ease the family's financial burden. He was twenty-one years old at the time and working as a blacksmith, probably for the carriage maker, as four other blacksmiths were also boarding with him. Blacksmithing was the occupation Samuel Eddy would follow for the rest of his life.

Ten years later, the family had moved westward again, this time to Bay City, Michigan. Bay City, at the time the Eddys arrived, was a thriving community of saw mills and small businesses. Now thirty-one and still unmarried, Samuel again lived apart from his family and plied his trade as a blacksmith.

Samuel Eddy's Civil War service was short-lived. He enlisted in the 1st United States Lancers, a cavalry battalion, at Bay City on December 31, 1861. The Lancers were organized by Colonel Arthur Rankin between November 30, 1861, and February

20, 1862. Exactly one month later, on March 20, 1862, the Lancers were mustered out of service in Detroit for reasons unknown. Eddy, who had held the rank of corporal in Company E for that brief period, was one of 686 men recruited before the unit was disbanded and never saw active service. There is no record of Eddy reenlisting, so it appears that his Civil War service lasted three months.

Eddy remained in Michigan after his brief stint in the cavalry. He had just turned thirty-five when he married Sarah Ann Hutchinson on November 15, 1864. Sarah, a Michigan native, was eleven years his junior. They were married in White Rock, Illinois, some four hundred miles from Bay City. If they were living there, it wasn't for long, because in 1867 their only child, Ralph Lewis Eddy, was born back in Bay City.

They remained in Bay City until 1870, during which Samuel continued working as a blacksmith, and Sarah cared for three-year-old Ralph. By the following spring, they had moved west to Elk Horn, a small farming community near Stockton, California, where, once again, Eddy found work as a blacksmith.

Perhaps the hot, dry summers of the region did not agree with him, and he was lured to the milder climate of southern California. Whatever the reason, as early as 1877, the Eddys were living in Tustin, then a part of Los Angeles County. Samuel Eddy owned and operated a blacksmith shop in partnership with G.W. Freeman, located on Main Street. It was later moved to the corner of Third and B streets, facing B. The family lived in a house across the street, on the southeast corner.

The blacksmith with his anvil and forge was an essential part of any agricultural community. In addition to repairing wagons and carriages and shoeing horses, the village blacksmith also forged custom tools and farm implements. Samuel Eddy served the needs of Tustin for about a dozen years, a number of those as the town's only blacksmith.

The Eddys quickly became involved in the community. Samuel served for several years as a trustee of the Sycamore School District, and both he and Sarah were members of St. Paul's Episcopal Church. Samuel was a member of the building committee for the church, which opened on September 5, 1881, on First Street near A Street.

From an 1886 city directory, we learn that at the time Eddy was the only blacksmith in Tustin and that he was no longer in partnership with Freeman:

"SL EDDY is the proprietor of the sole blacksmith shop in Tustin, located just north of the post office, about one square block. He is an enterprising man, a first-class workman, and does a good business."

In the same directory, we learn that Miss Martha Tustin, the founder's daughter, is the town's postmistress.

Two years after this city directory entry, Samuel Eddy was dead. He passed away on September 17, 1888, in Tustin at the age of 58. He had only been ill a short time, and his death came as a shock to family and friends. He was buried by his fellow Masons at Santa Ana Cemetery.

Ralph, undoubtedly trained by his father, took over the blacksmith shop for several years. He eventually sold it to Frank Van Kamp, and in the early 1890s, Ralph moved to the Inland Empire. He married in 1895 and, at various times, lived and worked as a blacksmith in San Bernardino, Temescal, and Lake Elsinore. He died in Riverside in 1940.

Sarah Eddy lived in the house on Third Street for several years. She filed for Samuel's Civil War pension on July 31, 1890, but it is not clear if she received it. Sometime after 1910, tired of living alone, she eventually moved in with a friend, Julia Douglas, in Santa Ana. She was on an extended visit to her son in Lake Elsinore when she fell ill and died of pneumonia on January 15, 1917, at the age of 75. Ralph, his wife Nellie Mae, and their son

Henry accompanied the body back to Orange County for the funeral, held on January 18. Sarah was buried next to her husband at Santa Ana Cemetery.

George W. Hale

Private, Co. B 27th Illinois Infantry

Private, Co. I 129th Illinois Infantry

George Hale entered the Union Army at the tender age of sixteen and eventually served in two different Illinois infantry regiments. He served for three years, then returned and spent the majority of his life in his home state before becoming the last Civil War veteran to move to Tustin, arriving in 1931.

George Washington Hale was born February 22, 1845, in Naples, Scott County, Illinois, the seventh of Allison and Rachel Hale's eight children. Both parents were from Tennessee, but by 1850, they had moved their large family to a farm in southwest Illinois.

Just before the outbreak of the Civil War, fifteen-year-old George Hale was already on his own. The 1860 census found him working and living on the Dugger farm in Scott County, Illinois.

At some point, he returned to Naples, where the now sixteen-year-old farm boy enlisted as a private in Company B, 27th Illinois Infantry Regiment, on September 21, 1861. The regiment was organized at Camp Butler the previous month, and Company B was comprised primarily of men from Scott County.

The regiment's first clash with the enemy came at the Battle of Belmont, fought on November 7, 1861, in Mississippi County, Missouri. The 27th Illinois was on the far-right wing of the Union forces under Gen. John McClernand and helped drive the Confederates away. The Union troops then stopped to loot the rebel camp, and to put a stop to this, the overall commander, Gen. U.S. Grant, ordered the camp burned. In the smoke and confusion, some Confederate prisoners were burned to death in their tents. It was certainly an ugly baptism of fire for the teenager from Scott County.

Southern reinforcements then surprised the Union soldiers and drove them back to their original lines. The battle was considered a draw, although both sides claimed victory. In Hale's first and only battle with the 27th Illinois, the Union forces lost 120 men killed in action, 383 wounded, and 104 captured or missing. Three of the four Union regiments involved in the battle were from Illinois, and Belmont Avenue in Chicago is named for the battle.

Belmont was the only battle George Hale fought with the 27th because on March 4, 1862, the day the regiment was ordered to occupy Columbus, Missouri, he was discharged due to disability.

Most casualties in the Civil War were the result of non-combat-related diseases. For every three soldiers who were killed in battle, five more died of disease. The infectious diseases most responsible for these deaths were pneumonia, typhoid, diarrhea/dysentery, as well as measles, mumps, malaria, and influenza. With thousands of men crowded into unsanitary camps with a poor diet and often tainted water, the spread of disease was inevitable.

It is not known what disease led to George Hale's disability discharge, but after four months of recuperation, he reenlisted as a private in Company I, 129th Illinois Infantry Regiment. He enlisted on August 2, 1862, for a period of three years and was mustered in at Pontiac, Illinois, on September 8, 1862.

On September 22, the regiment left Pontiac with 927 officers and men and reported to Louisville, Kentucky. The regiment spent the remainder of 1862 and much of 1863 at various posts in Kentucky, guarding railroads and repelling Confederate attacks. From August 1863 until February 1864, the 129th Illinois was stationed in Nashville.

The 129th then participated in all the major battles in the campaign leading up to and including the capture of Atlanta. It fought in the battles of Resaca, Lost Mountain, and Peachtree Creek, and in the taking of Atlanta. The regiment then joined General Sherman on his march across Georgia. After the war, the 129th Illinois marched in the grand review in Washington.

George Hale, after seeing three years of active campaigning, was mustered out in Chicago with the rest of the regiment on June 8, 1865. He had served for over three years and was only twenty years old at the time of his discharge.

He returned to Scott County after his discharge, and there he married Rebecca L. Braham on October 11, 1865. It is ironic that Hale had been at war fighting Southerners for three years, only to come home and marry a girl from Memphis, Tennessee. George was still only twenty, and Rebecca was seventeen.

George and Rebecca would remain living in or around Bluffs Village, Scott County, Illinois, until her death over fifty years later. The couple had five children: Horace, James, Lucien, Daisy Mae, and Clayton. George made his living as a teamster, driving a horse-drawn wagon.

Rebeca Hale passed away on March 17, 1918, in Bluffs Village. She was seventy years old, and she and George had been married for fifty-three years. After the death of his wife, George moved in with his daughter, Daisy Mae, and her husband, Ira

Price, first in Sefton, then later in Decatur, Illinois. In Decatur, George was a member of the GAR's Dunham Post 141.

George Hale was eighty-six years old in 1931 when he moved to Tustin with Daisy Mae, Ira, and his twelve-year-old granddaughter, Doris. His stay in Tustin was short, for he died two years later on March 3, 1933, at the age of eighty-eight. He was buried at Fairhaven Memorial Park in Santa Ana.

Daisy and Ira Price lived in Tustin for over twenty-five years. They owned a home at 535 Main Street, and Ira worked at various times as a bus driver and a janitor. He was working for the US Navy at the El Toro Marine Corps base at the time of his death in 1958. Daisy was living with Doris and her family in Glendora, California, at the time of her death in 1960, and the ***Tustin News*** ran a small obituary on the front page. Daisy and Ira are both buried at Fairhaven Memorial Park.

Orrin Hanlon

Private, Company G

26th Indiana Infantry

Orrin Hanlon was a twenty-one-year-old married man when he enlisted in an Indiana infantry regiment at the beginning of the war, and his unit saw much heavy fighting during his three years of service. After the war, the oft-married Hanlon eventually made his way to Tustin, arriving around 1912.

Orrin Hanlon was born on November 20, 1839, in Indiana, the first of Matthias and Margaret (Jones) Hanlon's thirteen children. Matthias was a carpenter, and the family moved often, a tradition Orrin would carry on as an adult.

Orrin was twenty-one years old when he married fifteen-year-old Sarah Ann Daugherty on January 20, 1860, in Tippecanoe County, Indiana. Later that summer, the couple moved east to Clinton County, where

Orrin worked as a day laborer for a personal estate estimated at just $25.

The following year, Orrin Hanlon answered his country's call to arms when he enlisted as a private in Company G, 26th Indiana Infantry Regiment on August 30, 1861. Orrin's younger brother, James, was also a private in Company G and was listed as a deserter in June 1863. Company G was comprised mostly of young men from Tippecanoe County.

The 26th Indiana was organized in Indianapolis in August 1861 and trained at nearby Camp Morton. The regiment was assigned to the Army of the West, and all the battles and skirmishes in which it participated were fought in the Western Theater of Operations.

The regiment's first few encounters with the enemy all took place in Missouri at Springfield, Sedalia, and Newtonia. The 26th then moved into Arkansas, where it engaged the Confederates at the Battle of Pine Grove on December 27, 1862. The battle resulted in 1,251 Union casualties but was considered a victory because it allowed them to gain control of northwestern Arkansas. The Confederates were forced to leave many of their dead on the field of battle. They piled the bodies in heaps and covered them with makeshift barriers to keep feral pigs from eating the corpses of their dead comrades.

In the summer of 1863, the 26th Indiana was part of the Union force that besieged and eventually captured Vicksburg, Mississippi. The regiment then spent several months in Louisiana before moving to Texas in the fall, where it participated in the capture of Brownsville on November 6, 1863. The Confederates abandoned the city and tried to set it to the torch as they left. By occupying the city, Union forces effectively cut off a main point of entry for rebel blockade runners.

The regiment remained in the Gulf Coast area for the remainder of its service. Over the course of the war, the 26th

Indiana lost 96 men killed in action or died of wounds, and another 3 officers and 265 enlisted died of disease for a total of 364 fatalities. Private Orrin Hanlon was discharged from the regiment on September 21, 1864, having fulfilled his three-year enlistment.

It is unclear whether Hanlon's marriage survived their wartime separation, but in 1867, Sarah married Charles E. Hershman. Two years later, on March 21, 1869, Orrin married Mary Elizabeth Harney. Orrin was twenty-nine, and his new bride was nineteen. The following year, the couple was living in the small town of Lost Creek, near Terra Haute, Indiana. Orrin worked as a day laborer while Mary cared for their infant daughter, Mary Margaret. Mary Elizabeth Hanlon died around 1877 at the age of twenty-seven.

Three years later, Orrin Hanlon is single, living with his younger brother, William, in Terra Haute, and working at a whisky distillery.

On October 20, 1890, Orrin again tied the knot, this time to Georgeann Hathaway in Martinsville, Illinois. The couple had a son, Arthur, followed by two daughters, Millie and Emma.

It seems that each new Federal Census found Orrin with a new wife, and 1900 was no exception. Georgeann was gone, dead or divorced, and by the turn of the century, Orrin was married for a fourth time. He was married to Nettie V. Kirby on September 7, 1898, in Paris, Edgar County, Illinois. Orrin was fifty-eight, and his new bride was twenty-six. Nettie gave birth to a daughter, Thelma, in 1907 and apparently helped raise Millie and Emma from Orrin's previous marriage.

Orrin and Nettie were still in Edgar County in 1910, but just a year or two later, they relocated to Tustin. Orrin was among the last of the Civil War veterans to settle in Tustin, most of whom had arrived before the turn of the century. Orrin worked as a farm laborer even in his seventies, and Nettie brought in additional income as a housekeeper. While living in Tustin, the family rented a house on D Street (now El Camino Real), and Thelma attended the local schools. Orrin, who was granted a military pension in the summer of 1892, joined the Sedgwick Post-17 of the GAR.

After about a dozen years in Tustin, the Hanlons moved to Santa Ana in 1923. They were living at 1324 E. Third Street when Orrin died on May 26, 1928, at the age of eighty-eight. He was buried at Santa Ana Cemetery on May 28 with graveside ceremonies provided by members of his GAR Post.

Nettie Hanlon was fifty-six at the time of her husband's death, and she and Orrin had been married for thirty years. She was left with his small military pension but soon moved in with her daughter Thelma's family, first in Los Angeles, and later, when they moved back to Santa Ana. Nettie Hanlon died on August 5, 1943, at the age of seventy-one and is buried at Fairhaven Memorial Park in Santa Ana.

The children of Orrin Hanlon were:

- Mary Margaret Hanlon was born February 24, 1869, in Indiana, the only child of Orrin and his second wife, Mary. On November 3, 1889, Mary Margaret married Solomon Wesley Dodd in Clark County, Illinois. The couple eventually had seven children. Solomon farmed in Clark County for thirty-nine years before moving his family to Santa Ana around 1920. In Santa Ana, he ran a grocery store on East First Street. Solomon died in 1930, and Mary Margaret was living with her daughter Estelle in Oakland, California, when she passed away on December 6, 1956, at the age of eighty-seven.

- Arthur Hanlon was born around 1890 in Illinois, a son of Orrin and his third wife, Georgeann. Arthur was living in New York at the time of his father's death, but beyond that, not much is known about him.

- Millie Hanlon was born August 4, 1891, in Illinois, a daughter of Orrin and Georgeann. She was about 21 when she moved to Tustin with her family. Shortly after the move, she married George Williams. George worked as a mechanic, and the couple lived on 17th Street in Tustin, where they raised a large family. In 1940, the family moved to South Flower Street in Santa Ana, where they lived with seven of their eight children. George died at age 67, and Millie died on January 5, 1975, at age 83. They are both buried at Fairhaven Memorial Park.

- Emma Hanlon was born July 6, 1893, in Illinois, a daughter of Orrin and Georgeann. She was eighteen years old when she married Vaughn Maynard in Tustin on April 4, 1912. The couple lived for a time on D Street in Tustin, next door to her father, before moving to Santa Ana. Their family would eventually include six children, four sons and two daughters.

  Vaughn, also a native of Illinois, had moved to California in 1908. He first worked on the Irvine Ranch as a mule driver and farmer, and later was a water-well contractor. The family lived on Sullivan Street in Santa Ana for many years before purchasing a citrus ranch in San Diego County in 1943. Emma died on April 6, 1976, at the age of eighty-three, and Vaughn passed away in 1984 at the age of ninety. Both are buried at Fairhaven.

- Thelma E. Hanlon was born on September 19, 1907, in Paris, Illinois, the daughter of Orrin and his fourth wife, Nettie. Thelma was just a young girl when the family moved to Tustin. At the age of seventeen, she married Leroy D. McCament, a railway clerk for the Post Office. The couple had two sons and a daughter. They lived in Los Angeles for a short time before settling in

Santa Ana, where they lived for many years at 417
Wakeham Avenue. They were living in Pala, San Diego
County, when Thelma died on August 24, 1989, at the
age of eighty-one. Leroy passed away the following
year in Pala at the age of eighty-six.

**The back of this photograph is captioned "Lemon Heights, Cal" but
the age and number of children would indicate it was probably taken
in Illinois before the family moved to California.**

William L.G. Haskins

Sgt. Co. C 51st Massachusetts Infantry

Pvt. Battery F 4th Massachusetts Heavy Artillery

W.L.G. Haskins, named for the most prominent abolitionist of the era, was raised in New England, surrounded by anti-slavery sentiment, and during the war served in two Massachusetts regiments. After the war, he spent many years in the Boston area before moving to Tustin in the early 1890s, where he quickly established himself as a respected member of the business community.

William Lloyd Garrison Haskins was born on November 30, 1840, in Putnam, Muskingum County, Ohio. Despite his birthplace, William was a New Englander to the core. His nativity in the Midwest appears to be the result of his father's one venture at pioneer life. (Putnam also happened to be an area of strong abolitionist sentiment.) Before William was a year old, his father, Robert Haskins, and mother, Lucretia (Child), had moved the family back to Worcester County, Massachusetts.

William grew up in West Boylston, Worcester County, and his parents lived there for the rest of their lives. It can be presumed that the Haskins opposed slavery since they named their son after the fiery Massachusetts abolitionist newspaper editor, William Lloyd Garrison.

Haskins was also a nephew of Lydia Child, one of the most well-known female authors of the time. She supported and spoke out for radical ideas like Native American rights, women's suffrage, and the immediate abolition of slavery. In fact, she wrote the most popular anti-slavery novel of the period until Harriet Beecher Stowe published *Uncle Tom's Cabin* in 1854. Today, Child is best remembered for her poem "Over the River and Through the

Wood." With these radical influences, it is not surprising that Haskins volunteered to preserve the Union and end slavery.

The outbreak of the Civil War found the twenty-one-year-old Haskins working on a farm near West Boylston. He enlisted as a private in Company C, 51st Massachusetts Infantry Regiment on September 25, 1862. The regiment was organized at Worcester from September 25 to October 30, 1862, for a nine-month enlistment. Thomas Wentworth Higginson, a Unitarian minister and well-known abolitionist, served as a captain in the regiment.

The 51st Massachusetts was assigned to the Department of North Carolina under General John G. Foster. The regiment was involved in the battles of Kinston, White Hall, and Goldsboro Bridge, all of which were fought in December 1862.

After its early battles, the regiment settled into guard and outpost duty. It was stationed at various spots in North Carolina, Virginia, and Maryland before returning to Worcester, where Haskins was mustered out with the rest of the regiment on July 27, 1863, having fulfilled the nine-month enlistment. By the time of his discharge, Haskins had been promoted to the rank of sergeant. The 51st Massachusetts lost no men in combat, but forty-four enlisted men died of disease. (William's older brother, George T. Haskins, died of disease at Nashville on January 25, 1863, while serving with the 90th Ohio Infantry.)

Haskins took a year off from the war, and on January 17, 1864, he married Alice M. Ross in Princeton, Massachusetts. His twenty-year-old bride was a native of Lancashire, England. One week after the birth of their first child, a daughter, William rejoined the army. There is no record of how Alice felt about this.

On August 15, 1864, Haskins enlisted as a private in Battery F, 4th Massachusetts Heavy Artillery. During the Civil War, heavy artillery was used in fixed fortifications to defend cities, forts, and seaports. It was also used in siege operations against enemy forts and was usually of large caliber. The state recruited fourteen companies of heavy artillery in the summer of 1864 to defend the Massachusetts coastline. However, in September, they were ordered to Washington, D.C. to man the forts protecting the capital. It was there that William Haskins served out the last year of his Civil War service. The 4th Heavy Artillery was mustered out of service in Washington on July 17, 1865. The 4th had lost no men in battle, but twenty-one men died from disease or accidents.

After leaving the artillery, Haskins attempted to enlist as an officer in the famous 54th Massachusetts Colored Infantry regiment (its story was chronicled in the movie *Glory*), and his obituary credits him with being a 2nd Lieutenant in that unit. But the official roster of the 54th Massachusetts shows that 2nd Lt. Haskins was never mustered into the regiment and that his commission was canceled.

William Haskins was twenty-four when the war ended. He returned home to Alice, baby Florence, and a farm near West Boylston. Within a few years, the family, now with two more daughters, Mary and Edith, had moved to Worcester, where Haskins worked as a grocer. By 1880, they were back on the farm near West Boylston, and the family was completed with the addition of a son, George. For many years, Haskins was commander of the GAR post in West Boylston.

William Haskins moved his family to Tustin in 1891, probably for his health. He put in for and received a pension as an army invalid, citing rheumatism, bronchitis, and heart problems, possibly contracted from sleeping on damp ground in the service down south. He bought a house and some acreage on Bryan Street near Redhill Avenue. In addition to farming, he also sold real estate, underwrote fire insurance, arranged loans, and served as a notary public.

He and Alice were devout Unitarians, and in April 1896, Haskins found himself in heady company when he was named to the first board of trustees for the new Unitarian church in Santa

Ana. On the board with him were A.C. Bowers and J.W. Towner, the latter the first Superior Court Judge of Orange County. In 1898, Haskins was elected a trustee of the Tustin Elementary School District.

Haskins survived the war but almost met an untimely end in a train accident. On Friday evening, April 14, 1899, Haskins, with several female family members in his carriage, was crossing the railroad tracks at Fourth Street in Santa Ana when the evening train from Los Angeles approached. Rather than continue across, Haskins stopped and then attempted to back the carriage off the tracks. The engineer put the train into reverse, but it couldn't stop in time. The locomotive knocked the horses off the tracks, and, according to a newspaper account of the accident, the women in the carriage jumped out, one of them landing hard on the street. The ladies were not named, but it is assumed they were female members of the Haskins family. There was no mention of William sustaining injuries, although the article implied the accident was his fault.

Shortly after arriving in Tustin, Haskins opened a real estate office in partnership with William B. Artz, a local merchant and farmer. Their offices were located in the bank building. By 1908, he had a new partner, David Cobau, who also owned a pool hall and cigar store. Their office was at 320 E. Main Street.

An advertisement from the 1908-1909 Santa Ana City Directory

William Haskins was apparently a well-respected member of the small Tustin business community. In 1905, he was elected vice-president of the newly formed Tustin Mutual Improvement

Association. This committee was somewhat of an early Chamber of Commerce. It had been organized by fellow realtor E.M. Wheeler and launched a campaign to have homeowners clean up their lots and beautify their property with flowers. The group held a fundraiser, and the proceeds were used to purchase the first street signs in Tustin. Haskins was also appointed a lieutenant of the home guard unit created in Tustin during the war hysteria created by the sinking of the USS Maine in Havana Harbor in 1898.

Tragedy struck the Haskins family when, about noon on March 4, 1909, Alice suffered a heart attack and died almost instantly. She was just two weeks shy of her sixty-sixth birthday, and she and William had been married for forty-five years.

One year later, William Haskins would find big changes in his life. On March 8, 1910, slightly over a year after Alice's death, he remarried. His new spouse was Dora Ironmonger. Dora, like Haskins' first wife, was a native of Lancashire, England. She was the sixty-five-year-old widow of Joseph J. Ironmonger, who had died in 1895. Their nuptials took place in Santa Ana, and five days later, an article appeared in the local paper stating that Mrs. Haskins was resigning as a Sunday school teacher at the First Methodist Church in Santa Ana. The reason given was that she was moving (presumably to Tustin), but perhaps it was because she had married a Unitarian.

Another big change was that after almost twenty years, Haskins was no longer in the real estate business. Apparently, his partnership with Cobau did not work out, and by 1910, Haskins, at the age of seventy, had returned to farming. Later records would list him as a rancher (undoubtedly a citrus ranch), and his home was still on Bryan Street, east of Newport Avenue. No photograph of Haskins has been found, but a Tustin "old-timer" remembered the realtor as having a flowing beard down to his belt.

Haskins became a widower for a second time when Dora passed away on July 11, 1915, at the age of seventy-one. The couple had been married just five years, and she was buried at

Diamond Grove Cemetery in Jacksonville, Illinois, next to her first husband.

In poor health for the last few years of his life, William Lloyd Garrison Haskins died at his home in Tustin on November 19, 1919. He was just eleven days short of his 79th birthday. He was buried at Santa Ana Cemetery next to his first wife, Alice.

The Haskins children all remained in the area. Florence, the oldest, stayed on at the house on Bryan Street until eventually moving to a house on Tustin Avenue. She never married, worked as a nurse, and at some point, in the late 1920s or early 1930s, opened a nursing home in Tustin. She worked up until about a year before her death and passed away in Tustin on January 27, 1944, at the age of 79.

Mary Haskins married a Canadian, Charles W. Gordon. They lived in Los Angeles, where Gordon died in 1923 at the age of 50. Mary spent her final years in Laguna Beach and died in 1947 at the age of 79.

Edith Haskins married David Dudley Field on January 11, 1905, in Tustin. According to the memory of Tustin "old-timer" William Huntley, Edith taught at Tustin Grammar School before her marriage. She and David had two children, Ross and Lydia. For many years, they lived on a citrus ranch at 17th Street and Holt Avenue in Tustin. Edith and David passed away within two days of each other in April 1937. A double funeral was held before their burial at Santa Ana Cemetery.

George M. Haskins never married. For a time, he lived in Santa Ana and worked as a box maker in an orange packinghouse. He passed away in Los Angeles in 1927 at the age of 49 and is buried next to his parents in Santa Ana Cemetery.

Benjamin F. Hennacy

Private

United States Marine Corps

Benjamin Hennacy was just a teenager when he enlisted in the Marine Corps early in the second year of the war. After his service, he returned home to Pennsylvania and then began a series of moves westward that would land him in Tustin just before the turn of the century.

Benjamin Franklin Hennacy was born on March 25, 1844, in Pennsylvania. His father, George Hennacy, was born in Ireland, but nothing is known about Ben's mother.

Benjamin Hennacy was eighteen years old when he enlisted in the United States Marine Corps at Philadelphia on September 3, 1862. The Marine Corps was a relatively small branch of the service during the Civil War, with only about 4,000 officers and men. Marines were primarily assigned to duty aboard Navy ships blockading southern ports. The Marines enforced discipline on the ship and, during battles, went aloft and acted as snipers, picking off officers and gunners on enemy ships.

In March 1863, Private Hennacy was part of a fifteen-man Marine detachment assigned to the USS Florida. The detachment consisted of a sergeant, two corporals, and twelve privates. The Florida was a 215-foot side-wheel steamship that was commissioned into Union service on October 5, 1861. The detachment sharpened its marksmanship by periodically firing at a barrel placed in the water about 300 yards from the ship.

In April 1863, the Florida was part of a fleet commanded by Admiral DuPont that unsuccessfully attempted to capture Charleston, South Carolina. The side-wheeler was then stationed off the coast of North Carolina as part of the North Atlantic Blockading Squadron.

An artist's rendering of the *USS Florida*

One afternoon in June 1863, off Cape Fear, North Carolina, the Florida intercepted and captured the blockade runner Calypso after firing several shots across her bow. When sailors from the Florida boarded the blockade runner, they discovered its crew had tried to destroy the ship by blocking the safety valves on the boiler. The Florida sailors quickly unblocked the valves, ending the threat of a disastrous explosion. The Florida later captured another blockade runner off the coast near Wilmington, North Carolina.

The blockade was critical to the Union strategy for winning the war. By cutting off imports and exports, the southern economy would be slowly strangled. But blockade duty could be very monotonous for the sailors and marines aboard the blockading ships. Spending months at a time patrolling the southern coastlines while enduring poor food, cramped quarters, and the unpredictable weather at sea, drove some crews close to mutiny. In November 1863, during stormy weather off the coast of North Carolina, a seaman was swept off the deck of the Florida, and efforts to rescue him proved unsuccessful.

Benjamin Hennacy served aboard the Florida from March 1863 until October 1864, when his Marine detachment was transferred to the Brooklyn Navy Yard. Shortly after his transfer to

Brooklyn, Hennacy was discharged after two years of service, most of that time spent at sea.

Hennacy returned to Pennsylvania and, around 1866, married Sarah L. Calvin. Over the next twelve years, they would have five children: George, John, Benjamin Jr., Nellie, and Minnie. The family lived in Beaver Falls, northeast of Pittsburgh, and Ben worked as a shoemaker. At some point after 1880, the family moved 23 miles west, just across the state line to Columbiana County, Ohio. Sarah passed away there in 1882 at the age of 36 and is buried at Achor Valley Cemetery.

The following year, on April 7, 1883, Benjamin Hennacy married Rachael A. Graves in Tipton, Iowa. Rachael was the 31-year-old widow of Civil War veteran Stephen Graves, a native of Tipton. She had one son, Fred Graves, who lived in Tustin for several years after the turn of the century. Ben and Rachael had one child together, a son, Phil Sheridan Hennacy. The boy, named after the Civil War general, was born in Tipton in 1884.

Ben and Rachael moved often, always westward. The year 1889 found them in Lincoln, Nebraska, while two years later, they were living in Denver. By 1896, they were in Los Angeles, and in each place, Ben plied his trade as a shoemaker. Finally, around 1898, the Hennacys arrived in Tustin, but their stay there was short. On the 1900 Federal Census, enumerated on June 5, the family was living in Tustin, where Ben was employed as a fruit peddler. By December of that same year, they had moved and were living on Fourth Street in Santa Ana.

Ben and Rachael would spend the rest of their lives in Santa Ana. Ben worked first as a grocer and then ran a small hotel/boarding house called The Waverly on Fourth Street. He was active in the Odd Fellows and the GAR, and Rachael served at least one term as president of Women's Relief Corps, an auxiliary of the GAR.

Rachael Hennacy passed away from spinal meningitis on April 16, 1913, at thc agc of 62.

Benjamin Hennacy, who suffered from painful rheumatism in his last years, passed away in Santa Ana on March 24, 1918, one day before his 74th birthday. He and Rachael are buried at Santa Ana Cemetery in the Odd Fellows section.

Phil Hennacy, the only child of Ben and Rachael, was a corporal in the army, serving at nearby Camp Kearney, and was able to make it home to be with his father at the time of his father's death. Phil appears to have been the "black sheep" of the family, often in trouble with the police, usually in incidents involving excess use of alcohol. Fred Graves served as executor and received his stepfather's entire estate, which amounted to only $290.

An uncredited photo of five Civil War-era Marines with their NCO at left.

Henry H. Higley

Corporal, Company E

15th Iowa Infantry

H.H. Higley was an Iowa farm boy when he enlisted to serve in the Civil War, and after three years of hard campaigning, his health was broken. After many years in Iowa, he migrated to Tustin in the late 1890s, staying about five years before moving on to Long Beach.

Henry Harvey Higley was born on April 4, 1842, in Danville, Iowa. He was the third of the five children of Ezra Cogswell Higley and Amanda Anna Messenger, and their only son. Ezra was a native of Massachusetts, a descendant of Mayflower passenger Joseph Higley. Ezra had migrated west to Ohio with his parents, and he and Amanda were married there in 1835. In the spring of 1839, they traveled by wagon with their two small children to the new territory of Iowa.

Henry Higley was raised working on the family farm and attending a one-room log schoolhouse near Danville. Danville, in Des Moines County, is in southwest Iowa near the Mississippi River. Henry was twenty years old when, on August 26, 1862, he enlisted in the 15th Iowa Infantry regiment. The regiment had been organized at Keokuk in February 1862 and mustered in for three years' service. There was a Lieutenant Mortimer A. Higley of Cedar Rapids, Iowa, in the regiment, but it is not known if he was related to Henry.

By joining the regiment in August Henry missed the Battle of Shiloh, fought on April 6, 1862. He did participate in all the other major engagements with the regiment, including the Battle of Corinth, the siege of Vicksburg, the campaign for Atlanta, and the battles of Jonesboro and Bentonville, as well as Sherman's March to the Sea. The regimental history states that during the siege of Atlanta, the 15th Iowa was in the front lines or under fire for ninety-seven days.

He was with the regiment when it marched into Savannah and went with Sherman into North Carolina, capturing Raleigh. Higley witnessed the surrender of General Johnston's army, effectively ending Confederate resistance in the east.

Higley was never wounded in battle but did contract smallpox and was confined to a military hospital in Duckport, Louisiana, for three months. He recovered from the smallpox, but the disease permanently damaged his eyesight. He also suffered other ailments during his service that affected his overall health for years. He was discharged on August 5, 1865, fulfilling his three-year enlistment. He was to receive a $4 monthly pension for his disabilities, about $114 in current (2021) dollars.

By the end of the war, the 15th Iowa had lost 8 officers and 118 enlisted men killed in combat. Also, one officer and 260 enlisted men succumbed to disease for a total of 387 regimental fatalities.

Henry Higley returned to Iowa after the war and, on January 29, 1866, married Mary Elizabeth Minson. The groom was twenty-three and his bride twenty-one. Their first child, Amanda, was born in 1869 and died in 1878 at the age of nine. The Highleys remained in Danville for the next thirty years, farming on land adjacent to his father's farm. Eventually, two more children were born, both sons: Henry Franklin Higley on August 2, 1880, and Pearl Minson Higley on May 15, 1887.

After a lifetime in Iowa, Henry Higley sold his 156-acre farm near Danville and moved the family to Tustin in 1897. It is highly probable that his decision to move west was influenced by Samuel A. Marchant, a friend and neighbor from Danville. Marchant had moved to Tustin in 1894 and owned a 17-acre walnut and apricot ranch. When Higley arrived in Tustin three years later, he purchased twelve acres on West Sixth Street next to the orchards belonging to his old friend from Danville. Higley grew oranges, walnuts, and apricots on his Tustin property.

The Higleys stayed in Tustin for only about five years, but during that time, they were active in the community. Henry was involved with the local GAR post and served as a deacon at the Santa Ana Congregational Church. Mary was a member of the Women's Relief Corps of the GAR, active in the Ladies' Missionary Society of the Congregational Church, and also taught Sunday school. She was also an active member of the Tustin branch of the Women's Christian Temperance Union.

While they were living in Tustin, their son, Henry "Frank" Higley, served as a private in Santa Ana's Company L of the 7th California Infantry Regiment during the Spanish-American War. By 1902, the family had relocated to Long Beach. Perhaps advancing age and his wartime disabilities were making farming more difficult for Henry. In Long Beach, he worked as a realtor and in 1911 served a term as commander of the Long Beach Post 181 of the GAR.

Mary Higley passed away at the age of seventy on August 21, 1914. At the time of her death, the newspapers were full of articles about the looming war in Europe. Henry survived his wife by almost twenty years. He was living with his son, Pearl, and his family in Lynwood, California, when he passed away on January 15, 1934, at the age of 91. He was buried beside his wife in Sunnyside Cemetery in Long Beach.

Henry Franklin "Frank" Higley almost died from lockjaw around Christmas, 1901. He was treated by a Santa Ana doctor, received a series of shots of anti-tetanus serum over six straight days, and eventually recovered. He went on to graduate from college and, in 1907, married Elma Risser. They had four children: John Devore, Wayne, Ray, and Fay. They lived in Canada for several years before returning to the United States, where Frank worked as a chemist in the oil fields of Long Beach for many years. Elma passed away in 1946, and Frank Higley died on June 8, 1963, and is buried at the National Cemetery in Los Angeles.

Pearl Higley attended the University of Pennsylvania for a year before returning to California, where he married Ruth Luse in 1909. The couple had four children: Harvey, Doris Helen, Emma, and Barbara. They lived at various times in Long Beach, Compton, and Lynwood. Pearl often worked as a carpenter or salesman. Ruth died in 1956, and Pearl passed away in Long Beach on March 12, 1961.

Lewis H. Hillyard

Private, Company D

25th Iowa Infantry

As a young man, Lewis Hillyard was involved in some of the fiercest fighting of the Civil War. After the war, he returned to Iowa and the peaceful occupation of farming and gradually moved west, eventually arriving in Tustin just after the turn of the century.

Lewis Henry Hillyard was born on March 1, 1843, in Monroe County, Ohio, one of eight children of Quaker Jacob and Martha (Eviston) Hillyard. Jacob was a native Pennsylvanian who moved west to Ohio, where he met and married Martha. When Lewis was just five years old, the family traveled by covered wagon to Grant County, Indiana. By 1860, the family had moved west again, this time to Henry County, Iowa, where Jacob and Martha would live the rest of their lives.

Lewis Hillyard was 19 years old when he enlisted for three years' service as a private in Company D, 25th Iowa Infantry. He was mustered in at nearby Burlington, Iowa, on September 12, 1862, along with older brothers George and Paren and younger brother Landen. Paren and Landen would serve with Lewis in Company D for the duration of the war, but sadly, 30-year-old George died of pneumonia at an army hospital in St. Louis on March 8, 1863.

The regiment was first sent north to Minnesota because of recent troubles there with the Sioux. (See the chapter on Harvey B. Lewis for details of the Great Sioux Uprising.)

The regiment then traveled south down the Mississippi River on riverboats and, for the next three years, participated in many of the major battles of the Western Theater; these included the siege of Vicksburg and the battles of Lookout Mountain, Missionary Ridge, Resaca, Kennesaw Mountain, and the campaign for Atlanta. During the siege of Atlanta, Hillyard was less than a hundred yards from General James B. McPherson when the latter was killed by an enemy bullet.

The 25th Iowa was part of Sherman's March to the Sea, then, upon reaching the Georgia coast, traveled through the Carolinas and into Virginia at the close of the war. The regiment then participated in the Grand Review of the Armies in Washington, D.C. Lewis Hillyard was discharged in Rock Island, Illinois, on June 18, 1865, after almost three years of continuous action.

Hillyard participated in some of the fiercest battles of the war, but it was in what can be considered a minor skirmish that he received his only wound. He suffered a gunshot wound in the leg at Cherokee Station, Alabama, on October 21, 1863. The skirmish was small by Civil War standards, with the victorious Union forces suffering only 7 dead and 28 wounded. Hillyard's wound must have been slight, for he quickly recovered and returned to service.

By the end of the war, the 25th Iowa had suffered the loss of 2 officers and 63 enlisted men killed in action or died of wounds. In addition, 2 officers and 207 enlisted men died of illness, making the total fatalities for the regiment 274.

Lewis Hillyard returned to Henry County, Iowa, after the war and on January 19, 1866, married 19-year-old Sarah Jane Kenyon. Lewis and Sarah would spend the next twenty-five years farming in Henry County, and Sarah would give birth to nine children. At some point in the early 1890s, Lewis moved the family to Long Island, Kansas. His older brother Henry had been there since 1884 and was the proprietor of a bakery and lunchroom in town. Lewis and Sarah farmed in Kansas for most of the decade, and while living there in 1898, they lost two of their grown children, a 29-year-old married daughter and a 25-year-old married son.

The Hillyards were back living in Henry County, Iowa, when Sarah passed away on May 29, 1900, at the age of 53. Lewis was left a widower with three children still at home. Shortly after his wife's death, Lewis moved to Tustin. Around the same time, a number of people, including his brother Henry, moved from Long Island, Kansas, to Tustin. Among the transplanted Kansans was a 46-year-old widow, Lovina Franklin. Lovina was part of the social scene in Long Island, and she and Lewis were undoubtedly acquainted.

Lewis and Lovina were married in Tustin on Valentine's Day, 1901. Lovina H. Pugh was born in Indiana and was the widow of Civil War veteran John F. Franklin. She had two grown children at the time of her marriage to Lewis Hillyard.

Lewis and Lovina purchased a citrus ranch on West Main Street in Tustin, near the P.T. Adams ranch. They later moved to a ten-acre walnut ranch on Glen Avenue (later renamed Tustin Avenue). Living with them were the three youngest children from Lewis's first marriage, Della, Vida, and Warren.

Lewis was very involved with the Methodist Episcopal Church in Santa Ana. He not only taught Sunday School but also organized the classes and trained new teachers. He was also an active member of the local GAR post. Lovina was active in the temperance movement and hosted meetings of the Tustin Women's Christian Temperance Union (WCTU) at her home.

In 1910, Lewis sold the Tustin property and moved the family to a house on Main Street in Santa Ana. Two years later, he bought back the same property in Tustin and moved back to the walnut ranch. The family remained in Tustin, except for a year in Utah for Della's health, until moving to Santa Ana for good just before 1920.

By 1920, Lewis and Lovina were making their home on an orange ranch on East Seventeenth Street in Santa Ana; it was there that Lewis Hillyard passed away on October 13, 1928, at the age of

85. His funeral service was performed by the pastor of the Four-Square Gospel Church of Santa Ana, and his graveside ceremony at Santa Ana Cemetery was conducted by members of Sedgwick Post 17 of the GAR.

Five of Lewis Hillyard's nine children preceded him in death. Of the four who survived him, three are buried near him in the family plot at Santa Ana Cemetery. His youngest son, Warren, went on to become prominent in Orange County government. Warren Kenyon Hillyard was born September 27, 1885, in Henry County, Iowa, and was a teenager when he arrived in Tustin with his father. He graduated from Santa Ana High School in 1905 and, in his senior year, was the starting shortstop in a legendary sixteen-inning, 0-0 tie against Fullerton High. The Fullerton pitcher who struck out 35 batters was Walter Johnson, who would go on to pitch many seasons for the Washington Senators and was one of the first players inducted into the Major League Baseball Hall of Fame.

Warren went on to study mining engineering at the University of California and spent three years in Mexico working on an irrigation project. While in Mexico, he survived one of that country's many revolutions. He returned to Orange County in 1912 and began working at the county engineer's office. His work was interrupted while he served as a lieutenant in the 27th Engineers of the 1st Army Corps during World War One, spending seven months overseas in France. He returned home and was appointed County Surveyor in 1923, a position he held until his retirement in 1954. Warren "Cap" Hillyard passed away on January 12, 1965, at 79, and is buried in the family plot at Santa Ana Cemetery.

Upton C. Holderman

Private, Company A

22nd Iowa Infantry

Upton Holderman entered the Union ranks as a teenager
and saw much action in his three years of service. After the war, he
married and spent twenty years in Nebraska before moving to

Southern California in 1893, where he soon became a successful grower and prominent citizen of Tustin.

Upton Christian Holderman was born December 6, 1844, in Rochester, Cedar County, Iowa, to Christian and Mary Ann (Coe) Holderman. Iowa was a territory and considered part of the West at the time of Upton's birth and would be admitted as the twenty-ninth state in the Union two years later.

Christian Holderman died in October 1846, and Mary Ann, who was a widow when she married Holderman, took a third husband, Edwin Morse, in April 1849. In 1851, the new family moved to nearby Johnson County, Iowa. In two subsequent federal census records (1850, 1860), Upton is listed as Upton Morse, although he never legally changed his name to his stepfather's. Edwin and Mary's five daughters, along with Mary's daughter from her first marriage, gave Upton Holderman six half-sisters but no brothers.

Upton Holderman was seventeen years old and working as a farm laborer when he enlisted as a private in Company A, 22nd Iowa Infantry Regiment in August 1862. The 22nd was organized at Iowa City and mustered into Federal service on September 9, 1862. The 22nd was also known as the "Johnson County Regiment", since that county furnished the majority of its recruits. The regiment drilled at Camp Pope near Iowa City in the late summer of 1862 before being sent to Missouri on garrison duty. In 1863, the 22nd Iowa served under Gen. U.S. Grant in the Vicksburg Campaign, where it fought in the battles of Port Gibson, Champion Hill, and Black River Bridge.

After the siege of Vicksburg ended in a Union victory, the regiment was sent to the Texas Gulf Coast and later to Louisiana.

In May 1864, the 22nd was ordered to Virginia, one of only three Iowa regiments to serve in that state. It participated in Gen. Philip Sheridan's Shenandoah Valley Campaign and fought in the bloody third Battle of Winchester and at the Battle of Cedar Creek.

Following Lee's surrender, the regiment served several months of occupation duty in the Carolinas and Georgia before being mustered out of service on July 25, 1865, in Savannah, Georgia. By the end of the war, the 22nd Iowa had lost 6 officers and 108 enlisted men killed in combat. An additional 1 officer and 135 enlisted died of disease for a total of 250 regimental fatalities.

Although on many bloody battlefields during his three years of service, Upton Holderman was never wounded, he did spend a short time in the hospital with mumps. He had close calls, having both his hat and coat punctured by bullets in the heat of battle.

The twenty-year-old veteran returned to Iowa and, on Christmas Day 1867, married Almira Morse. "Myra", a native of Malcom, Iowa, was a second cousin of Upton's Morse half-sisters but no blood relation to him. Their first two children, Ethel (always known as Uppie) and Emma, were born in Iowa in 1869 and 1873. The couple spent the first years of their marriage farming near Iowa City.

In 1873, the Holdermans moved west to Adams County, near Hastings, Nebraska. Upton farmed and also ran a mercantile business. The Holdermans lived in Nebraska for twenty years, and in that time, four more children were born: Myron (1874), Lyda (1880), Nelson (1885), and Upton Grant (1888).

Upton C. Holderman

Myra Morse Holderman

Upton Holderman pulled up stakes after two decades in Nebraska and moved to Tustin in 1893. He purchased twenty acres on Laguna Road, east of Newport Avenue. Of those twenty acres, five were planted to oranges, five to apricots, and ten to walnut trees. He later purchased another ten acres of walnuts about a mile away, near Seventeenth Street and Holt in Tustin.

Holderman was described as well-informed on politics, and, though a Republican, he considered himself a non-partisan on many issues. He cast his first presidential ballot in 1864 for Abraham Lincoln while serving in the army. While in Iowa and Nebraska, he served as a delegate to Republican County conventions. After moving to Tustin, he sat on the Orange County Republican Central Committee for a dozen years and served a four-year term (1903-1907) on the County Board of Supervisors, representing the 5th District. Holderman was also very active in the local Sedgwick Post-17 of the GAR.

Upton C. Holderman died on June 13, 1913, at the age of sixty-eight. He had spent the last two decades of his life in Tustin, where he had become a respected member of the town's agricultural, political, and social circles. He was buried several days later on June 17 at Fairhaven Memorial Park in Santa Ana.

Five years later, Myra married another Civil War veteran, Elwood C. Coate. (Coate had served with the 2nd Iowa Cavalry.) The couple made their home in Orange until Elwood's death on April 22, 1923. Myra was 83 and living with her daughter, Lyda, in San Pedro, California, when she passed away on April 18, 1929. Myra had remained involved in GAR activities over the years and was proud that both of her husbands and two sons were veterans.

Myra was buried at Fairhaven Memorial Park beside her first husband.

Myra & Upton in the family grove, Tustin, c.1913

The following is a brief summary of the lives of Upton and Myra Holderman's six children:

Ethel "Uppie" Holderman married Walter E. Parker on September 21, 1888, in Hastings, Nebraska. The couple had one son, Claude, and lived most of their married life in Omaha, Nebraska. They were still in Omaha as late as 1942, but at some point, they moved to southern California, where Uppie died in 1950. Walter died in Tacoma, Washington, in 1962, and both he and Uppie are buried at Fairhaven Memorial Park in Santa Ana.

Emma Mary Holderman married John C. Lamb in 1900. They had one son, Dana. John was the Orange County Tax

Collector for many years. The couple lived in Santa Ana for a number of years, but by 1925, they had moved to a house on Redhill Avenue north of Irvine Boulevard in Tustin. John Lamb passed away in 1940, and Emma lived another quarter century, passing away on October 25, 1965. She and her husband are buried at Fairhaven.

Myron Charles Holderman served in the Spanish-American War. He was a musician in Company L, 7th California Infantry Regiment. In 1901, he married Grace Tucker, but they divorced in 1911. In 1914, Myron married Alma Leffew of Santa Ana. Both the bride and groom were thirty-nine years old. In 1921, they had their only child, Elwood. The family lived in San Diego, where Myron worked as a carpenter. Alma died in 1933, and Myron passed away on December 4, 1959, and is buried at Fort Rosecrans National Cemetery in San Diego.

Lyda Holderman married fellow Tustin resident William W. Cooker in 1908. They lived for a time in Boise, Idaho, and were together in Seattle in 1916, but then William disappeared from the records. He either died or they were divorced, for in December 1918, Lyda married Eugene Marsh. The couple lived in Los Angeles. Eugene died in 1938, and Lyda passed away on September 21, 1959.

Nelson Miles Holderman married Margaret Arminda Talbott around 1909. The couple had two sons, Charles and Armind, and two daughters, Dorothy and Myra. After starting his military career as a bugler for the local National Guard unit, Nelson Holderman went on to become one of the most decorated American soldiers of World War One. As a Captain in the famous "Lost Battalion," his exploits earned him the Congressional Medal of Honor, the Silver Star, the Purple Heart with two oak clusters, as well as decorations from France, England, and Belgium. He was wounded three times and eventually received a disability retirement. His exploits during the war warrant a book of their own. From 1926 until his death in 1953, he was the Commandant of the Veterans' Soldiers Home in Napa, California. He is buried at the Golden Gate National Cemetery in San Bruno, California. Margarite Holderman passed away in 1969.

Upton Grant Holderman, always known as Grant, married Mina Alice Halderman in 1912. They settled on the fifteen-acre family walnut and orange ranch at Seventeenth and Holt in Tustin. They had two sons, Lloyd and Eugene, and lost an infant daughter in 1915. Grant ran the ranch until his death in 1951. Mina passed away in 1992 at the age of 102. Holderman Park, a small park at Seventeenth and Holt streets, marks what was once the driveway to the Holderman ranch.

L to R: Mina & Grant Holderman, Margarite & Nelson Holderman, Myra, John & Emma Holderman Lamb, William & Lyda Holderman Cooker, seated Upton with grandsons left Charles N. Holderman, right Dana Lamb.
Picture is circa 1913 in Holderman Grove, Tustin.

George W. Hubbard

Private, Co. I 16th New York Infantry

Private, Co. I 121st New York Infantry

George Hubbard was one of only three Tustin Civil War veterans who lived in California before the war. During the war, he served in two New York infantry regiments and endured a stint in a notorious southern prison camp. He returned to California in the early 1880s and, for many years, was a large property owner and citrus grower in Tustin.

George Washington Hubbard was born on February 18, 1832, in Putney, Vermont, one of six children of Abel and Sophia (Miller) Hubbard. Abel was a house painter and a farmer, and George grew up working on the family farm.

By the age of eighteen, George was on his own, living and working on a neighboring farm. In 1852, at twenty, the lure of the Gold Rush led him to California. He sailed from New York to Panama, crossed the isthmus on foot, and then took a boat up the Pacific Coast to California. Rather than prospecting, Hubbard worked for a year on a farm near San Jose, perhaps saving money towards his mining efforts. But his California adventure was cut short after only one year when he received word of his father's death and returned home to help support the family.

In 1857, George married Marcia Wood, a native of Malone, New York. By 1860, the couple was settled on a farm near Malone, and their household included one-year-old son, Clinton, and George's widowed mother. Malone, in northeast New York, is only about ten miles south of the Canadian border.

George W. Hubbard was thirty years old when, on August 30, 1862, he enlisted as a Private in Company I of the 16th New York Infantry Regiment. He enlisted for three years at Malone and was not mustered into the regiment until October 5. The 16th New York had been organized earlier from small towns, assembled at Albany, and mustered into Federal service for two years on May 15, 1861. The regiment was originally known as the "1st Northern New York Infantry." Company I was made up primarily of recruits from Malone.

Because he enlisted over a year after the regiment was formed, George missed the battles the 16th New York fought during the Peninsula Campaign in early 1862 in Virginia. He joined the regiment several weeks after it had participated in the Battle of Antietam, still the single bloodiest day in United States military history.

The first big battle for George Hubbard was the disastrous Union defeat at Fredericksburg in December 1862. Luckily for the 16th New York, it was on picket duty during the battle and avoided much of the slaughter. But Hubbard and the regiment did suffer on the infamous Burnside "Mud March" after the battle.

On May 3 and 4, 1863, the regiment suffered heavy losses at Salem Church, part of the Chancellorsville Campaign, with 20 killed, 87 wounded, and 49 missing. This was undoubtedly the heaviest fighting Hubbard saw while serving with the 16th New York. The 16th, having fulfilled its two years' service, was mustered out on May 23, 1863, at Albany. Those men who had enlisted later for three years, including George Hubbard, were transferred to the 121st New York Infantry regiment at this time.

The 121st New York Infantry Regiment had been mustered in for three years' service in August 1862. Hubbard and his fellow three-year men from the 16th New York were with their new regiment at Gettysburg in July 1863. Hubbard's luck held, as the 121st New York, part of the VI Corps, was held in reserve and suffered no casualties in the greatest battle ever fought on the North American continent. Later, in November 1863, the regiment lost 25 men at the Battle of Rappahannock Station, Virginia.

Beginning in May 1864, the regiment was in one major battle after another as Gen. Ulysses S. Grant used the Army of the Potomac to pound away at the Confederate forces of Gen. Robert E. Lee in Virginia. The 121st New York fought and suffered heavy casualties at The Wilderness and Spotsylvania. At the latter battle, their Corps commander, Gen. John Sedgwick, was killed. He had just remarked, "They couldn't hit an elephant at this distance", when he was struck by a bullet below the left eye. The GAR post in Santa Ana, California, was named in his honor. The 121st was then engaged in the battles of North Anna, Totopotomy, Cold Harbor, and the first great assault on Petersburg.

When Confederate General Jubal Early threatened Washington in July 1864, the VI Corps, with the 121st New York, was ordered to stop him. The regiment was involved in a sharp fight at Fort Stevens. Abraham Lincoln visited the fort and is the only president to come under fire in a battle. The regiment then followed Early's forces up into the Shenandoah Valley. It was in the valley, near Middletown, Virginia, that George Hubbard was captured by Confederate forces on September 24, 1864. A biographical sketch of Hubbard, written in 1911, states that he was captured at the Battle of Strasburg, fought on August 17, 1864. The 121st New York was not at the Battle of Strasburg, and regimental records place his capture at Middletown in September.

Wherever he was captured, George Hubbard was sent to the notorious Libby Prison in Richmond. The prison was a three-story brick warehouse on the James River waterfront. The second and third floors housed the prisoners, and the windows were barred but open to the elements. The overcrowded, unsanitary conditions, combined with malnutrition, made for a mortality rate second only to Andersonville Prison in Georgia.

George Hubbard spent two months or several weeks in this hell-hole, depending on the true date of his capture. On October 9, 1864, he was sent along with over 1,000 other prisoners to Salisbury, North Carolina. With continual new arrivals, Salisbury Prison soon held over 10,000 Union prisoners. Vastly overcrowded, disease ran rampant, and the death rate soared from 2% to 28%. Most of the dead were buried in mass graves. By the end of the war, over 50,000 men had died of disease in prison camps, both North and South.

George Hubbard survived six months of the deplorable conditions at Salisbury Prison before being paroled on March 2, 1865, at North East Bridge, North Carolina. He returned to his unit and was finally discharged at Annapolis, Maryland, on June 26, 1865, completing his three-year enlistment.

The 121st New York finished the war having lost 15 officers and 213 men killed in battle, while 4 officers and 114 men died of disease, including 20 who perished in Confederate prison camps. The high casualty rate of the regiment was undoubtedly due to the heavy fighting it endured during the spring of 1864; Grant's forces had suffered 65,000 casualties in about seven weeks.

George Hubbard returned to civilian life in the summer of 1865. Three years of arduous service and six months confinement in an enemy prison must have surely affected his health. (He would apply for a disability pension in 1877.) He returned to Malone, to his wife, Marcia, and six-year-old Clinton, and to his farming life. Their second and final child, Emma was born in 1867. The

Hubbards would remain in Malone for the next fifteen years and turn their farm into a prospering enterprise.

Apparently, the West still called to him for in 1883 George sold his New York property, put his family on a train, and returned to California, the state he had reluctantly left thirty years earlier. He must have made a nice profit on his New York land, for shortly after arriving in southern California, Hubbard purchased forty acres on Laguna Road in Tustin and a town block of twelve lots. He planted his large acreage to oranges, apricots, and walnuts. He also planted oranges on his town lots.

The Hubbards bought a house in Tustin on the corner of Third and A streets. Built in 1876, the property was originally owned by Barbara Lewis, a sister of town founder, Columbus Tustin. George and Marcia were members of the Baptist church, and in addition to his agricultural pursuits, George was active in the local GAR post.

Daughter Emma married Willard Day in Tustin in January 1889 and was already a widow by the time of her own death in January 1894. She died at her parents' home in Tustin after a lingering illness and was buried at Mount Hope Cemetery in San Diego.

Six years later, on May 27, 1900, Marcia Hubbard died at her home at the age of sixty-five. She and George had been married for forty-three years. She was buried at Fairhaven Memorial Park in Santa Ana.

At the time of Marcia's death, her sister, Alice Macomber, was living with the Hubbards. Perhaps Alice, a widow, was helping to care for her ill sister. Eventually, Alice and George (who was sixteen years her senior) were married. The couple continued to make the house at Third and A Street their home.

Marcia Hubbard

George continued to maintain a prosperous orchard business and a local newspaper article described him as a wealthy hop buyer who spent part of each year in Oregon buying hops. The only place to sell the hops was to breweries, and this almost got him discharged from the Santa Ana Baptist church, which supported the prohibition of alcohol, and actually caused a schism that split the congregation. He also appears to have embraced the conservative politics of his adopted county and on one federal census he described his occupation as "Capitalist." As the years progressed, George turned over the day-to-day operations of his ranch to his son, Clinton.

George W. Hubbard died at his home on A Street on July 22, 1922, at the age of ninety. He had lived an adventurous life; as a youth, he traveled to California for the Gold Rush, fought in many great battles of the Civil War, survived imprisonment, and eventually returned to California to prosper and grow old among the orange blossoms. His funeral was held on July 24, and he was buried beside Marcia at Fairhaven Memorial Park.

Alice Hubbard remained at the house in Tustin, living with Clara, a daughter from her first marriage. Clara Macomber, a teacher, was part of the inaugural faculty of Tustin High School in 1921 and taught at the school for the next twenty-four years. Clara and her mother were still living together when Alice passed away on April 17, 1942, at the age of ninety-three. Clara lived to the age of 100, passing away on February 25, 1978, in Los Angeles. She and her mother are buried at Fairhaven.

George and Marcia's son Clinton S. Hubbard was already a widower by 1900. He had three children: Edith, George, and Ernest. Clinton continued to farm, raising walnuts in Tustin and on leased land in Irvine. He remarried but was a widower again at the time of his death in 1944 at the age of eighty-five. His son, Ernest, remained in Tustin and can be seen in an early group photo of the volunteer fire company.

Clinton S. Hubbard

William A. Jerome

Private, 1st Pennsylvania Cavalry

William Jerome's life is possibly the most interesting and controversial of all the Tustin Civil War veterans. An immigrant from England, after an undocumented Civil War service, Jerome re-enlisted, deserted, and allegedly re-enlisted under an alias. He then served in the cavalry out west and was awarded a Medal of Honor for action against the Apaches in Arizona. A jack-of-all-trades, he came to Tustin in the early 1880s and eventually served as the town's first constable.

William Ambrose Jerome was born July 21, 1846, in London, England. Nothing is known of his parentage or his childhood in England, but we can assume from the quality of his later literary efforts that he received a better-than-average education for a boy of that era. He came to the United States either in 1864, at the age of 18, or around 1861, near the beginning of the Civil War, depending on which source is correct.

The story of William Jerome's military service is in many ways just that- a story. Most of his military information is based on Jerome's family history, much of it not confirmed by records and some of it directly contradicted by those that do exist. The following account of his Civil War and Indian Wars service is based on family lore, with contradictions noted as they occur.

William Jerome enlisted in the 1st Pennsylvania Cavalry regiment shortly after his arrival in America and shortly after the outbreak of the war. He would have been around fifteen years old at this time, and he served with the 1st Pennsylvania throughout the entire war.

The 1st Pennsylvania was organized from July to September 1861. By the end of the war, the regiment had participated in some sixty-six engagements, from small skirmishes to major battles such as Cedar Mountain, Second Bull Run, Fredericksburg, Gettysburg, and Cold Harbor; it was also present at Lee's surrender at Appomattox Courthouse. The regiment suffered a total of 537 casualties by the end of the war, a combination of killed, wounded, missing, captured, and died of disease.

A search of each company roster of the 1st Pennsylvania Cavalry failed to yield a William Jerome or any similar-sounding name. There was a second organization and recruitment drive for the regiment in 1864, and if the 1864 arrival date in America for William Jerome is correct, perhaps he joined the regiment for the final year of the war, and his records have somehow fallen through the cracks.

According to the family story, after the war, William re-enlisted in the regular army only to desert and then re-enlist again under the alias Charles H. Ward. He was supposedly hoping to go west with his new regiment, the 1st US Cavalry, and he was sent to the West Coast to replace the First California Volunteers, who were battling Native American tribes in the region. Jerome/Ward sailed to Panama, crossed the isthmus, and then traveled by boat to San Pedro, California. He moved with his company across the desert to Yuma, Arizona, and eventually to Fort Bowie in southeastern Arizona.

Private Ward, with Troop G of the 1st Cavalry, was one of sixty-one men in a detachment under Capt. R.F. Bernard is pursuing Apaches under Cochise in the Chiricahua Mountains. The troopers were surprised by their prey in a rocky canyon near Chiricahua Pass, and in the initial volley, two troopers were killed and one wounded.

The Apaches held the high ground and were embedded in the rocks. A fierce firefight ensued, lasting from noon until just before sunset. The troopers were then ordered to withdraw to safer positions, and while coming downhill, Ward fell over some rocks and broke his leg.

Darkness ended the battle. The cavalry claimed eighteen dead Apaches, with Ward credited with one of the kills. The army lost two troopers killed and three wounded, including Ward and his broken leg. Lt. John Lafferty had his entire lower jaw shot off, but survived.

In January 1870, Charles H. Ward received the Medal of Honor for "Gallantry in action with Indians at Chiricahua Mountains, Arizona, October 20, 1869." The Battle of Chiricahua Pass saw 33 of the 61 soldiers involved receive the Medal of Honor, more than any other battle in the history of the U.S. Army.

Ward's Medal of Honor, along with its documentation, was donated to the Tustin Area Museum in 1980 by William A. Jerome's grandson. An accompanying letter stated that Jerome chose the alias Ward because it was his wife's maiden name. One theory is that Jerome knew his wife's family in England and sent for her when he left the service, marrying her in 1875, the year she arrived in America.

An army enlistment register lists William Jerome, age 21, from England, who enlisted on August 19, 1867, in Company G, 3rd US Artillery, in New York. He was described on the enlistment rolls as 5 feet 10 inches tall, with a fair complexion, light hair, and green eyes; his occupation was listed as a casket maker. That same enlistment register lists Jerome as a deserter as of June 26, 1868.

Charles H. Ward enlisted in Co. G, 1st US Cavalry, on June 23, 1868, in Philadelphia, three days prior to Jerome's reported desertion date. It is hard to reconcile these two dates with the Jerome/Ward assumed-name story, unless his desertion occurred earlier and was not officially recorded until the June date. The last record of Charles H. Ward is the 1870 Federal Census, where he appears with the other members of Troop G at Fort Bowie, Arizona Territory. He was twenty-three years old and a native of England. William Jerome was exactly twenty-three years old in June 1870 and was a native of England. Also, Ward's enlistment papers listed him as 5 feet, 11 inches tall, very close to Jerome's height. Once again, it should be stated that there are too many similarities and too many contradictions to make a positive determination of the validity of the Jerome/Ward alias story. It should be noted that after his discharge for disability in 1870, Charles H. Ward disappears from the records; even the Medal of Honor Society has no record of his death or burial site.

**Fort Bowie, Arizona Territory, nestled among
the Chiricahua Mountains.**

Regardless of the true story of his military service, William Jerome resurfaced in Los Angeles in the mid-1870s, where he joined the growing city's police force. Los Angeles in the 1870s was just coming out of its wild frontier phase, but was still a dangerous place to live, boasting one of the highest murder rates in the country.

By all accounts, Jerome was a capable and well-liked police officer. The Los Angeles newspapers of the era were filled with stories describing Jerome arresting robbery suspects, disarming a bayonet-wielding attacker, nabbing burglars in the act, staking out would-be gold thieves, and raiding an illegal gambling den; he was even credited with foiling two suicide attempts. He was also injured in the line of duty in 1878 and couldn't work for a month. He performed all these dangerous duties for $95 per month.

In September 1875, William married Martha F. Ward in Los Angeles. It was a busy year for Martha, like her husband, a native of London. She had left England, landed in San Francisco, moved down to Los Angeles, and married William Jerome, all in 1875. Martha, born in London on September 25, 1854, was sent to America by her brothers for her health.

The couple's first two children, both sons, were born in Los Angeles: William C. (1876) and Benjamin W. (1878). In 1879, the family left Los Angeles and moved to Olive, near Orange. Their first daughter, Martha Louisa, was born there in 1880. The following year, on September 25, 1881 (Martha's twenty-seventh birthday), they moved to Tustin.

Shortly after arriving in town, William built a house on A Street that would remain their home for most of their years in Tustin. Their last two children, daughters Nellie (1883) and Estelle (1887), were born in Tustin.

William was employed as a plasterer, a trade he learned in Philadelphia. In addition, he worked as a cement contractor and probably laid some of the first cement sidewalks in Tustin. He was a jack-of-all-trades who reportedly excelled at any job he took on. He was also Tustin's first constable, serving from January 1890 to January 1891. Undoubtedly, patrolling the quiet village of Tustin lacked the excitement of his law enforcement days in Los Angeles. It has been reported that he never arrested anyone in Tustin but kept an eye on possible troublemakers.

Apparently, William possessed a sharp wit and lively sense of humor and cultivated a wide circle of friends in town. One local "old-timer", when asked to name the most unforgettable character he knew in Tustin, didn't hesitate when he answered, Mr. Jerome. He was also a popular member of several fraternal organizations and an active member of Sedgwick Post 17 of the GAR in Santa Ana.

Perhaps it was his local popularity, combined with his law enforcement experience, that earned him the Republican nomination for sheriff in the inaugural election for the newly formed Orange County in 1889. His run was unsuccessful, as he lost to R.T. Harris, but he ran again three years later on the same Populist Party ticket that sent fellow Tustin veteran Charles F. Bennett to the state legislature. Jerome's election bid failed again, losing this time to Theo Lacy of Santa Ana.

Jerome was also a prolific writer. Under the pen name MUM, he supplied local newspapers with newsworthy items from Tustin and also wrote a weekly column recounting incidents from the early days in southern California. His writing was stylish and sprinkled with literary and historical allusions, demonstrating that he was well educated and possessed an impressive vocabulary.

On August 20, 1900, William Jerome was putting the finishing touches on the cement sidewalk in front of the Westcott place in Tustin when he was stricken with a fatal heart attack. The popular veteran had just turned fifty-four the previous month. He was buried at Fairhaven Memorial Park in Santa Ana, with fellow Civil War veteran Upton C. Holderman among the pallbearers. Jerome, Tustin's first peace officer, had certainly led a colorful, exciting, and intriguing life in his adopted country.

William Jerome is at the far left in the back row. A jack-of-all trades, he was apparently working at a packinghouse in 1900, shortly before his death.

Martha Jerome survived her husband by just over twenty years. She was well known and popular in the Tustin, Irvine, and Santa Ana communities. She had a reputation for always being willing to nurse a sick neighbor, no matter the distance involved. Martha was a charter member of the Sycamore Rebekah Lodge 140, a women's fraternal organization associated with the Odd Fellows, established in 1888. She was living with her daughter, Louisa Jerome, in Irvine when she passed away on January 28, 1921, at age 66. She was buried beside her husband at Fairhaven Memorial Park.

The children of William A. Jerome and Martha F. Ward were:

- William Centennial Jerome was born in Los Angeles on July 4, 1876, the one hundredth anniversary of the signing of the Declaration of Independence, hence the unique middle name. He was five years old when his father moved the family to Tustin, and he grew up attending Tustin schools and was an active member of the Tustin Boys Brigade.

Around the turn of the century, William married Annie R. Gould, who, like his parents, was a native of England and came to America in 1886 at the age of twelve. The couple eventually had four children, two sons, Donald and William C. Jr., and two daughters, Anita and Muriel. In the early years of their marriage, they lived in Tustin, then in Irvine, where William was a bean farmer in partnership with his younger brother Benjamin. In 1914, William ran for and was elected Auditor of Orange County, holding the position until 1931. (The primary responsibility of an auditor is to prepare the county budgets, assign tax values to properties, and issue vendor licenses.) He was a county supervisor from 1933 to 1937, and then served as the Santa Ana purchasing agent and auditor from 1942 until his retirement in 1947. For many years, the family lived on North Poinsettia Street in Santa Ana. Annie passed away on March 17, 1945, one week shy of her seventy-first birthday. William C. Jerome died on December 4, 1954 at the age of seventy-eight. He and Annie are both buried at Melrose Abbey Memorial Park in Anaheim, California. Jerome Park in Santa Ana is named for William C. Jerome and his son, William Jr., in recognition of their many years of service in city government.

- Benjamin W. Jerome was born January 15, 1878, in Los Angeles. He was just three years old when the family moved to Tustin. Like his older brother, he attended Tustin schools and was also a member of the Tustin Boys Brigade. In 1902, he married Effie Smithwick, a young school teacher from Santa Ana. Effie was the

granddaughter of Noah Smithwick, a legendary Texas
frontiersman and a contemporary and acquaintance of
Davy Crockett, Sam Houston, and Jim Bowie. Known
for his storytelling abilities, Smithwick described early
Texas as "Heaven for men and dogs, hell for women
and oxen."

For a number of years, Benjamin, Effie, and their only
child, Benjamin E. Jerome, lived on a 320-acre ranch
north of Irvine. In partnership with his brother William,
he ran a farming operation on 800 acres of leased land
at Whiting Ranch. The brothers also owned and farmed
200 acres of their own, 160 in the Imperial Valley, and
40 near Tustin.

At some point in the early 1930s, possibly driven by the
economic realities of the Great Depression, Benjamin
moved the family to Carlsbad, New Mexico, where he
owned and operated a fertilizer plant. It was truly a
family affair, with their son, his wife, and three children
living with them, and the younger Benjamin working
for his father.

Sadly for Benjamin and Effie, their only son passed
away in December 1949 at the age of forty-four.
Benjamin W. Jerome died on October 13, 1960, at the
age of eighty-two. Effie followed him five years later
and was buried beside her husband and son at Carlsbad
Cemetery in Carlsbad, New Mexico.

- Martha Louisa Jerome was born on October 26, 1880,
  during the family's short time in Olive, near Orange,
  California, and was just an infant when the Jeromes
  settled in Tustin. Always known by her middle name,
  Louisa never married and, over the years, supported
  herself with a number of different jobs. In 1910, the
  thirty-year-old was the live-in housekeeper for the
  James Irvine family, owners of the large Irvine Ranch.

Ten years later, Louisa was leasing and farming 200 acres of the Irvine Ranch with help from her brothers. By 1930, she was living in Santa Ana with her brother William and his family and working as a clerk in the sheriff's office.

She continued to work for the county and lived with her brother for a number of years. She passed away on August 10, 1960, at seventy-nine and is buried at Fairhaven Memorial Park in Santa Ana.

- Nellie Jerome was born on May 17, 1883, in Tustin. She was 27 when she married Chester E. Stone in Los Angeles. In the early years of their marriage, they lived in Irvine, where Chester worked as a ranch foreman for his brothers-in-law. By 1930, the Stones had three sons and were living in Los Angeles. Perhaps hard hit by the Depression, Chester was now employed as an elevator operator. The couple remained in Los Angeles the rest of their lives and both died relatively young. Chester passed away on November 20, 1941, at the age of 60, and Nellie died two days before Christmas in 1946, at the age of 63. They are both buried at Forest Lawn Cemetery in Glendale, California.

- Estelle Jerome was born on Christmas Eve, 1888, in Tustin and was only eleven years old when her father died in the summer of 1900. She was twenty-three years old when she married Donald Rudd in Los Angeles on February 25, 1912. Donald was born in England and came to America with his family in 1893, at age 5. The couple had two daughters, Elizabeth and Martha. Donald worked his entire career as a projectionist at movie theaters, first in Los Angeles and then for a time in Seattle before returning to Southern California. Donald Rudd died December 28, 1948, in Los Angeles at the age of sixty. Estelle passed away on May 15,

1971, at the age of eighty-two and was buried beside
her husband at Forest Lawn Cemetery in Glendale,
California.

Lorenzo B. Kiser

Private, Co. B, 1st Battalion

17th United States Infantry

Lorenzo Kiser answered the call of his country at the tender age of sixteen, and his service sent him to the battlefields of Virginia, to a fort in New York Harbor, and to the swamplands of south Texas. After the war, he spent three decades on the plains of Nebraska before moving to Tustin early in the new century, where he would live out the rest of his life.

Lorenzo Brown Kiser was born April 15, 1847, in Somerset County, Pennsylvania, the oldest of John and Isabella (Allen) Kiser's six children. In Somerset, John Kiser worked as a carpenter, but by 1860, he had moved his family to a farm near Dixon, in Lee County, Illinois. (Dixon would later serve as the hometown for a future US president, Ronald Reagan.)

Lorenzo Kiser was two months shy of his seventeenth birthday when he traveled to nearby Amboy, Illinois, and enlisted for three years as a private in Company B, 1st Battalion, 17th United States Infantry. Army regulations required recruits to be 18 to enlist, but this could be circumvented by a note from a parent or by simply lying about one's age. It is not known which method young Lorenzo used, but it should be noted that recruiting officers were usually more concerned about filling their quotas than following regulations to the letter. His enlistment papers from February 16, 1864, described him as 5'8" tall with blue eyes, dark hair, and a light complexion. The 17th US Infantry was a regular army unit, created by an act of Congress and organized in 1861. It was assigned to the Fifth Corps of the Army of the Potomac and suffered heavy casualties at the Battle of Fredericksburg in late 1862 and at the Battle of Gettysburg in July 1863.

Kiser's Company B joined the regiment in the field on June 8, 1864, during the Battle of Cold Harbor in Virginia, but most of the heavy fighting of the battle had taken place days earlier. The 17th Infantry then participated in the Siege of Petersburg and, in August 1864, fought at the Battle of Weldon Railroad.

By October 1864, the regiment was so reduced in numbers from both casualties and illness that it was removed from the front in Virginia and sent to garrison Fort Lafayette in New York Harbor. At Fort Lafayette, the men of the 17th served as guards at the military prison located there.

The prison held Confederate POWs as well as political prisoners. The fort was built on a rock island between Staten Island and Long Island and at one time housed Confederate naval officer William T. Glassell, a brother of Andrew Glassell, one of the founders of Orange, California.

The regiment served at Fort Lafayette for a year and then, in October 1865, was transferred to a post on Long Island Sound. The war had ended in April 1865, and a year later, the 17th Infantry was ordered to Texas and traveled by sea, landing in Galveston in late April 1866.

The various companies of the regiment spread out to different points in Texas on Reconstruction Duty, protecting the newly freed slaves and northern sympathizers from the wrath of the defeated Texans. Kiser's Company B was sent to Hempstead, a small town northwest of Houston. In 1867, a Yellow Fever epidemic broke out in the area and killed 120 men of the 17th Infantry. Fortunately for Kiser, he had been discharged in February 1867, having fulfilled his three-year enlistment.

An artist's rendering of Fort Lafayette in New York Harbor

Although he had served for three years in the war, Lorenzo Kiser was still two months shy of his twentieth birthday when he was discharged and returned to his parents' farm in Dixon.

On March 7, 1875, Lorenzo married Catherine "Kate" Berkey in Dixon. Kate was also a native of Somerset, Pennsylvania. She was the daughter of Henry Berkey, a minister of the Reformed Church, and Louisa Lucy Philson. Her parents remained in Somerset, so it is unclear how Kate came to be in Illinois, though she was 28 at the time of the wedding.

Lorenzo and Kate stayed in Dixon for three years, then in 1878 moved to Seward County, Nebraska, where they would remain for the next thirty years. The couple had six children: Lucy,

Olive, Edmund, Harry, Dudley, and John. Lorenzo supported his family by farming and doing carpentry work.

In January 1908, Lorenzo and Kate visited their married daughter Lucy at her home in Tustin. They stayed several weeks and, perhaps comparing the winter weather of southern California to the frigid Midwest, moved to Tustin before the end of the year. Lorenzo and Kate were both 61 years old when they moved to Tustin, first renting a house on Glen (now Tustin) Avenue. Lorenzo plied his trade as a carpenter, and his sons, Henry and John, took odd jobs to help support the family. Eventually, they would own a home on C Street, where they would live for the rest of their lives.

The family finances must have been in order, for local newspapers articles of the time mention a number of trips to Catalina Island and several long vacations back to see relatives.

One vacation lasted three months, and in 1914, Lorenzo and Kate spent eight months visiting relatives and friends in Nebraska, Kansas, Illinois, and Pennsylvania. So, although he was still working as a carpenter, it appears Lorenzo may have been semi-retired.

Kate Kiser passed away at the home on C Street on August 4, 1924, at the age of seventy-seven. Her funeral service was conducted by Rev. W.S. McDougall, the pastor of the Tustin Presbyterian church, and she was buried at Fairhaven Cemetery in Santa Ana. Lorenzo survived his wife by just five months, dying on January 25, 1925, at the age of seventy-seven. Rev. McDougall once again performed the services, and Lorenzo was laid to rest beside his wife at Fairhaven. Lorenzo was a member of Sedgwick Post 17, so it is surprising that his fellow veterans did not perform the graveside ceremonies.

The children of Lorenzo Kiser and Catherine "Kate" Berkey were:

- Lucy Belle Kiser was born November 24, 1877, in Dixon, Illinois. On June 4, 1903, she married a cousin, Ira F. Kiser, in Lincoln, Nebraska. Ira had enlisted in the army in 1899 and served in the Philippines. The marriage was short-lived, with Ira dying on February 5, 1905, at the age of twenty-seven, at their home in Pleasant Dale, Nebraska.

  Two years later, on May 25, 1907, Lucy married Charles Martin Pilgrim in Tustin. Charles was born in Buffalo, New York, but raised in Nebraska, and that is probably where he and Lucy met. On the morning of the wedding, Charles met her at the train station in Los Angeles, and they were married at their future home at Newport Road and McFadden Street by the pastor of the Tustin Presbyterian Church. The couple did not stay in Tustin long. By 1910, they were farming in Tulare County, California, but within two years, they had settled in Oceanside, California. The couple had no children, and Charles passed away on June 21, 1942, at the age of seventy-four, at their home in Oceanside. Lucy died five years later on August 17, 1947, at the age of sixty-nine and was buried beside her husband at Oceanview Cemetery in Oceanside.

- Olive May Kiser was born July 9, 1880, in Nebraska. On March 5, 1901, twenty-year-old Olive married Theodore W. Bose in Lincoln, Nebraska. For the next twenty years, the couple farmed near Emerson, Harlan County, Nebraska. The couple had three children, Frank Verne, June Catherine, and Theodore John. By 1924, they had joined the rest of the Kisers in southern California, living on First Street in Santa Ana. Theodore Bose died in 1945, and Olive passed away six years later, on May 9, 1951, and was buried beside her husband at Fairhaven Memorial Park in Santa Ana.

- Edmond Lee Kiser was born March 1, 1883 in Nebraska. Ed was twenty-two when he married Rosetta Kopies on March 30, 1905, in Lincoln, Nebraska. Their son Lee was born in 1907 in Emerald, Nebraska, and shortly after, the family moved to Tustin - around the same time as Ed's parents. Their other child, Bernice, was born in Tustin in 1909, and shortly after, Ed moved the family back to Nebraska. Their return to Nebraska was short-lived, for in the fall of 1911, they returned to Tustin, and this time they stayed. Ed was a carpenter and contractor who built many houses in the Tustin area, some in partnership with William Bowman.

  Ed Kiser was also involved in a number of civic activities. He was an early member of the Tustin volunteer fire department, and a 1940 city directory lists him as the fire chief. When Tustin was incorporated in 1927, Ed was elected to the first city council that met in the Knights of Pythias building. Ed Kiser passed away on November 28, 1946, and was buried at Fairhaven Memorial Park. Rosetta died on November 16, 1971, at the age of 90 and was buried beside her husband.

- Harry Thomas Kiser was born May 19, 1885, in Seward County, Nebraska, and came to Tustin with his parents in 1908. On December 12, 1912, in Tustin, he married Florence Virginia Brookbank, a twenty-four-year-old native of Iowa. Shortly after the wedding, they moved to Orange, where Harry was employed as an engineer at the Orange waterworks. By 1920, the couple, who had no children, were back in Tustin. At one time, Harry owned and operated a restaurant in town, worked as a salesman, and also served on the volunteer fire company with his older brother, Ed. Harry and Florence owned a home on San Juan Street, but by 1940, they had moved to Anaheim, where he worked as a farm laborer, and she was employed as a sorter in a packinghouse. Harry Kiser died on July 18, 1960, at the age of seventy-five. Florence passed away five years later on September 8, 1965, and was buried beside her husband at Fairhaven Memorial Park.

- Dudley Cameron Kiser was born November 19, 1888, in Nebraska, and as a young man came to California with his parents in 1908. On May 5, 1914, he married Alice Ruth Matthews in Tustin. The couple had two children, Charles and Barbara. At the time of his wedding, Dudley was employed by the Tustin Lumber Company, but he held many jobs over the course of his life: carpenter, aluminum salesman, and store manager, to name a few. In the 1930s, Alice helped out, working in the local citrus packinghouses. In 1915, Dudley had a house built on C Street, across from the new schoolhouse, but from 1920 on, he and Alice lived on Redhill Avenue in Tustin. Dudley Kiser died on October 18, 1959, at the age of seventy. Alice passed away on April 10, 1984, at ninety-one and was buried beside her husband at Fairhaven Memorial Park.

- John Russell Kiser was born in Milford, Nebraska, on December 31, 1890, and came to Tustin with his parents as a teenager. On October 22, 1912, John married Jessie E. De Baun. Jessie, a native of Passaic, New Jersey, was working as a live-in maid for the Charles Artz family in Tustin, and John was employed by the Tustin Lumber Company. The couple had three children, Bonnie, Lois, and Warren. John was a cabinetmaker for 50 years and was employed by various lumberyards in the area. The family lived on 2nd Street, but for the last twenty years, made their home at 240 S. Prospect in Tustin. John Kiser died on August 7, 1966, at the age of seventy-five. Jessie

passed away three years later on March 6, 1969, and
was buried beside her husband at Fairhaven Memorial
Park.

Henry Kissel

Private, Company C

192nd Pennsylvania Infantry

Henry Kissel's service in the Civil War was short; he spent just seven months in uniform before being mustered out. Like many of the Tustin Civil War veterans, Henry moved to Nebraska after the war, eventually moving to Tustin in the early 1880s.

Henry Kissel was born February 21, 1839, in Pennsylvania, the sixth of Henry and Catherine (Morningstar) Kissel's seven children. By 1860, the twenty-one-year-old Henry was married and working as a blacksmith in Lower Swatara, Dauphin County, Pennsylvania. His wife was fellow Pennsylvania native Catherine Tyler. The couple's first child, Mary Catherine, was born in November 1861.

Henry registered for the draft in June 1863 but was apparently not called to serve at that time. Congress had just passed the country's first military draft law in March, and it proved very unpopular. In fact, a violent draft riot occurred in New York City in July 1863, and President Lincoln was forced to send troops fresh from the battlefield at Gettysburg to quell the disturbance. It is estimated that over one hundred people were killed in the riot, mostly African-American citizens of the city.

Henry Kissel was just days shy of his twenty-sixth birthday when, on February 9, 1865, he enlisted as a private in Company C, 192nd Pennsylvania Infantry regiment. Company C was one of nine new companies organized at Harrisburg. The regiment soon moved to Harpers Ferry, West Virginia, and then proceeded to Staunton and Lexington, Virginia. By this time, the war was almost over, and the 192nd saw little or no fighting. Henry Kissel was mustered out with the rest of his regiment on August 24, 1865, having served seven months. In that short time, the 192nd Pennsylvania suffered no combat fatalities but did lose sixteen enlisted men who died of disease.

Shortly after the war ended, Henry and Catherine headed west, settling in Blue Springs, Nebraska. Blue Springs is in Gage County in the southeastern portion of the state, near the Kansas border. Their second and final child, Anna, was born there in 1868. Their oldest daughter, Mary, was 16 when she married Herbert D. Godfrey in Blue Springs on November 14, 1876.

By 1880, the Kissels had moved again, this time some 260 miles south to Wellington in Sumner County, Kansas. It is unclear how the family supported itself because the 1880 federal census lists Henry as unemployed and blind.

The Kissel family moved to Tustin in 1881, where on February 1, 1887, Annie married Thomas Cummins. The minister who married the young couple was Gardner Godfrey, Mary's father-in-law, so it appears Mary and her family had relocated to California by this time. Annie's husband had a younger sister, Maggie Cummins, who eventually became the second wife of C.E. Utt, a prominent Tustin grower and businessman. (In 1880, the large Cummins family was also living in Sumner County, Kansas, so Annie and Thomas may have known each other before marrying in California.)

At the turn of the century, Henry and Catherine were residing on McFadden Avenue in Tustin. Catherine passed away on May 13, 1902, at the age of sixty-three. At some point after the death of his wife, Henry moved in with his widowed daughter, Mary Godfrey, at her home in Los Angeles. He was still living with Mary, blind and eighty-one years old, when he died on March 23, 1920. The local GAR post assisted at his burial when he was laid to rest beside Catherine at Santa Ana Cemetery.

Mary Catherine (Kissel) Godfrey was widowed when her husband, Herbert Godfrey, died on August 29, 1897, in Los

Angeles. She and Herbert had two daughters, Myrtle Chloe Godfrey and Mabel Claire Godfrey. Mary passed away on April 12, 1953, in Santa Monica at the age of ninety-one and was buried at Rosedale Cemetery in Los Angeles.

Anna Idella (Kissel) Cummins divorced Thomas Cummins sometime before 1910. They had two children, Carl C. Cummins and Irene Cummins. Anna died on April 10, 1936, in San Diego at the age of sixty-eight. She is buried beside her parents in Santa Ana Cemetery.

**Henry and Catherine Kissel's
tombstones in Santa Ana Cemetery**

Henry Leck

Private

5th Iowa Militia

German-born Henry Leck served with a state militia unit in Iowa during the war. After the war, he farmed for many years in southeast Nebraska before moving to Tustin around 1890.

Henry Leck was born in Germany on November 15, 1835, the son of Frederick and Martha Leck. When he was five years old, Henry sailed with his family to America, arriving at Philadelphia on August 12, 1841. The family settled near Plumcreek, in Armstrong County, Pennsylvania, where Henry was raised working on the family farm.

At some point in the mid-1850s, Henry moved west to Illinois, where he married Mariah Scott around 1856. Mariah was born in Pike County, Ohio, in 1837, but grew up in Illinois. The first of Henry and Mariah's five children was born in Illinois, the second in Kansas Territory, before the couple settled in Iowa. They were living on a farm near Indian Creek, in Story County, at the outbreak of the Civil War.

During the war, Leck served as a private in a state militia unit. Being a married man with three young children at home (a second son was born in 1862) may have kept him from enlisting in a federal army regiment. Over the course of the war, Iowa enlisted two militia brigades. The Northern Border Brigade served from September 1862 to September 1863 and was called up over fear that the Sioux uprising in Minnesota would spread south. The Southern Border Brigade, consisting of four battalions, was called out to protect the southern portion of Iowa from the depredations of southern sympathizers from Missouri.

Henry had two brothers, Adam and John, who served in Pennsylvania regiments during the war. The Leck brothers were just three of the 216,000 German-born men who served in the Union ranks during the Civil War, the largest body of foreign-born men, with immigrant Irish soldiers second at around 150,000.

After the war, Henry and Mariah moved to a farm in Nemaha County in southeastern Nebraska. Their family now consisted of four sons, James, Jasper, Emmet, and Andrew, and a daughter, Medora. Henry farmed in Nemaha County for twenty years, but at some point in the 1870s, he and Mariah divorced.

In 1880, Henry married Alice Muzzy, a thirty-year-old widow from Florida. The Leck farm in Nebraska prospered, but eventually Henry decided to move west. In September 1889, he held a public sale of his farm property that included 120 head of cattle, 85 hogs, 10 horses, 75 acres of corn in the field, as well as all of his furniture and farm implements.

The revenue from this sale must have financed his move west, and he first appears in Tustin on an Orange County voter registration list from 1892. At the time, the 56-year-old immigrant was described as 5 feet, 8 inches tall, with dark complexion, blue eyes, and gray hair.

Henry would live the rest of his life on his farm in Tustin. He passed away there on February 13, 1905, at the age of 69 and was buried at Santa Ana Cemetery.

Two of Henry Leck's sons also chose to make Southern California their home. Oldest son John, born in March 1857 in Illinois, arrived in Santa Ana in 1891 and eventually owned his own machine shop there. He was visiting a daughter in Long Beach when he passed away on August 24, 1937, at the age of 80 and was buried at Santa Ana Cemetery.

Henry's second son, Jasper, became well known in Orange County politics, serving as County Supervisor representing the 5th

District from 1911-1919. Born November 28, 1862, in Story County, Iowa, Jasper came to Tustin in the early 1890s. He was a farmer and lived with his wife, Catherine, for many years at 340 W. Main Street in Tustin before eventually moving to Laguna Beach. Jasper Leck passed away on March 21, 1943, at the age of 80 and is also buried at Santa Ana Cemetery.

Harvey B. Lewis

Corporal, Company H

30th Wisconsin Infantry

Harvey Lewis spent much of his Civil War service fighting Native Americans rather than Confederate soldiers. After the war, he became one of the early settlers of Tustin and eventually was the first postmaster of the town who was not a member of the Tustin family.

Harvey Boardman Lewis was born in 1841 in upstate New York to Chauncey and Mary Lewis. The Lewis family eventually moved west, and in 1860, Harvey was working on the family farm near Greenbush, Sheboygan County, Wisconsin. Although Wisconsin had achieved statehood in 1848, it was still considered part of the Northwest Frontier when the Lewis family arrived.

On August 18, 1862, twenty-one-year-old Harvey Lewis answered President Lincoln's call for 300,000 volunteers and enlisted in Company H of the 30th Wisconsin Infantry Regiment at Auroraville in Waushara County. Company H was made up of men primarily from that county.

The regiment was organized at Camp Randall in Madison and officially mustered into Federal service on October 21, 1862. The majority of the men in the 30th Wisconsin were lumbermen, farmers, miners, and even a number of Native Americans from the Chippewa Reservation.

The 30th Wisconsin had a very diverse service record during the war. The regiment was seldom together at one time, and it never participated in any significant battle against Confederate forces. In the summer of 1863, various companies of the regiment were sent to different parts of the state to maintain order during disturbances caused by the unpopular draft. The draft law allowed men to furnish a substitute or pay $300 to be exempted. The $300 was beyond the means of most workingmen and gave rise to the feeling that it was a "rich man's war and a poor man's fight." $300 in 1863 had the same buying power as $6,564 current dollars. In the Confederacy, a man was exempted from the draft if he was an overseer on a plantation or owned over twenty slaves, and was equally unpopular among the working class.

One who evaded the draft by fleeing to Canada was a young student at the University of Wisconsin, the future naturalist John Muir.

In the spring of 1864, detachments from the regiment were sent to the Dakota Territory and northwestern Minnesota to aid in the campaign against the Sioux and took part in several engagements with the rebelling tribe. Company H, along with three other companies of the 30th Wisconsin, built and garrisoned Fort Rice in Dakota Territory along the Missouri River.

Two summers prior to this, in August and September 1862, settlers in Minnesota fought the Dakota Sioux in what became known as the Great Sioux Uprising. When it was over, some 800 settlers, mostly German immigrants, and an unknown number of Sioux were dead. It is second only to the terrorist attacks of 9/11 in terms of civilian casualties on US soil.

In a sad postscript to the uprising, the army rounded up 303 Sioux warriors and a military tribunal found them all guilty of murder and sentenced them to hang. President Lincoln commuted most of the sentences but left 38 stand, and on December 26, 1862, all 38 Sioux were hanged in a single drop, the largest legally sanctioned execution in American history.

On October 12, 1864, Lewis and Company H left Fort Rice in Dakota Territory and floated down the Missouri River on flatboats they had built, arriving on November 2 at Sioux City, Iowa. (They were replaced at Fort Rice by a unit consisting of former Confederate prisoners who had pledged allegiance to the

Union to avoid further captivity.) From Iowa City, they continued their descent down the river, but their way was blocked by ice, and Company H had to abandon their boats and march the final few miles to St. Joseph, Missouri, arriving on November 17. They left St. Joseph the next day by train and eventually arrived at Louisville, Kentucky, by the end of the month.

The remainder of the 30th Wisconsin's service was spent in Kentucky. They acted as guards for the military prison in Louisville, were garrisoned at Bowling Green, and also engaged in chasing and capturing rebel guerrillas in the region.

The regiment was mustered out in Louisville on September 20, 1865, but by then Harvey Lewis was already gone. He had been discharged four months earlier on May 23, 1865. Perhaps he was ill or otherwise incapacitated. This is highly probable, for on June 14, 1865, less than a month after his discharge, he applied for a disability pension.

Shortly after the war, Lewis moved west to Goodhue County, Minnesota, where he married Theresa Hilton, a native of Maine, on October 24, 1867. She was the daughter of Ebenezer and Eliza Hilton. Harvey and Theresa had two sons, both born in Kenyon, Minnesota: Percy in 1868 and Perry in 1869. Harvey and Theresa lived with her parents, but each owned their own parcel of land. The two families moved to Tustin together in 1876, becoming among the town's early settlers.

Lewis initially purchased a ten-acre tract of land north of the future high school site, but sold it during the land boom of the 1880s. (After the boom collapsed, he bought back the entire ten-acre tract.) In 1884, he bought 20 acres at Main and Newport Road in Tustin, and this became the family's permanent home, first known as the Lewis Addition and later as the Lewis Ranch. The Lewis home was a two-story house at the southeast corner of Main Street and Newport Road.

Lewis was active in the new community. In 1879, he became a member of the three-person Sycamore (Tustin) School Board and, in 1889, acted as a poll inspector at the election to create Orange County. Also, in 1889, he was appointed Postmaster of Tustin, succeeding Martha Tustin, the town's founder's daughter. For the first two years of Lewis' tenure as postmaster, the mail was delivered to the Santa Fe depot on Newport Road, but in 1891, the Railway Post Office was taken off the Tustin route, and Tustin's mail was then dropped off at Aliso Station, about a mile southwest of town. Franklin Crawford and his son, Ernest, had the job of transporting the outgoing mail to the Aliso Station and returning with the mail destined for Tustin residents.

The job of postmaster in a small town was not well compensated. The postmaster received as a salary only what he collected from selling stamps; for a small town like Tustin, this could not have been much. The original post office was on the ground floor of the two-story Columbus Tustin building. About the time of Lewis' appointment, the post office moved to a small building next door, with the post office lock boxes located on the right wall as you entered. The citizens of Tustin were required to pick up their mail at the post office until Rural Free Delivery (RFD) began in the early 1900's, but home delivery in the city limits did not begin until 1948.

While serving as postmaster, Harvey continued his ranching operations with the help of his son Perry. Older son Percy had died of typhoid fever on October 21, 1885, at the age of seventeen.

On June 19, 1898, four years after his term as postmaster ended, fifty-seven-year-old Tustin Civil War veteran Harvey Lewis was stricken with a fatal heart attack at his home. He was buried at Fairhaven Memorial Park in Santa Ana. Theresa Lewis stayed on at the Lewis Ranch, living with her son Perry, and passed away on March 17, 1925, at the age of eighty. She was buried next to Harvey at Fairhaven Cemetery.

**The Tustin Post Office in center with the two-story
Tustin Building on right**

Harvey and Theresa's surviving son, Perry Lewis, went on to become a successful grower and businessman in Tustin. For a time, he ran a general store in partnership with C.E. Utt on Main and D Street in Tustin. Later, he opened a candy and ice-cream shop in Santa Ana. Following his father's death, he took over the family's ranching operations and lived in the family home with his mother. He also expanded his acreage, purchasing land in north Tustin, and was a member and leader of numerous fraternal and agricultural organizations.

Three years after the death of his mother, fifty-eight-year-old Perry finally married. His bride, also fifty-eight, was the renowned artist and author Minnie Childs. The couple had endured a thirty-five-year courtship, their romance having begun at the

Chicago World's Fair in 1893! Their home became the center for arts and literature in Tustin. Minnie passed away in Tustin on December 23, 1942, and Perry Lewis was eighty-four when he died at the Lewis Ranch on June 7, 1954.

The Lewis house in Tustin on the southeast corner of Main and Newport, pictured in 1957.

Noah S. Long

Private, Company C

44th Indiana Infantry

Noah Long was a native of Indiana and served in an infantry regiment from that state during the war. After the war, like several other Tustin Civil War veterans, he spent many years living in Nebraska before eventually moving to Southern California.

Noah Salathiel Long was born November 8, 1845 in Coesse, Whitley County, Indiana, the sixth and last child of Jesse Witt Long and Hannah Heggler. Noah's mother died two weeks after his birth, undoubtedly a victim of complications of childbirth. His father remarried two years later, and Noah was raised in part by his stepmother, Ann Mariah Ruch. Noah grew up working on the family farm in Whitley County and was seventeen years old when his father died on January 26, 1863.

The month after his father's death, Noah and a neighborhood friend, Eli Meiser, went off to Kendallville and on February 14, 1863, enlisted as privates in Company C, 44th Indiana Infantry Regiment. Noah and Eli would be tent mates and serve together for the duration of their enlistment.

The 44th Indiana, which would earn the nickname "The Iron Regiment", was organized at Fort Wayne in the first year of the war. By the time Long joined the regiment, it had already seen hard fighting at the battles of Fort Donelson, Shiloh, and Stones River. The regiment was stationed in Tennessee when Long joined Company C, and he first saw action at the Battle of Chickamauga in northwestern Georgia, near the Tennessee border. The battle, fought September 18-20, 1863, was considered the worst defeat of the Union forces in the Western Theater. It produced the second most combined casualties of any battle after Gettysburg; 34,624 killed, wounded, missing, or captured between the two armies.

Following the bloodbath at Chickamauga, the 44th Indiana next participated in the Battle of Missionary Ridge. Fought on November 25, 1863, it was a Union victory highlighted by an assault that captured what was considered an unconquerable Confederate position. The victory at Missionary Ridge led to the Union occupation of Chattanooga, where the 44th Indiana spent most of the remainder of the war on provost (police) duty.

Noah Long, like thousands of soldiers on both sides, fell ill during his service. In April 1864, he was unable to return from a furlough due to lung issues. He eventually did return to his unit, but in June, he was admitted to the military hospital in Chattanooga with chronic diarrhea. He recovered sufficiently to serve out his enlistment and was mustered out in Nashville on September 15, 1865, having served two years and seven months. In 1890, Noah applied for an invalid pension, stating lung disease as the cause of his disability.

Noah returned to Indiana after the war but soon moved west to Nebraska, where he married Lois Palmer on June 30, 1872, in Gage County. Lois Amanda Palmer was born in Indiana in 1847, a daughter of William and Amanda (Dorsey) Palmer.

Noah and Lois spent the next thirty-five years in Nebraska, with a brief stay in Iowa, where their first child, Frank, was born in 1876. Frank was followed by Lois, who was born in Nebraska in 1884 and died in 1887, and Louise, who was born in 1886. Noah, perhaps kept from farming by his disabilities, worked at various times as a store clerk or as a salesman. The family lived in Fairbury, Nebraska, for many years, where, in addition to clerking in a clothing store, Noah owned several houses and cottages that he rented, as well as nearby farmland that he leased out.

The Longs left Fairbury around 1905 and moved to Long Beach, California. By 1909, they had settled in Tustin, where they would reside for the next dozen years. They lived at 208 A Street, and Noah was employed as a real estate agent. He was a member of the local GAR post, and Lois was involved with the Women's Relief Corps; their daughter, Louise, gave music lessons at the house. Their son Frank died of pneumonia at the house on A Street on May 6, 1921, at the age of 44.

In 1923, Noah and Lois moved to Beverly Hills to live with their daughter, Louise, an aspiring screenwriter. Beverly Hills began as an agricultural suburb of Los Angeles and was not yet the exclusive enclave it is today. In 1920, three years before the Long's arrival, it had a population of just 674; but in 1919, Douglas Fairbanks and Mary Pickford built a mansion there, and by 1930, the population had exploded to over 17,000.

Noah Long died at home in Beverly Hills on October 18, 1928, at the age of 82, after an illness of several months following a stroke; he had come a long way from his days as a farm boy in Indiana. He was buried at Fairhaven Memorial Park in Santa Ana with Sedgwick Post 17, GAR conducting the graveside service. Lois was in poor health at the time of her husband's death and was still residing with her daughter in Beverly Hills when she passed away on June 15, 1930, at the age of 83. She was buried beside Noah at Fairhaven with the Women's Relief Corps of the GAR conducting her graveside service.

Louise Long, the surviving child of Noah and Lois, had a short but successful career as a Hollywood screenwriter. Born October 16, 1886, in Merrick County, Nebraska, Louise gave music lessons from her home on A Street during her early years in Tustin, but around 1917, she moved to Los Angeles. She eventually began writing scripts for silent films, and by 1930, she was doing well enough to have a live-in servant and a live-in nurse for her mother at her Beverly Hills home. Between 1926 and 1933, she was credited with writing eighteen screenplays.

In August 1931, the 41-year-old writer married Max Freedom Long. Max Long had just returned from almost fifteen years living in Hawaii, where he had become fascinated with the Native Hawaiian practice of magic and spiritualism, called Huna. He spent the rest of his life studying and writing about Huna, and his papers and books became part of the Max Freedom Long Library and Museum at the Huna Research Center at Fort Worth, Texas.

A few years into the marriage, Louise gave up writing for the movies and concentrated on producing religious tracts and books. For a number of years, she ran her own publishing house that printed many of her husband's works. Louise Long passed away in San Diego on July 14, 1966, at the age of 79. Max Freedom Long died five years later from a self-inflicted gunshot wound.

George W. Mason

Private, Company G

63rd Ohio Infantry

George W. Mason served two enlistments, totaling four years, with an Ohio infantry regiment during the war. He returned to the Midwest, where he lived for the next twenty years before relocating to Southern California in the early 1887.

George Winchester Mason was born July 8, 1842, in Washington County, Ohio, the fourth of John and Rosannah Mason's seven children. George was just nine years old when his father died, leaving him to help his mother run the family farm. George was nineteen when he left the family farm and traveled to nearby Marietta to enlist as a private in Company G, 63rd Ohio Infantry; he was mustered in three weeks later on November 24, 1861.

The 63rd Ohio was organized from August 1861 to February 1862, and served exclusively in the Western Theater of operations. The regiment participated in the battles of New Madrid, Island No. 10, and the siege of Corinth, all in 1862.

The regiment did not see action again until the spring of 1864. In the time between battles, George Mason must have gone home on furlough, for in August 1863, he married Nancy L.

Allison back in Washington County. Mason returned to his unit, his enlistment ended, and he was mustered out at Prospect, Tennessee, on December 31, 1863. Possibly feeling the need to finish what he started, Mason re-enlisted in Company G the very next day. Men who re-enlisted were considered veterans and entitled to an immediate furlough; this allowed George to return home once again and spend more time with his new bride before reporting back for duty.

The 63rd Ohio next participated in the campaign to take Atlanta, fighting in the battles of Resaca, Dallas, Kennesaw Mountain, Decatur, and, eventually, the siege and capture of Atlanta; all these battles were fought in Georgia in the spring and summer of 1864. Following the capture of Atlanta, George Mason and the 63rd Ohio participated in Sherman's March to the Sea, leaving a path of destruction through Georgia. The march culminated in the siege and capture of Savannah in December 1864.

Sherman then turned his army north through the Carolinas, where the 63rd fought its last battle at Bentonville, North Carolina, March 19-21, 1865. The war ended the following month, and after participating in the Grand Review of the Armies, the regiment traveled by train to Louisville, Kentucky, where George Mason was mustered out on his 23rd birthday, July 8, 1865.

Over the course of the war, the 63rd Ohio lost 2 officers and 91 enlisted men killed in action; 5 officers and 259 enlisted died of disease, for a total of 357 fatalities.

After the war, Mason returned to his wife and son, Charles, who was born in 1864. The couple would eventually have two more children, daughters Nellie and Clara. In 1880, the family was living in Jeffersonville, Wayne County, Illinois, where George was employed as a carriage maker. He became a man of some importance in the small village when, in 1884, he was elected police magistrate and two months later was appointed postmaster.

In 1887, George moved the family west, traveling by train to Southern California. He homesteaded 120 acres in Silverado Canyon, a remote area in the Santa Ana Mountains. There, he built the family a fine house. Later, a spa was opened at the sulphur springs on the property, which became a popular resort known as Mason's Springs or Mason's Chateau.

In the summer of 1890, George and Nancy divorced after twenty-six years of marriage. Two years later, George married Cecelia Rosa Martin on December 10, 1892, in San Bernardino. They would remain together only five years, divorcing in January 1898, but did produce a daughter, Lourena, born in 1893. George purchased a tract of land in the small San Bernardino County community of Moreno and built several houses there.

At the turn of the century, George, his two ex-wives, and all his children were settled in Southern California. He was farming in Riverside County, his first wife, Nancy, and daughter Clara were living in Orange, his second wife, Rosa, and daughter Lourena were in Riverside, and his son, Charles, was in Los Angeles.

At some point, George moved to Orange, possibly to be closer to his daughter. While in Orange, he served a term as commander of the Gordon Granger Post of the GAR. By 1910, he was working as a carpenter and living alone in Tustin on 17th Street near Newport Avenue, but three years later, he was at home on a citrus ranch west of Santa Ana and married for the third time.

His new wife was 65-year-old widow Amelia Crabb. They were married on September 19, 1913, in Santa Ana, but this marriage would also be short-lived. Less than a year later, George was admitted to the Soldiers Home in Sawtelle, near Santa Monica; on the admission form, he was listed as married-separated.

The Soldiers Home in Sawtelle was one of many similar homes across the country established in the latter part of the nineteenth century to house disabled and indigent veterans. The Soldiers Home in Sawtelle was established in 1887, and admission was open to all honorably discharged officers, soldiers, sailors, and marines who had served in the regular or volunteer forces of the United States.

The home, situated on 300 well-maintained acres, at its peak, housed over 2,000 needy veterans. These veterans wore uniforms, slept in barracks, ate at mess halls, and were subject to military discipline for infractions of the many rules. Many aging veterans chafed at this discipline, and a number were evicted for repeated infractions, and some disillusioned veterans left of their own accord. George Mason fell into the second category; he was admitted to the home on July 14, 1914, and left of his own volition three months later on October 31.

**The chapel of the Soldiers Home still stands,
but is in need of renovation.**

**The National Soldiers Home is now part
of the West Los Angeles VA Campus.**

Mason returned to Orange but was in ill health. His admission form to the Soldiers Home listed his disabilities as defective vision and hearing, heart trouble, and chronic pain from an old gunshot wound in his left leg. This is the only record of his being wounded in the war.

Six months after leaving the veterans home, George Mason died at the county hospital in Orange, on April 3, 1915, at the age of 72. Funeral services were held at the Orange Christian Church, where he had been a member, and the graveside ceremony at Santa Ana Cemetery was conducted by twenty-six members of the Gordon Granger GAR post.

Mason's daughter Nellie would follow him to the grave only one year later, passing away in Tustin on August 29, 1916, at the age of 46. She left a husband, Neil McTaggert, and three children. Mason's son Charles also died young, passing away in Laguna Beach on January 19, 1918, at 54.

Mason's daughter, Clara, began teaching school in Silverado Canyon at 18 and then married George K. Fox. She and George lived on a citrus ranch in El Toro. Clara was quite an accomplished woman; she studied art at Cooper Union in New York City, wrote poetry, and later designed a Craftsman home in Laguna Beach. In 1939, she published a history of the city of El Toro and had her botanical art on display at the Huntington Library in San Marino. The couple were living at 148 N. B Street in Tustin when George passed away in 1951. Clara Mason Fox passed away on March 11, 1959, at 85 and is buried at Santa Ana Cemetery.

Lourena, George's daughter with his second wife, Rosa, married Frank L. Green. Frank was a box maker at a packinghouse, and the couple had three children. Frank died in 1943, and Lourena Cecelia (Mason) Green died on May 16, 1960, in Lindsay, California, at age 66.

James R. McCloud

Private, Company G

3rd Illinois Cavalry

James McCloud's service in the Civil War was short. He joined the cavalry just months before the war ended and served out the remainder of his enlistment fighting the Sioux in Minnesota and the Dakota Territory. He was one of the first Civil War veterans to arrive in Tustin, and his life was marked by family tragedy. His own death was the result of an accident.

James R. McCloud was born on April 3, 1845, in Plattville, Illinois, the sixth of John and Paulina (Ricketson) McCloud's ten children. James grew up working on the family farm, first in Kendall County and later near Odell, in Livingston County, Illinois.

James was nineteen years old when he was mustered into the 3rd Illinois Cavalry regiment at Springfield on January 22, 1865. His enlistment papers listed him as 5'8" tall with black hair, blue eyes, and a light complexion. At this point, the war was winding down, and James enlisted for one year of service. By the time James joined the 3rd Illinois Cavalry, the regiment had already built a distinguished service record during the war. Organized and mustered into service in August 1861, the regiment had participated in such major battles as Pea Ridge, Port Gibson, Champion Hill, Vicksburg, and Nashville. The regiment had suffered 234 fatalities, both killed in action and died from disease.

At the time James joined the regiment it was stationed in Alabama. It then moved to Mississippi before being transferred west, where it operated against the Sioux in Minnesota and the Dakota Territory. Much like Harvey Lewis with the 30th Wisconsin, James McCloud's Civil War service was primarily spent skirmishing with Native American tribes rather than fighting the Confederate forces in open rebellion against the government. McCloud was mustered out of service at Fort Snelling, Minnesota, on October 10, 1865, having completed ten months of active duty. Still only twenty years old when the war ended, McCloud returned to Illinois. In 1870, he was working on the farm of his older brother John near Saunemin in Livingston County.

James McCloud decided to move west, and on May 17, 1875, he arrived in Tustin, one of the first Civil War veterans to do so. For a short time, James worked on Andrew Mills' 200-acre ranch. He then went into business for himself, purchasing and operating a corn sheller. (In 1880, before citrus became dominant, corn and barley were the main crops in Tustin.) He did this for ten years and also farmed on a small scale. Eventually, he purchased four acres south of Tustin where he first planted fruit trees. Not happy with their production, he tore them out and replaced them with walnuts, which produced well enough to provide him a comfortable living.

Less than a year after his arrival in Tustin, on February 24, 1876, he married Mary Alice Weekley. The groom was thirty, his bride nineteen. For the next several years, James' life in Tustin would be tinged by tragedy.

In 1878, Mary gave birth to a daughter, Attie May. Two years later, Mary died at the age of twenty-three. Later that same year, on June 11, 1880, James married Mary's younger sister, eighteen-year-old Etta Caroline Weekley.

The following year, Etta gave birth to a son, James Morton McCloud, and in 1882, to a daughter, Maud. In 1883, Etta died, perhaps from complications from Maud's birth. To add to the tragic turn of events, in 1884, two-year-old Maud passed away. In a span of four years, James McCloud lost two wives and an infant daughter.

McCloud never remarried but had help raising his young children; his son was raised by the M.H. Bear family in Old Newport. Old Newport was an area of Gospel Swamp that is now Costa Mesa, bordered by southwest Santa Ana. By the turn of the century, James was on his own. Attie May was living elsewhere, and James Morton was serving in the army.

McCloud lived on the northwest corner of Tustin Avenue and McFadden, an area known as South Tustin. Fittingly for a former cavalryman, he raised and raced horses up and down the state. A popular sport of the day, he entered two of his mares in the races at the inaugural Orange County Fair in October 1890.

On Tuesday afternoon, January 28, 1902, James was harrowing a field, stopped to adjust a harness, and was kicked in the stomach by the horse. Although painful, he didn't consider the injury serious and continued working; later, the pain became so bad that a doctor was summoned. The kick had caused internal injuries, and two days later, McCloud died at his home in Tustin at the age of fifty-six. His son James was still in the Philippines, but Attie May came down from Los Angeles for the funeral.

Although James McCloud was not among the more prominent or successful of the Civil War veterans who settled in Tustin, his story illustrates the fragility of life in pioneer times. The loss of two wives at very young ages and an infant daughter, combined with his own death in a farming accident, illustrates how precarious life was in the latter years of the nineteenth century.

Attie McCloud married Edward Tharp in Los Angeles on November 24, 1906. Tharp was a bartender from Missouri, and it is not surprising that the marriage did not last. Two weeks before they were married, Tharp attacked Attie and was arrested and charged with attempted murder. She refused to testify against him, was held in contempt of court, and then married Tharp. At that time in California, a wife could not testify against her husband in court. By 1920, Tharp was remarried and living in Arizona, and Attie disappeared from the records.

James McCloud was buried at Santa Ana Cemetery with graveside ceremonies provided by the Odd Fellows and members of Sedgwick Post 17 of the GAR.

James Morton McCloud was born January 27, 1881, and was only three when his mother died. Following his mother's death, he was raised by the Bear family in Old Newport. He attended Sunday school at the Advent Christian Church in Tustin and served in Company F of the 35th US Infantry from 1899 to 1901 in the Philippines. Afterwards, he stayed in the Philippines, serving in the constabulary forces of the islands, rising to the rank of Captain. When World War I broke out in Europe in 1914, McCloud resigned from the service and enlisted in the British Army in Hong Kong. He was wounded but survived the Battle of Gallipoli and when the United States entered the war, he was commissioned a major. McCloud was a company commander when he was killed by an artillery shell at the Battle of Soissons on July 19, 1918. He is buried in Arlington National Cemetery.

United States Casualty List

Pershing's Army Heroes

WASHINGTON, July 30.—One hundred and forty-five army casualties today included:

Killed in action, 17; died of wounds, 11; died of disease, 15; died of accident and other causes, 3; wounded severely, 95; wounded slightly, 1; missing in action, 3.

Major Goodwin Compton, Memphis, and Major Theodore Roosevelt, Jr., were listed as severely wounded and Major James M. McCloud, London, was killed in action.

(Major McCloud was born at Tustin and attended school at Old Newport and Tustin. He was raised by Mr. and Mrs. M. H. Bear of Old Newport.)

Note that the son of former President Teddy Roosevelt was on the same casualty list as James M. McCloud. Teddy Jr. recovered and went on to serve as a general in the Second World War and was awarded the Congressional Medal of Honor.

James W. Northcross

Private, Company D

7th Tennessee Cavalry

Raised on a large slave-worked plantation in Tennessee, James Northcross served in a Confederate cavalry regiment and was wounded and captured by Union forces. In the late 1880s, he followed family members to southern California, and in the 1890s, he lived and farmed in Tustin.

James Wolf Northcross was born in September 1837 in Trenton, Gibson County, Tennessee. He was the third of the eight children born to Northern Nelms Northcross and Margery Ann Marshall. James' father, with the alliterative name, was a large landowner and by 1860 possessed plantations in two counties worked by numerous enslaved people. N. N. Northcross had inherited land from his parents and had numerous siblings in the area and in nearby northern Mississippi.

James Northcross was twenty-four years old when he enlisted as a private in Company D, 7th Tennessee Cavalry regiment on June 20, 1862. The regiment was organized in April of that same year and was sometimes referred to as "Duckworth's Cavalry" after its commanding officer, Col. William L. Duckworth.

The regiment saw action soon after James enlisted, participating in a raid behind enemy lines that resulted in the capture of fifty-seven Union soldiers and the destruction of a locomotive and a train of cars on June 25, 1862. The regiment next fought at the Battle of Corinth in October 1862 and then was engaged at Grenada, Mississippi in August 1863.

In November 1863, the 7th Tennessee Cavalry was transferred to the force commanded by Gen. Nathan Bedford

Forrest. Forrest was a successful, almost legendary, cavalry leader who had been a slave trader before the war and, after the war, was a founding member of the Ku Klux Klan. In February 1864, the regiment fought well at the Confederate victory at Okolona, Mississippi.

Northcross and the 7th Tennessee were on detached duty at Union City, Tennessee, when the rest of Forrest's troops attacked and captured Fort Pillow, north of Memphis, on April 12, 1864. Therefore, Northcross was not involved in the infamous massacre of the black Union soldiers who had surrendered the fort. The exact number of black troops killed is not known for certain, but it is generally believed that as many as 200 were slaughtered after laying down their arms. The regiment next fought at the battles of Tishomingo Creek and Harrisburg before participating in the Battle of Franklin.

The Battle of Franklin, fought on November 30, 1864, south of Nashville, was a disastrous defeat for the Confederate forces under General John B. Hood. When it was over, six Confederate generals were dead, the Southern Army retreated and was virtually destroyed as an effective fighting force the following month at the Battle of Nashville. The 7th Tennessee Cavalry under Forrest was part of a rearguard action protecting Hood's retreat from Nashville when James Northcross was captured by Union forces on December 17, 1864.

He was initially housed at the military prison in Louisville, Kentucky, where Tustin Civil War veteran Harvey B. Lewis was stationed at that time as a guard. On January 4, 1865, Northcross was transferred to Camp Chase military prison in Columbus, Ohio. Fortunately for Northcross, he did not stay long at the crowded Camp Chase, being transferred to Point Lookout, Maryland, on February 17, where he was soon paroled or exchanged.

Northcross was admitted to Wayside Hospital, also known as Hospital No. 9, in Richmond, Virginia, on February 28, 1865. It is not known if he was recovering from a wound received in battle or suffering from a disease brought on by his imprisonment. One account has Northcross losing an arm to amputation, but voter registers from the 1890s under the category for distinguishing marks or scars consistently listed none for James. These registers were very detailed, listing moles, scars, limps, and, in one case, even a crooked index finger. It seems unlikely a missing limb would be overlooked.

Wayside Hospital in Richmond. A former tobacco warehouse, James Northcross was treated here after his release from a Union prison camp.

Six miles west of downtown Columbus, Ohio, the Camp Chase Cemetery is on the site of the former prisoner of war camp. Nine thousand Confederate soldiers were imprisoned here, and 2,206 died of disease and are buried here. James W. Northcross was fortunate that his stay here was brief.

Camp Chase Confederate Cemetery

James Northcross returned from the war to Trenton, where, later that year, on November 11, 1865, he married Lenora "Nora" Irwin. Twenty-five-year-old Nora was also a native of Trenton. Her father died when she was just five years old, and her mother soon remarried to a local planter, Henry Davis Harper. Nora grew up on Harper's large, slave-worked plantation. In later years, she would reminisce about her privileged childhood, where all the chores were done by servants (enslaved people) and she never even had to dress herself, that task performed by her beloved "Mammy".

**Lenora Northcross, shown as a Southern Belle when
she was 20 years old.**

It appears James' father was able to retain much of his
property after the war, and with his unpaid labor force set free, he
turned to signing his former enslaved people to sharecropping
contracts. It is not unreasonable to believe James resorted to the

same practice in order to run his farm. Both father and son also remained active in local Democratic politics, often acting as delegates to the state conventions.

James and Nora remained in Gibson County for the next twenty years. As those years went by the family grew with a new child arriving every few years, until the family numbered eight children: William, Margery, Thomas, Ruth, Kathrene, Sallie, Dorothy, and Nelms (Nellie).

After a life spent in Tennessee, the couple moved their family to Southern California around 1887, first settling in the city of Orange. James' father, Northern Nelms Northcross, had visited California as early as 1868 and had moved to Orange with his wife Margery sometime after June 1880. N.N. Northcross died in Orange in 1881, and James' brother Marshall went west to settle his father's estate and stayed on. So there was already a Northcross presence in Orange (and a Northcross building on the Plaza) when James and Nora arrived in 1887.

James farmed and may have dabbled in real estate. The local papers of the time contained numerous land title transactions under his name. For a few years in the early 1890s, James also ran an orchard fumigation business. He also became locally active, serving for a time on the executive committee of the Orange County Farmers' Alliance.

In the summer of 1891, James moved the family to Tustin. Perhaps he felt a change of residence would help ease the pain of the loss of their daughter Sallie, who had died earlier in the year. James registered to vote in Tustin, and from that record, we have a description of him: farmer, 5 feet 10 inches tall, light complexion, blue eyes, gray hair, with no visible scars or marks.

We know one of the crops James grew in Tustin because a 1897 newspaper article reported that Nora fell off their hay wagon and broke her kneecap while helping James bring in the crop. (She was long removed from the days when servants did all her work.)

Just a few years after Nora's mishap on the hay wagon, the family was no longer in Tustin. By the turn of the century, they were back in Orange, where James was growing citrus. Their son Thomas and his wife were in Orange, as were James' brothers, Marshall and William.

James' return to Orange was short-lived. In the spring of 1902, he, Nora, and their oldest daughter, Margery, were stricken with typhoid fever. James died on April 12, 1902, in El Modena at the age of sixty-four. He was buried two days later beside his father and mother at Santa Ana Cemetery. Two weeks later, thirty-one-year-old Margery succumbed to the fever and was buried beside her father.

Nora survived her bout with typhoid fever and lived another forty-two years, most of that time residing at 273 N. Center Street in Orange with her two unmarried daughters, Kathrene and Nellie. Nora was active in her church and was a member of the United Daughters of the Confederacy, often attending the annual Robert E. Lee dinner.

On her one hundredth birthday in 1940, the local newspapers ran articles about the event, and Nora shared stories from her childhood in the antebellum South and about the hardships she endured pioneering in early Orange County. She maintained her faculties until the very end. In 1943, a local paper solicited her opinion, having lived through five wars, on the internment of Japanese-Americans. (She approved of the camps.)

Nora Northcross died on November 11, 1944, at the home of her daughter Ruth in Laguna Beach. She was 104 years old. Her obituary made much of the fact that she had recently registered as a Republican for the first time in her life. Perhaps she was tired of the New Deal or wary of Franklin D. Roosevelt winning an unprecedented fourth term. Whatever her motivation, she cast her first vote for a Republican presidential candidate, Thomas Dewey, and died a week later. Nora was buried beside her husband at Santa Ana Cemetery.

James and Lenora Northcross' Tombstones

The children of James W. and Nora (Irwin) Northcross, all born in Gibson County, Tennessee, were:

- William L. Northcross was born December 15, 1866. Rather than move with the family to California, William chose to remain in Tennessee. In May 1898, he enlisted in Company K, 2nd Tennessee Infantry, and served in the Spanish-American War. He returned to Gibson County after the war and worked as a teamster.

William moved to California sometime after his father's death, probably around 1907. William never married. Over the years, he lived in Orange, Anaheim, and Garden Grove, and he was a citrus grower. He was a resident of Laguna Beach when he died at Santa Ana Community Hospital on March 13, 1950, at the age of eighty-three. He was buried with military honors in the Northcross plot at Santa Ana Cemetery.

- Margery Northcross was born in 1870 and was about seventeen years old when the family moved to Orange, California. Margery never married and was thirty-one years old when she died of typhoid fever on May 1, 1902, in El Modena. She was buried in the family plot at Santa Ana Cemetery.

- Thomas Jefferson Northcross was born February 21, 1873, and was around fourteen years old when he moved with his family to southern California. He was living with his parents in Tustin when he married Belle Murray of Long Beach in February 1897. By the turn of the century, the couple was living in Orange, where they ran a bakery. They eventually had four children, Olive, Carl, Mabel, and Isabel. Sadly, Carl died of tetanus on May 8, 1908.

It seems the marriage dissolved after the death of their son. By 1910, Thomas was gone, and Belle, who carried on running the confectionery, listed herself as a widow on the census that year. By 1917, Thomas was remarried to a woman named Rose and living in San Francisco. It seems that marriage was short-lived, for by 1920, Thomas was living without Rose in a boarding house and working at a sugar refinery, still in San Francisco. Thomas Northcross eventually returned to Orange County, where he died on January 23, 1938, at the age of sixty-four. He is buried with his parents and siblings at Santa Ana Cemetery.

- Ruth Northcross was born April 11, 1877, and was about ten years old when she came to Southern California with her family. On June 16, 1903, she married William E. Harper in El Modena. Harper, a native of Iowa, was the Northcross family's next-door neighbor. Will and Ruth had two sons, Thomas and Robert. The family first lived in Orange, where Will worked as a carpenter. By 1932, Will and Ruth had moved to Laguna Beach, where they lived for the rest of their lives. Ruth died on June 25, 1947, at the age of seventy. Will passed away less than a year later, on April 19, 1948. Both are buried at Santa Ana Cemetery.

- Kathrene Northcross was born January 12, 1878, and was around nine years old when she moved to Southern California with her family. Kate never married and lived with her mother for most of her life in the house on Center Street in Orange. She worked for many years as a dressmaker and seamstress and belonged to many community groups. Her name was often on the society page for her involvement with her Methodist church group, the Orange Women's Club, the United Daughters of the Confederacy, and a bridge club. Kate began to experience heart problems in the early 1940s and died in Orange on March 18, 1946, at the age of sixty-eight. She is buried in the Northcross plot at Santa Ana Cemetery.

- Sallie Northcross was listed on the 1880 federal census as two years old. Above her name is Kathrene, listed as five, when in fact Kate was actually two in 1880. Perhaps their ages were accidentally switched, which would make Sallie's birth year about 1875. In fact, all the Northcross children's ages are slightly off on that census sheet. Nora giving birth, probably in the house while the census was being taken, may have contributed to the errors. The only other documented appearance of Sallie is from a single line in the *Orange News* of December 31, 1890: "Miss Sallie Northcross is quite ill." It is probable that Sallie died shortly after this notice. In the 1900 federal census, Nora Northcross is listed as the mother of eight children, seven of whom are living. Since the other seven children lived to adulthood and are accounted for, it is apparent that Sallie is the deceased child.

- Dorothy Northcross was born June 4, 1880. (She was the baby born the same day the census was being enumerated at their house.) Dorothy would have been about seven years old when the family moved to California. On June 2, 1904, just two days shy of her twenty-fourth birthday, Dorothy married Irvin H. Cammack at the Northcross home in El Modena. Cammack was a 54-year-old widower, originally from Indiana, who had moved to the Quaker community of Whittier, California. At the time of the marriage, Irvin was the superintendent of the Friends (Quaker) Training School in Los Angeles. Irvin and Dorothy had two children, Lenora and William.

In 1917, the family traveled as missionaries to Tegucigalpa, Honduras. Earlier that year, Dorothy had been recorded as a minister of the gospel by the East Whittier Monthly Meeting of Quakers. Twelve years later, on October 26, 1929, Irvin died in Tegucigalpa at the age of seventy-nine. He was buried there but later disinterred and buried at Rosehill Memorial Park in Whittier. Dorothy and the children returned home and were living in Huntington Park, near Los Angeles, the year after Irvin's death. Dorothy returned to her missionary work in Honduras in the early 1930s and was still there at the time of her mother's death in 1944. By 1946, she was back in Orange and then lived with her daughter Lenora for a number of years in the desert at Twenty-Nine Palms, California. Dorothy was back in Orange at the time of her death on May 22, 1977 at the age of ninety-six. She was buried at Fairhaven Memorial Park in Santa Ana with her daughter, who had died in 1973.

- Nelms Northcross was born February 12, 1886 and was an infant when the family moved to southern California. It was a Northcross family tradition to name a son after the family patriarch, Northern Nelms Northcross. Nora Northcross was forty-five when her last daughter was born, correctly figuring this would be their last child; she and James named her Nelms. She was always known to family and friends as Nellie. Nellie never married and never moved out of the family home, living with her mother and sister Kathrene for most of her life. After her mother and Kate died, Nellie moved to Laguna Beach, where Ruth and William lived. She was living in Laguna Beach but was visiting a friend on Cambridge Street in Orange when she died on October 30, 1956, at the age of seventy. She was buried in the Northcross family plot at Santa Ana Cemetery.

Joseph Pollock

Landsman

United States Navy

Joseph Pollock enlisted to serve the Union at the age of fifteen and spent the last year of the war serving on Navy ships blockading the southern coastline and patrolling the James River in Virginia. After the war, he spent thirty years farming in Minnesota before relocating to Southern California shortly after the turn of the century.

Joseph Pollock was born June 10, 1849, in Washington County, New York, the fifth of William and Rheuamy (Kinney) Pollock's eight children. Joseph grew up working on the family farm near the village of Argyle in upstate New York, on the border with Vermont.

In July 1864, one month after his fifteenth birthday, Joseph enlisted at Argyle as a private in the Union army. His enlistment papers list him as sixteen, but he probably lied about his age. Most of the other men who enlisted from Argyle, in their twenties and thirties, were mustered into the 123rd New York Infantry. Joseph, however, perhaps due to his youth, was assigned to the Navy ship USS Minnesota as a Landsman.

Landsman was the lowest rank in the United States Navy in the 19th Century; it was given to new recruits with little or no experience at sea, and this would certainly describe Joseph, who had spent his life on a farm in upstate New York, far from any ocean. Approximately fifty percent of any Civil War crew was made up of Landsmen, usually boys under seventeen years of age. They required close supervision to learn their new trade, while doing the menial, mundane tasks such as holystoning the wooden decks and keeping the ship clean, all for a salary of $12 per month.

After three years' experience, or upon re-enlistment, a Landsman could be promoted to ordinary Seaman; the rating of Landsman was abolished in 1921.

Pollock's first ship, the Minnesota, was an old frigate that had played a part in one of the most famous sea battles in history, albeit two years before Pollock came aboard. On March 8, 1862, the Minnesota was run aground by the Confederate ironclad CSS Virginia, also known by its former name, the Merrimack. The Virginia returned to her harbor, intending to return the next day and finish off the Minnesota. However, the next morning, the Virginia was intercepted by the USS Monitor, and the first naval battle in history between two ironclad warships was fought to a draw in Hampton Roads, Virginia. The Virginia eventually withdrew, and the Minnesota was saved.

During Pollock's time on the Minnesota, the ship was part of the blockading squadron commanded by Admiral Albert Lea. The ship patrolled the southern coastline and was berthed off Fort Monroe, Virginia.

The USS Minnesota

Later, Pollock served aboard the USS Agawam, at Deep Bottom on the James River, also in Virginia. The Agawam was a double-sided, side-wheel gunboat built for service on the inland rivers of the South. In one engagement on the James River, the Agawam dueled with Confederate shore batteries for over four hours and lost three men killed and four wounded in the battle. A young lieutenant on the Agawam was George Dewey, who as an admiral would become a hero of the Spanish-American War when his ships destroyed the Spanish fleet at Manila Bay in 1898.

When Joseph Pollock was discharged from the Navy at Norfolk, Virginia, in July 1865, he had served for a year at sea and was still just sixteen years old when he returned to the family farm in New York. He didn't stay home for long; perhaps the drudgery of farm life was no longer bearable to Joseph, for after a stint as a customs clerk in New York, he spent the next ten years traveling throughout the Midwest and the West. He farmed for a few years in Iowa, then went west again, working in mining camps in Illinois, Colorado, Wyoming, and Utah before returning to the family farm in New York in 1875.

Pollack finally decided to settle down and returned to Hinckley, Illinois, where, on November 30, 1876, he married Amanda Strever. Amanda was born in New York in 1853 and, as a child, moved with her family to DeKalb County, Illinois. It was there that the twenty-three-year-old met and married the twenty-seven-year-old Navy veteran.

The year after their wedding Joseph and Amanda moved to southern Minnesota, settling on a farm four miles west of the town of Austin. They remained there for almost thirty years, and eventually the farm grew to 220 acres; in addition to the usual crops of the area, Joseph also raised and sold prize-winning Angus cattle.

The couple's first child, a daughter, was born on December 6, 1880, and was named Rheuamy, after Joseph's mother. Sadly, the child did not reach her fourth birthday, passing away on June 9,

1884. Their only other child, Roy, was born in 1882; he lived to reach adulthood and, years later, would accompany his parents to Southern California.

After many years on the farm, Joseph purchased a lot in the nearby town of Austin and had a large house built on the property, but the family did not move into town; instead, Joseph rented the house to provide another source of income. When he finally decided to move, Joseph chose a destination much farther away: California.

Joseph began preparing to move west in the fall of 1905. He and Amanda had suffered various illnesses in the previous few years, and both felt the warmer climate on the West Coast would be better for them in their later years. In early December, Joseph traveled by train from Austin to Los Angeles and began the search for a new home, leaving Amanda and Roy at home to care for the farm.

Pollock eventually purchased property in Orange, California, that already contained a mature orange grove. He sent a picture postcard back to an Austin newspaper showing him picking an orange from a tree and stating he planned to build a house in the grove. He put his livestock and farm machinery back up for sale in Minnesota, but retained the farm itself, planning to lease it out. Even without selling his farm property, Pollock was able to bring $15,000 (the equivalent of $523,000 in 2023 dollars) to start his new life in California.

Amanda and Roy left Minnesota for their new home in Orange on May 1, 1906. Joseph and Amanda lived in Orange for the next ten years, moving several times within the town limits as Joseph bought and sold various properties.

Joseph Pollock, like many Union veterans, was a staunch supporter of the Republican Party. In 1912, Pollock supported Theodore Roosevelt in his unsuccessful attempt to regain the presidency, running against the incumbent, fellow Republican

William Howard Taft. (Roosevelt's "Bull Moose" party split the Republicans, and Democrat Woodrow Wilson won the election.) Pollock even started a Roosevelt Republican Club of Orange County, with many Civil War veterans as initial members.

In December 1915, Pollock purchased a twenty-acre tract in Anaheim that was planted with Valencia oranges. His son Roy and his family moved to Anaheim and took over management of the ranch; Joseph and Amanda moved to the home Roy's family had occupied on East Santa Clara Avenue in Tustin.

By the time Joseph moved to Tustin, he was 66 years old, and this would be his last move. He had been living on the Santa Clara Avenue citrus ranch for ten years when he passed away at home on January 6, 1926, at the age of 76. He had been a member of the Gordon Granger GAR Post in Orange, and also of Sedgwick Post-17, which performed the graveside ceremonies at Fairhaven Memorial Park. Amanda Pollock survived her husband by eight years. She died at the ranch home on Santa Clara on March 5, 1934, after an extended illness. The minister of the First Methodist Church of Santa Ana, where she and Joseph had been longtime members, conducted her funeral service, and she was buried beside her husband at Fairhaven.

Roy Nelson Pollock, the only surviving child of Joseph and Amanda, was born July 9, 1882, in Austin, Minnesota. When his father decided to move west, Roy traveled to Southern California with his mother in 1906.

Roy then returned to Austin, where he married Carrie Evelyn White on April 8, 1909. Roy brought his bride back to Orange County, where they first farmed in Westminster and later in Garden Grove. By October 1911, they had moved to the five-acre citrus ranch on Santa Clara Avenue in Tustin.

The couple had three children, Joseph, Hazel, and Lucille; Joseph died in 1935 at the age of nineteen. For many years, the family lived on their citrus ranch on Sunkist Avenue in Anaheim, but Roy and Carrie were living in Orange when he passed away on December 2, 1953, at the age of 71. Carrie passed away eighteen years later, on May 27, 1971, at 90, and was buried beside her husband at Fairhaven.

David N. Robinson

Private, Company I

8th Indiana Infantry

David Robinson joined the Union Army as a teenager and served for three years, participating in some of the war's fiercest battles. After the war, he re-enlisted in the regular army and served in the force that occupied the South during Reconstruction. He came to Tustin from Michigan at the turn of the century and stayed for a decade before living his final years in Los Angeles.

David Nathaniel Robinson was born in May 1846, in Wabash County, Indiana to Reuben and Lodema Robinson. Both of his parents were born in Vermont, and both were relatively old at the time of David's birth; Reuben was fifty-five and Lodema forty-three. David, like most of the other Tustin Civil War veterans, was raised working on the family farm.

David Robinson was sixteen years old when, on August 30, 1862, he was mustered in as a private in Company I, 8th Indiana Infantry Regiment. The 8th Indiana was organized in April 1861 as a three-month regiment; at the time, many people on both sides expected a short war. When the original enlistments expired, the 8th was reorganized in August 1861 with a three-year enlistment term.

When David Robinson joined the regiment, it was operating in southeast Missouri, where it would remain through the fall and winter of 1862 and the early part of 1863. In the spring of 1863, the regiment became part of the XIII Corps of the Army of Tennessee. Beginning on April 29, 1863, at the Battle of Grand Gulf, the 8th Indiana seemed to be in constant combat in the following battles (all in Mississippi): May 1, Port Gibson; May 16, Champion Hill; May 17, Big Black River Bridge; May 18-July

4, the siege of Vicksburg. The regiment was also part of the two failed frontal assaults on Vicksburg, on May 21 and May 22, that led to the siege. There was no rest for the Hoosiers even after Vicksburg fell on July 4; they then swung east and were part of a force that besieged Jackson from July 5-25, forcing the surrender of the state capital.

In August, the 8th Indiana and the rest of the XIII Corps were ordered to New Orleans, where they performed garrison duty before being sent to Texas in November. The regiment then took part in the Battle of Fort Esperanza, fought on Matagorda Island off the coast of Texas. The battle, fought November 27-30, 1863, resulted in few casualties on either side as the Confederate force eventually evacuated their fort.

From Texas, the Hoosiers went to Washington, D.C., where they remained on garrison duty until July 1864, when they were attached to the XIX Corps as part of the Army of the Shenandoah. They then participated in General Phil Sheridan's Shenandoah Valley campaign, where they saw action in the Battles of Berryville, Third Winchester, Fisher's Hill, and Cedar Creek, all fought between September 3 and October 19, 1864.

Cedar Creek was the last major engagement for the 8th Indiana. By the end of the war, the regiment had lost 7 officers and 84 enlisted men killed in action; 5 officers and 166 enlisted also died from disease, for a total of 262 fatalities. David Robinson was mustered out on June 14, 1865, having served just under three years.

David Robinson's whereabouts just after his discharge are unknown, but within two years, he was back in uniform. The now twenty-one-year-old farmer was in Logansport, Indiana, on August 6, 1867, where he enlisted for three years as a private in Company K of the 24th United States Infantry Regiment. His enlistment record describes him as 6'3" tall, with hazel eyes and light- colored hair. The average height of a man of that era was about 5'7", so Robinson must have towered over most of his fellow soldiers.

Robinson's second hitch in the army was spent as part of the occupation forces sent south during the Reconstruction period to protect the lives and property of freed slaves and their white sympathizers. In 1869, as part of an army reorganization in which some units were eliminated and others merged, Robinson became a private in Company C, 11th United States Infantry Regiment. He was discharged in Waco, Texas, on August 6, 1870, exactly three years to the day of his enlistment.

Robinson's whereabouts after his second discharge were also hard to track. He does not appear again in any records until 1884, when he tied the knot in Michigan. Robinson, now thirty-eight, married thirty-one-year-old Abigail Tyrrell on November 25, 1884, in Escanaba, Michigan. Abigail was a native of Canada and immigrated to the United States just three years before her marriage to David Robinson.

The couple's first child, Edwin, was born one day after their first wedding anniversary. Another child was born but died in infancy. Escanaba is a port city on Michigan's Upper Peninsula, located on Little Bay de Noc. It was an area where iron ore was mined and where lumber was harvested and shipped. The Robinsons remained there until 1898, when they relocated to Southern California.

By the summer of 1900 David, Abigail, and fourteen-year-old Edwin were living on their citrus ranch on Holt Avenue just north of First Street in Tustin. They would remain there until moving to Los Angeles in 1910. Perhaps David's health prompted the move; neither he nor Abigail worked in Los Angeles, and they lived in a rented house with Edwin, who worked as a clerk at the Post Office.

Civil War veteran David Robinson was 71 years old when he passed away in Los Angeles on September 19, 1917. He was buried at Forest Lawn Memorial Park in Glendale. Abigail survived her husband by eleven years, passing away on November

14, 1928, in Los Angeles; she was 75 and was buried beside her husband.

Edwin Stanley Robinson, the only surviving child of David and Abigail, was born on November 26, 1885, in Escanaba, Michigan. He was twelve years old when the family moved to California, and he grew up on the family citrus ranch in Tustin. He graduated from Santa Ana High School in 1905 (Tustin did not yet have its own high school) and later enrolled in college. In 1910, he began a 37-year career with the United States Post Office, working as a clerk in Los Angeles. He would eventually work his way to an upper management position in the organization.

In 1913, Edwin returned to Tustin, where, on September 13, he married Julia Etta Crawford at her parents' home. Her parents, Thomas J. Crawford and Emma Frances Bishop, were longtime residents of Tustin. Edwin and Etta graduated together from Santa Ana High, and Etta went on to Occidental College and U.C. Berkeley, earning a high school teaching credential.

Etta and Edwin had no children and lived in Los Angeles. In addition to his job at the Post Office, Edwin produced travel films that were shown on television and was an active conservationist. Edwin Robinson died in Duarte, California on February 26, 1971, at the age of 85 and was buried beside his parents at Forest Lawn. Etta survived her husband by nine years, passing away on August 2, 1980.

Henry W. Smith

Corporal, Company A

13th Michigan Infantry

Henry Smith served in a Michigan infantry regiment and participated in some of the war's fiercest battles. Married three times, Smith fathered nine children. He came to Tustin around the turn of the century and served a term as Justice of the Peace of the township.

Henry William Smith was born September 29, 1841, near Canandaigua, Ontario County, New York. He was the second of Albert and Martha (Abbott) Smith's eight children. When Henry was about eight years old, his father moved the family to a farm outside Grand Rapids, Michigan. Later, they moved a little south, near Kalamazoo, Michigan, where Henry worked on the family farm and attended school when possible.

Henry Smith was twenty years old when he enlisted at Galesburg as a private in Company A, 13th Michigan Infantry Regiment. He enlisted for three years' service in November 1861 but was not mustered into service until January 1862, when the regiment was organized in Kalamazoo.

The 13th Michigan was first attached to the Army of the Ohio and was later reassigned to the Army of the Cumberland. The regiment was involved in many of the major battles of the Western Theater of Operations, and Henry saw action at Stones River, Chickamauga, Chattanooga, Missionary Ridge, and participated in Sherman's March to the Sea.

On December 21, 1864, Union troops occupied Savannah, Georgia, and General William T. Sherman sent his famous telegram to President Lincoln, "I beg to present to you, as a Christmas gift, the city of Savannah." Several weeks later, now a corporal, Henry W. Smith was discharged in Savannah, having fulfilled his three-year enlistment.

Smith, despite being in many major battles, had survived the war unscathed, but many in his regiment were not so fortunate. By the end of the war, the 13th Michigan had suffered 388 fatalities; 72 killed in action, and a staggering 316 men died of disease. These numbers are only the fatalities and do not include the wounded.

Monument to the 13th Michigan at the Chickamauga Battlefield.

Following his discharge, Smith returned to Michigan, where he again took up farming and also worked in the lumber business. On December 6, 1865, he married Mary Louisa Weatherby in Kalamazoo. Henry was twenty-four, his bride twenty-one. The couple moved to a farm near the town of Free Soil, in northwest Michigan. As the years passed, the family grew, eventually numbering eight children. Sadly, Louisa passed away on May 22, 1880, at the age of thirty-six, four days after giving birth to her eighth child in fifteen years.

A widower with seven children to raise (one child had died in infancy) Henry remarried the year after Louisa's death. His new bride was Emily (Butterfield) Daken, a widow with two children. She had previously been married to Stephan Daken who died in 1878. In 1882 Henry moved his family, now numbering nine children, to South Dakota. For almost twenty years they farmed near the town of Blendon in Davison County. To help support his large family Henry also ran a mercantile business in addition to working his farm. In their time in South Dakota Henry and Emily had two sons, raising the number of young mouths to feed to eleven.

In 1901 Smith gave up farming in South Dakota and moved to Tustin. Perhaps the Smiths were lured to Tustin by Emily's brother, Reverend G.C. Butterfield, pastor of the Tustin Presbyterian Church, who had come to Tustin the year before. Smith tried farming for a while but soon entered the real estate business where he apparently found some success. In 1909 Smith partnered in real estate with J.A. Phiney, a prominent Tustin businessman who would later be appointed town postmaster. Smith later branched out and added insurance sales to his real estate endeavors. Also, in 1919 Smith served as Justice of the Peace for Tustin township.

Emily Smith was an active member of the Tustin Presbyterian Church, the Women's Relief Corps of the GAR and for several years served as president of the Tustin Women's

Christian Temperance Union, a nationwide organization that lobbied for the prohibition of alcohol. Emily did not live to see her goal fulfilled. She passed away from heart disease on May 13, 1919; Congress passed the 19th Amendment on June 4, 1919 and it was ratified into law on August 18, 1920. At the time of her death, she and Henry had been married for thirty-eight years.

Once again Smith was a widower and once again, he wasted no time in remarrying. On September 14, 1919 he married another widow, seventy-one-year-old Isabel "Belle" O'Neil in Pomona, California. (The wedding announcement in the local newspaper shaved half a dozen years off both of their ages.) Belle's late husband, Dewitt Clinton O'Neil, had served with Henry in Company A of the 13th Michigan during the war.

Smith brought his new bride back to Tustin where they lived on the southeast corner of 3rd and Pacific streets. His real estate office was located on the west side of D street (now El Camino Real) just north of Main Street. He served as commander of Sedgwick Post 17 of the GAR in 1923.

Henry W. Smith was eighty-four years old when he passed away at his home in Tustin on January 22, 1926. He was buried beside Emily at Fairhaven Cemetery in a section that is now part of Santa Ana Cemetery. The graveside ceremonies were performed by members of the Sedgwick Post 17 of the GAR, with members of the Women's Relief Corps in attendance.

After the death of her husband, Belle Smith returned to Pomona and was living there with her son, C.I. O'Neil, when she passed away on June 19, 1935 at the age of eighty-seven. She was buried in the family plot beside her first husband in Kalispell, Montana.

The following is a brief accounting of the children of H.W Smith and Louisa Weatherby:

- Edward Ellsworth Smith was born in Free Soil, Michigan, on May 4, 1866. He and his wife Mollie

(Buckmiller) had three children. They lived on San Juan Street and then moved to 170 D Street in Tustin. Edward worked as a foreman at a citrus packing house and later as a tree pruner. Edward died on April 19, 1943, and Mollie followed shortly after on December 28, 1943. They are both buried at Fairhaven.

- Onadell "Ona" Smith was born September 27, 1867, in Free Soil. She married James Franklin Mays in 1892 in South Dakota. The couple had six children. They moved to Minnesota, back to South Dakota, and eventually to Saskatchewan, Canada, where Ona died on April 3, 1921. James passed away in Canada in 1932.

- Arthur Albert Smith was born in 1869 in Free Soil. In 1897, he married Ada Estell Illingworth, and eventually the couple had four children. They lived in South Dakota, where Arthur worked for the Post Office. Ada passed away in 1919, and Arthur married a woman named Sophia in 1926. By 1940, they had moved to Pasadena, where Sophia died in 1945. Arthur died in 1956 and is buried in Mitchell, South Dakota.

- Nina Jane Smith was born in Free Soil on August 29, 1872. She married Milton G. Swatman, and they farmed in Idaho, where they had 10 children. Milton died in 1926. Nina passed away in Moscow, Idaho, on October 12, 1937, at the age of sixty-five.

- Myrtie Belle Smith was born April 8, 1874, in Free Soil. In 1897, she and her husband, Alfred C. Davis, and their two children moved to Manitoba, Canada.

- Leon Smith was born May 3, 1878, in Free Soil. He married Lena Davis on February 24, 1904, in Mitchell, South Dakota. They farmed in Davison County for many years and had no children. Leon died in 1964, and Lena passed away in 1969.

- Louis Henry Smith was born May 18, 1880, in Free Soil. In 1905, he married Etta Mathis. They farmed in Davison County, South Dakota, and had three children. Etta died in 1939, and Louis passed away on August 20, 1944. They are both buried in Mitchell, South Dakota.

The children of H.W. Smith and his second wife, Emily (Butterfield) Daken were:

- Roy Irving Smith was born September 10, 1884, in Davison County, South Dakota. In March 1907, he married Sue Blackmore in Tustin. They had two children but eventually divorced. Sue later married Cecil Maudlin "Cye" Featherly, a longtime Orange County supervisor for whom Featherly Regional Park in Santa Ana Canyon is named. Roy then married Iris Williams in 1928. At one time, Roy worked on the Irvine Ranch and then grew nursery stock in Tustin. Roy Smith died on July 5, 1936, at age fifty-one, leaving a widow with three young children to raise.

- Charles Earl Smith was born on September 23, 1886, in Davison County, South Dakota. He married Vera A. O'Brien in Tustin in April 1911. The couple had no children. Charles grew citrus and also worked as a construction foreman for the Irvine Company. Vera passed away on August 29, 1967, and Charles died just a few months later on November 26, 1967.

Thomas H. Smith

Private, Battery G

1st Ohio Light Artillery

A native of England, Thomas Smith served his adopted country as an artilleryman in an Ohio regiment during the war. After the war, he farmed in Iowa and then spent a decade in Nevada before moving his family to Tustin in 1890, where he became a prosperous businessman.

Thomas H. Smith was born April 8, 1841, in Norton, Herefordshire, England. He was the eighth child born to John and Elizabeth (Jones) Smith. Both parents were born in Wales but spent the majority of their lives in Herefordshire.

Thomas was thirteen years old in 1854 when he came to the United States with a married sister. They departed Liverpool on a steamship and arrived in Boston two weeks later. Thomas quickly moved to Cleveland, Ohio, where he learned the marble cutting trade and then later worked as a clerk in a wholesale house.

Thomas H. Smith was twenty-one years old on August 15, 1862, when he enlisted as a private in Battery G, 1st Ohio Light Artillery, near Cleveland. Battery G had been organized at Camp Dennison, near Cincinnati, in September 1861 for three years of service.

A typical Union artillery battery during the Civil War consisted of four cannon and had a complement of around 100 men, commanded by a captain with two lieutenants. Ten soldiers manned each cannon, with the remaining men in charge of the horses, ammunition limber, and other equipment. Battery G used four small, six-pounder cannons (named for the weight of the cannonball.) Light Artillery was also sometimes known as "Horse Artillery" because they were required to keep up with swiftly moving cavalry units. Each cannon weighed approximately 800 pounds and was pulled by a team of four horses.

Battery G of the 1st Ohio Light Artillery was first assigned to the Army of the Ohio, where Smith participated in the Battle of Perryville, Kentucky. In 1863, the 1st Ohio L.A. was transferred to the Army of the Cumberland, where it fought at the Battle of Chickamauga. The battle, fought in northern Georgia on September 18-20, 1863, amassed the second-highest number of casualties in the war after the Battle of Gettysburg, with over 34,000 combined killed, wounded, and missing in action.

Thomas Smith then saw action at Missionary Ridge (November 25, 1863), Spring Hill (November 29, 1863), Franklin (November 30, 1864), and Nashville (December 15, 1864), all in Tennessee. At the Battle of Franklin, Battery G helped anchor the left flank of the Union line. It poured around 50 shots into the Confederates, silencing an enemy battery and contributing to the Union victory. Battery G then traveled through east Tennessee into North Carolina before Smith was honorably discharged and mustered out of service in August 1865 in Nashville. Smith had served three years, and by the end of the war, Battery G had lost thirty-three men, six killed in action, and twenty-seven had died of disease.

Smith returned to Cleveland, where, later in the year, he became a naturalized citizen. Smith was not alone as an immigrant-soldier. During the war, over 200,000 German-born and 150,000 Irish-born immigrants enlisted in the Union ranks. About 10,000 immigrants from England served in the war. Many of these men left their native lands to escape poverty and oppression and came to believe the freedoms provided by their adopted country were worth fighting for.

Soldiers & Sailors Monument in downtown Cleveland dedicated to those men who served in the war from Cleveland.
The four sides are adorned with statues depicting the infantry, cavalry, artillery, and the navy.

In the fall of 1865, Smith returned to England to visit his family. Four of his siblings moved to the United States, but his parents and other brothers and sisters never left England. Smith spent the winter in England and returned to Cleveland in the spring of 1866.

Shortly after he returned to the states, Smith purchased a farm in Washington County, Iowa. On December 13, 1869, the twenty-eight-year-old Smith married Sarah Stanley in Harlan, Iowa. Sarah, twenty-two years old, was a native of Illinois, and she and Thomas had only one child, Harry Roy Smith, born on September 28, 1872.

The Smiths remained on their Iowa farm for about ten years and for six of those years Thomas served as the local Justice of the Peace. In 1879, Smith sold the farm and sent Sarah and H. Roy to stay with her parents in Harlan, Iowa, while he went in search of a new home in the west.

Smith's search ended in Gold Hill, Nevada, where he boarded with a cousin, J.P. Jones, and other members of his extended family. He worked as a woodcutter before sending for Sarah and Roy, and once established in Gold Hill, Smith worked in the coal and lumber business and also hauled freight.

Gold Hill, just south of Virginia City, was a booming mining town at the time of Smith's arrival. It was part of the famous Comstock Lode and boasted major deposits of silver and gold ore. In its heyday, the population peaked at 8,000, one-third of whom worked in the mines. The majority of miners were Irishmen, along with a contingent of Cornishmen.

Smith, an English immigrant, left no record of how he fared among so many Irishmen, but their relations must have been peaceful, for he remained in Gold Hill for a decade. In that time, Smith served six years as president of the board of education, and his son Roy graduated from Gold Hill High School.

In 1887, Smith made his first visit to California. He was so impressed with the soil and climate that he eventually purchased an existing citrus ranch in Tustin. He moved his family there in August 1890, traveling by wagon from Nevada, bringing his livestock along.

The Smith ranch in Tustin was located on Prospect Avenue, north of First Street, and consisted of seventeen acres of oranges, lemons, apricots, grapefruit, and a few walnut trees. At some point, Smith purchased sixteen additional acres south of Tustin where he grew alfalfa.

Around 1900, Smith became director of the Santa Ana Valley Irrigation Company, a position he would hold for several years. He belonged to a fraternal organization known as the Ancient Order of United Woodmen and was also an officer of Sedgwick Post-17 of the GAR.

In politics, Smith was a loyal Republican, breaking with the party only in the 1896 presidential election, when he sided with those who supported Democratic candidate William Jennings Bryan. Bryan believed that a monetary standard relying on both silver and gold would revive the flagging economy. Smith was probably influenced by his years spent living in a silver-mining town.

In addition to running the ranch on Prospect Avenue, in 1912, Smith assumed the presidency of the Farmers' Mutual Fire Insurance Company of Orange County. Their son Roy and his family lived next door, so Sarah had her grandchildren nearby. The youngest grandchild was just an infant when Sarah passed away at home on the day after Christmas, 1922. Sarah was seventy-five years old and had been married to Thomas for fifty-three years.

Thomas was a widower for three and a half years before he passed away at the ranch after an illness of ten days. He died on May 17, 1926, at the age of eighty-five. At the time of his death, he was still president of the insurance company. He was buried beside Sarah at Fairhaven Cemetery in Santa Ana.

The English immigrant had spent three years fighting for his adopted country. In his long life, he had worked as a marble cutter, clerk, and farmer. He had sold coal, lumber, and insurance and owned thirty acres of land. It can certainly be said that Thomas H. Smith made the most of his opportunities in America.

Harry Roy Smith, the only child of Thomas and Sarah, was born September 28, 1872, in Iowa. On May 10, 1896, he married Flora Thomas of Tustin. The couple eventually had three children. They lived on Prospect Avenue in Tustin next to his parents. Roy grew citrus and also worked as a buyer and shipper for a large packinghouse. Roy died of a heart attack on October 20, 1932, at the age of sixty. Flora passed away on April 20, 1945, at seventy-one, and both are buried at Fairhaven Cemetery.

Horace C. Snow

Sgt., Co. H, 13th US Infantry

1st Lt., Co. D, 45th US Colored Infantry

Horace Snow was born and raised in New England, and after an adventure in the gold fields of California, was living in Iowa when he enlisted to serve the Union during the Civil War.

He was eventually commissioned as an officer and served with an all-black regiment. After the war, he returned to Northern California and later followed a younger brother to Tustin, where he became a successful grower in the local citrus industry.

Horace C. Snow was born on October 2, 1831, in Whitefield, New Hampshire. He was the oldest of James Porter Snow and Satira Hutchins six surviving children, an older daughter having died in infancy. James, a blacksmith, also had seven children with his first wife, making him the father of fourteen.

Horace attended the State Normal School in West Newton, Massachusetts. The school was a college that prepared its students for careers in education, law, and medicine, but Horace was expelled before graduating.

On September 5, 1853, Horace left his home in Bridgewater, Massachusetts, for the gold fields of California, carrying one suitcase and with just $40 in his pocket. He traveled by ship from New York Harbor to Panama, then crossed the Isthmus by canoe and mule. He then took another ship up the coast to San Francisco, arriving there on October 12, 1853, just ten days after celebrating his 22nd birthday. Horace soon met up with his younger brother, Hiram K. Snow, who, in 1849, at the age of 15, had sailed around Cape Horn on a six-month voyage to California.

Horace spent almost two years in California and wrote many letters home to a friend and former classmate named Charlie Fitz. Over a century later, these letters were collected and published in book form. The letters show Snow to have been well educated with a wonderful power of description and a lively sense of humor. The letters offer a fascinating look at daily life in a mining camp and an eyewitness account of the wild lawlessness of Gold Rush-era California.

Horace, Hiram, and a friend named Spears, who had accompanied Horace to California, staked claims and lived together for almost two years in a small cabin near the mining camp of Agua Fria, just south of the town of Mariposa. They dug and panned for gold every day except Sunday and shared the cooking and cleaning chores. It is not clear why, but Horace suddenly left California, arriving back in New York Harbor on June 11, 1855. He would not return to the Golden State until after his service in the Civil War.

By the following year, Horace had gone west again, but this time only as far as Iowa; according to the 1856 state census, he was living in the town of Osage and working as a carpenter, a job he had taken up shortly after arriving in California to help pay off his debts.

He traveled back to New England and on January 27, 1857, married Emily Lawrence in Ashburnham, Massachusetts. Horace returned with his bride to Osage, where they had a son, Alfred Fitz Snow, who died on May 30, 1858, only five months old. A little over a year later, on July 1, 1859, twenty-five-year-old Emily died in Osage. Her body, along with that of her infant son, was sent back for burial together in Ashburnham.

On February 10, 1862, the thirty-year-old widower enlisted as a private in Company H, 13th United States Infantry Regiment. The 13th Infantry, an old regular army unit, was reorganized at Jefferson Barracks, Missouri, in the fall of 1861. The regiment was first stationed at Alton, Illinois, and then moved to Memphis on garrison duty until November 1862. The regiment was then a part of General Sherman's Yazoo Expedition and participated in the battles of Chickasaw Bayou, Hayes Bluff, Jackson, Champion's Hill, and Black River, all in the spring of 1863.

The 13th US Infantry participated in the Siege of Vicksburg from May 18 to July 4, 1863. On May 19th, the regiment took part in the unsuccessful frontal assault on Vicksburg but was credited with being the only Union unit to plant its flag on the Confederate positions. When Vicksburg finally surrendered on July 4, 1863, the Confederacy was effectively cut in half.

During his stint with the 13th Infantry, Horace Snow was promoted to Commissary Sergeant, a position in which he assisted the commissary officer in receiving, storing, and issuing supplies for the regiment. Snow remained with the regiment through the remainder of 1863, including the Union victory at Chattanooga in November.

Horace Snow was mustered out of the 13th Infantry on August 31, 1864, and one week later was commissioned a First Lieutenant in the 45th Colored Infantry regiment in Philadelphia.

The 45th had been organized at Philadelphia from June to August, 1864, and was composed of free blacks from the north and former slaves. All the enlisted men were black but commanded by all white officers. It is not surprising that Horace sought service in a black regiment. As early as 1853, he had declared himself a dedicated abolitionist, and service in a black regiment would allow him to put his beliefs into action.

Since the war began, abolitionists and black leaders had been calling for the recruitment of black troops, but it wasn't until 18 months into the conflict that the Lincoln Administration and the War Department relented and began recruiting and organizing black regiments. This arose from the unpopularity of the draft and the manpower shortage as the war progressed.

Being a white officer in a black regiment was considered a choice assignment. Applicants were motivated by the chance for a quick promotion and a pay raise, but many were also motivated by idealism and a chance to help the black cause. A Bureau of Colored Troops was established to screen the candidates. The Bureau wanted only "intelligent white men with high morals who were willing to make a commitment to uplifting the black race." Horace Snow certainly met these qualifications.

Unlike in other regiments, where officers were chosen by the men or given command due to their ability to recruit, an interview and written examination were administered to those applying for a commission in a black regiment. Only 60% passed the exam, and then only a quarter of those were actually commissioned as officers in the United States Colored Troops. In fact, a school was established to help men prepare for the exam and served as a precursor to the Army's Officer Candidate Schools. (It is possible that Horace Snow was detached from the 13th Infantry to attend this school since he was commissioned only a week after mustering out.)

The Lincoln Administration wanted the experiment of black soldiers to succeed, believing it would combat negative racial stereotypes held by both Northern and Southern whites and ease the path of black citizenship after the war. For this reason, the black regiments were to be led by only the most qualified white officers.

The 45th Colored Infantry saw its first action at Chaffin's Farm and Darbytown Road, a part of the Petersburg campaign, fought September 28-30, 1864. The troops fought well in their first engagements but were then part of the Union defeat at the second Battle of Fair Oaks on October 27-28. The 45th stayed in the trenches before Richmond until March 1865. The regiment was then involved in the pursuit of General Lee's army that eventually resulted in his surrender at Appomattox Court House on April 9, 1865.

The 45th moved to Texas in May and June 1865 and performed garrison duty at Edinburg, near the Mexican border until September, and at Brownsville until mustered out on November 4, 1865. Texas was considered the worst place for black troops to serve with the occupation forces. Racism was rampant among the defeated Texans, and acts of violence were common against the black troops and their white officers.

It is unclear if Horace Snow accompanied the regiment to Texas. On the Company D roster, it was noted that Snow was absent and on detached duty when the regiment was mustered out. In fact, while the regiment was still in Texas, Snow was married in Philadelphia.

In all, some 180,000 black soldiers served in the war, and nearly 37,000 gave their lives. They had been involved in 449 separate engagements and fought well, with twenty-five black soldiers winning the Medal of Honor. They had certainly done their part to fight for their own freedom. General Ulysses S. Grant recognized the contribution of the black soldiers to the Union victory. As free black men poured into the Union Army late in the war, Grant wrote, "The problem is solved. The Negro is a man, a soldier, a hero." By the end of the war, two million men had worn the Union blue, but only 7,000 of those served as white officers in black regiments, making Horace Snow a member of an elite group.

Horace Snow was still in uniform when he married Margaret Fox Butcher at St. Paul's Episcopal Church in Philadelphia on September 28, 1865. Margaret was born in Philadelphia in 1845, and the couple's courtship undoubtedly began while Snow was stationed in the City of Brotherly Love.

Soon after their marriage, the couple headed west, first settling in Vallejo, California, just north of San Francisco. Their first three children were born there in Solano County: William (1867), Margaret Grace (1868), and Martha (1871). Horace supported his growing family as a dry goods merchant. Between 1865 and 1878, Horace's mother and three brothers, Hiram, Harvey, and Hubbard, all made their way to Solano County.

After almost a decade in Solano County, Horace moved the family north, to Eureka in Humboldt County. Their final two children were born there: Horace (1876) and Carrie Bessie (1879). Snow was in the mercantile business in Eureka with his brother Hiram and with Jonathan Freese, whose son would one day marry Grace Snow.

In 1877, Hiram Snow moved from Vallejo to Tustin, where he purchased fifty-six acres and became one of the early orange growers in the area. Five years later, Horace followed his younger brother to Tustin.

Horace purchased fourteen acres about a mile southwest of the town center. He diversified his acreage, planting six and a half acres to oranges, with the remaining acreage going to walnuts, lemons, apricots, and prunes, with a remaining half-acre reserved for home garden use. He also built a house and a barn that could also serve as a packing house.

Snow seemed to prosper in Tustin. By 1893, his oranges alone netted him $3,500, a sizable income for the time. He also operated a lumberyard on Fruit Street in Santa Ana in partnership with his son-in-law, Sherman Stevens. (Stevens was also Horace's nephew, the son of his sister Betsey.)

But Snow's years in Tustin were also tinged with tragedy. In November 1888, nine-year-old Carrie Bessie Snow died. In October 1891, Grace lost her husband in a terrible accident. Then, on February 12, 1893, sixteen-year-old Horace J. Snow passed away.

But the biggest blow to Horace came on August 25, 1893, when Maggie, his wife of thirty years, died of a heart attack while the couple was on a vacation at San Juan Hot Springs. Three years later, on November 7, 1896, Horace Snow passed away suddenly from a heart attack at the age of sixty-five. He was buried beside Maggie at Fairhaven Memorial Park in Santa Ana.

The Children of Horace and Maggie Snow:

- William Butcher Snow married Blanch Amanda Bullock in Eureka in 1889. They eventually moved to Santa Ana, where William farmed and then later ran a dry goods store. The couple had six children: Gertrude, Annie, Horace C., Sarah, Bertram, and Huestis. William passed away in Santa Ana on November 11, 1948, and Blanch died five months later on April 4, 1949.

- Margaret Grace Snow married Benjamin Franklin "Frank" Frees on July 20, 1887, in Tustin. They had two sons, Norman and Benjamin. Little Benjamin was just an infant when tragedy took his father away. Frank Frees was greasing a windmill, but failed to tie the blades down. A gust of wind caught the blades, which struck Frank, knocking him forty feet to the ground. He lived for five hours before succumbing to his injuries. (Ironically, sixteen years earlier to the day, his father had been killed in a logging camp accident in Humboldt

County.) Although widowed at twenty-three, Grace never remarried. She eventually moved to Los Angeles to live with her youngest son and his family, and she passed away in that city on March 1, 1948, at the age of seventy-nine.

- Martha "Mattie" Snow married Sherman Stevens on April 3, 1888, in Tustin; she was just shy of her seventeenth birthday, and the groom was twenty-four. The wedding took place at the Presbyterian Church on Main Street, and the guests walked across the street for the reception at the Queen Anne Victorian house Stevens had built for his new bride. Stevens was a large grower and businessman, at one time a director of the First National Bank of Tustin. Stevens also partnered with Ed Utt and the Irvine Company to form the San Joaquin Fruit Company, planting 1,000 acres of walnuts and oranges. He later joined C.E. Utt to develop 900 acres in Lemon Heights. Mattie and Sherman had two sons: Clarence, who died in 1906 at age 17, and Horace J. Stevens. Mattie died on May 15, 1947, and Sherman passed away the following year.

- Horace J. Snow was born April 23, 1876, and passed away in Tustin on February 12, 1893, just shy of seventeen. He was a sergeant in the Tustin Boys Brigade, and his comrades acted as pallbearers and honored him with a twenty-one-gun salute.

- Carrie Bessie Snow passed away from diphtheria at her home in Tustin on November 30, 1888, at the age of nine.

The Brothers Snow: Hubbard, Harvey, Hiram, and Horace.
Horace followed Hiram to Tustin.

Abraham H. Stutsman

Private, Company C

1st Iowa Cavalry

A.H. Stutsman went to war as a young man, was seriously wounded and was fortunate to survive. He recovered and went on to a long career as a lawyer and judge in Iowa. He relocated to Tustin in the 1890s, where he became a successful grower of citrus and walnuts.

Abraham Hutchinson Stutsman was born December 21, 1840, in Gosport, Owen County, Indiana, the sixth of Abraham S. and Sarah (Kern) Stutsman's eight children. In 1842, the family moved to a farm in Lee County, southeastern Iowa, where the elder Abraham passed away in 1845 at age 52. For a time, Sarah continued to operate the family farm with the help of her sons. Sarah received a pension because her husband served with Capt. Jacob Pearsall's Company in the War of 1812.

In 1860, the family was living near Elk Springs, Missouri, but by the following year, Abraham was back in Lee County, Iowa. Stutsman was twenty years old when he enlisted as a private in Company C, 1st Iowa Cavalry Regiment on July 13, 1861.

The 1st Iowa Cavalry was organized at Davenport, Iowa, in the summer of 1861 and mustered in for three years of Federal service, the first Union cavalry unit of the war to be accepted for a three-year term. It was also one of the few Union cavalry units in which the members supplied their own horses and equipment.

The regiment was first stationed at Benton Barracks near St. Louis, but eventually was spread throughout Missouri, where it skirmished with Confederate guerrillas, bushwhackers, and southern sympathizers. The regiment's first large engagement was at the Battle of Black River, where the Iowans captured about 1,300 Confederate recruits and their arms. On January 8, 1862, the regiment attacked and destroyed a Confederate camp at Silver Creek, Missouri.

Stutsman was first wounded on March 25, 1862, in a skirmish with rebel guerrillas at Roseville, Missouri. He received a flesh wound in the face that left a bad scar, but he quickly recovered and returned to his unit.

Stutsman was back with the 1st Iowa Cavalry on August 27, 1863, at the Battle of Bayou Meto. The battle, also called the Battle of Reed's Bridge, took place near present-day Jacksonville, Arkansas, and was part of the Union campaign to capture the state capitol at Little Rock. The Confederate forces were driven back across a bridge over the bayou. The 1st Iowa made a charge at the Confederate lines but was driven back, unsuccessful in its attempt to stop the rebels from burning the bridge.

The 1st Iowa lost two men killed and thirty-five wounded in the charge at Bayou Meto. Among the wounded was Private Abraham Stutsman. According to an unknown source, possibly a family account, Stutsman was left on the battlefield for dead but was discovered after three days to have a faint pulse by an intern who went looking for any signs of life. He was taken to a hospital in Little Rock, where his arm was amputated near the shoulder. An older brother, Dr. Samuel H. Stutsman, an assistant surgeon in the Iowa infantry, came to care for him and took him back to Iowa.

Stutsman was discharged for his wounds on January 13, 1864, in Davenport, Iowa.

Stutsman returned home to Iowa to recuperate from his wounds and to learn to live with the use of only one arm. Before the war, he had made his living as a farm laborer, but now he had to learn to use his brain rather than his brawn. He consequently read law for three years, then graduated from the University of Michigan Law School in 1868. The following year, he was elected and served a term in the Iowa State Legislature.

On April 15, 1870, the twenty-nine-year-old Stutsman married Frances Olivia "Fannie" Allen at Fort Madison, in Lee County, Iowa. By that summer, they were living in Chariton, Iowa, where Stutsman practiced law. A Chariton neighbor and fellow lawyer was Daniel Baker, who, years later, would also relocate to Southern California and become the owner and editor of the ***Santa Ana Bulletin***. Stutsman and Baker would remain lifelong friends.

Later in 1870, Abraham and Fannie moved to Burlington, Iowa, where all of their six children would be born: Carl Allen (1871), Carolyn "Carrie" (1872), Walter A. (1875), Elizabeth (1878), Samuel C. (1880), and Abraham H. Jr. (1884). Elizabeth died in 1881, and Samuel passed away in 1882.

Abraham prospered in Burlington, serving as city solicitor from 1874 to 1876. In 1878, he was elected judge of the district court and was re-elected for another four-year term in 1882. It is a mystery why an established attorney and judge would leave what appeared to be a comfortable life to move west. But that is just what A. H. Stutsman did, moving to Tustin in June 1892.

Stutsman must have purchased land with established orchards just a few months after the move. A newspaper article reported that Mrs. Stutsman earned $572 from the sale of her apricot crop. (Also, a month after moving to Tustin, Fannie badly injured her right eye with a large needle while attempting to sew up a sack of dried fruit.)

Abraham Stutsman in his Tustin orchard.

Judge Stutsman

Fannie Stutsman

It appears that Judge Stutsman did not close his law practice in Burlington, and for years after his move to Tustin, the local papers recorded his comings and goings to Iowa on business. It seems the family may have spent the entire year of 1894 back in

Iowa while still holding on to their property in Tustin. At some point, the Judge closed out his practice in Iowa; perhaps it was in 1905, when his son and law partner, Carl, moved to Southern California.

In Tustin, the Stutsman home was located on the east side of Newport Road, right across from McFadden Avenue. Stutsman was an orchardist, growing oranges, walnuts, and apricots, but also carried on a law practice with his son, Carl. Stutsman was also involved in various agricultural organizations. He was an agricultural commissioner in 1907 and, for a time, director of the Santiago Orange Growers Association and president of the Tustin Walnut Growers Association. He was also, for many years, the president of the Iowa State Society of Southern California and a frequent speaker at the society's annual picnic for transplanted Iowans.

Fannie Stutsman was also a civic-minded citizen of Tustin. She was an active member of the Tustin Literature Section, a women's group that discussed current events and articles from the Literary Digest magazine. She was also very active in the Baptist church and a member of the Ebell Club and the Daughters of the American Revolution.

The Stutsmans had been living in Tustin for almost forty years when Fannie passed away on August 8, 1931, at the age of eighty-four. (On the day of her death, 125,000 former Iowans gathered for their annual picnic at Bixby Park in Long Beach.) At the time of her death, she and the Judge had been married for over sixty-one years.

Judge Stutsman had retired from his law practice for over a dozen years at the time of his death on March 17, 1934, at the age of ninety-three. One newspaper reported his death as the result of a fall several days earlier that had caused a head injury. Another newspaper attributed his death to a paralytic stroke. At the time of his death, he was living on his Tustin ranch with his son Walter.

The Civil War veteran was paid military honors at his funeral by his fellow members of Sedgwick Post-17. Although Fannie had preceded him in death by three years, the funeral was a dual service, and afterward, both were buried at Inglewood Park Cemetery, near Los Angeles.

The children of A.H. and Fannie Stutsman were all born in Burlington, Iowa.

- Carl Allen Stutsman was born January 27, 1871. He graduated from the University of Iowa in 1891, then graduated from law school the following year and passed the bar. He came to California in 1905 and married Helen Buchanan of Pittsburgh, Pennsylvania. He practiced law with his father and was then appointed municipal court judge in Los Angeles in 1926. In 1931, he was promoted to the superior court and was re-elected repeatedly to that position until his death.

  Carl and Helen had two sons, Carl Jr. (1913-1985), who was also an attorney, and Stewart, who died in 1917 at only a year and a half old. Helen passed away on September 7, 1918, two months before her youngest son. Carl remarried in 1931 to Gertrude Mary Stephenson, and the couple had no children. Carl A. Stutsman died on July 14, 1950, at the age of seventy-nine.

- Caroline "Carrie" Stutsman was born December 4, 1872. She never married and, for many years, lived at home with her parents. She often appeared in the society columns of the local newspapers, usually in connection with one of her mother's various organizations. Carrie was living in Los Angeles when she died on July 11, 1928, at the age of fifty-five.

- Walter A. Stutsman was born February 28, 1875. He first married Abbie May Cartwright in 1906 in

Burlington, and she passed away two years later. He then married Ruth Elizabeth Wing on April 27, 1914, in Riverside, California. Walter and Ruth had three children: Ruth Elizabeth, Walter Jr., and Allen Wing. Walter Sr. worked for years as a mining engineer before moving to Tustin to take over his father's citrus ranching operation. Walter passed away at the Tustin ranch on June 15, 1936, at the age of sixty-one. Ruth died in Tustin in 1961.

- Abraham H. Stutsman Jr. was born on November 22, 1884. In 1910, he married Mildred Adams of Tustin. They moved to Los Angeles, where Abe worked in the hardware business. They had one daughter, Marion. Abe died on September 27, 1920, after a short illness. He was just thirty-five years old. Mildred passed away in Los Angeles in 1944 at the age of fifty-eight.

The Stutsman Family.
Left to right: Judge Stutsman, Walter, Carrie, Carl, Abraham Jr.,
Fannie. The photo was taken on March 1, 1901 in Santa Ana.

Henry L. Vanhise

Private, Company I

2nd New Jersey Cavalry

Henry Vanhise was just a teenager when he served in the final year of the war. After the war, he began to move west, first to Illinois, then to Kansas, before finally arriving in Tustin around 1890.

Henry Lane Vanhise was born on November 3, 1846, in New Jersey, the fourth of Isaac and Fannie (Johnson) Vanhise's eight children. Henry grew up in various towns around New Jersey because his father's work as a carpenter took them to many locations.

Henry was just seventeen years old when he enlisted as a private in Company I, 2nd New Jersey Cavalry Regiment. The regiment had been mustered into service in August 1863 at Camp Parker in Trenton, New Jersey. Vanhise mustered in one year later, on August 31, 1864, for a one-year enlistment. At the time of Vanhise's enlistment, the regiment was part of the Cavalry Corps of the District of West Tennessee. Then, from the winter of 1864 until the end of the war, the 2nd New Jersey served primarily in the Military Division of West Mississippi. Both Tennessee and Mississippi were largely under Union control by this period in the war.

The first action Vanhise would have seen with the 2nd New Jersey was at the Battle of Egypt Station, fought on December 28, 1864, at Egypt, Mississippi. The battle, a Union victory, was part of a cavalry raid led by Union General Benjamin Grierson. Early on the morning of the 28th, the 2nd New Jersey Cavalry charged and drove back a Confederate skirmish line. The Confederate forces eventually surrendered, and 500 prisoners were taken. The

2nd New Jersey lost nineteen killed and seventy-one wounded during the charge, by far the most Union casualties of the battle.

Sign Marking Battle of Egypt Station

Next, in early April 1865, the regiment participated in the siege and capture of Spanish Fort and Fort Blakeley, two of the forts in a ring surrounding Mobile Bay in Alabama. By the end of the war, the 2nd New Jersey Cavalry had lost 241 men; 3 officers and 48 enlisted men killed in action, and 190 men who died of disease. Henry Vanhise was discharged on June 29, 1865, in Vicksburg, Mississippi, having fulfilled ten months of his one-year enlistment.

Henry Vanhise was still just eighteen years old at the time of his discharge. He had lived his entire life in New Jersey, but after the war, he began a series of moves westward that, many years later, would end in Southern California. The summer of 1870 found him working as a farm laborer for a family in Richland County, Illinois.

Five years later, he was farther west, now working on a farm near the town of Doyle in Marion County, Kansas. It was in the Marion County town of Peabody that the now thirty-year-old Vanhise married Sarah Legate in 1877. Sixteen-year-old Sarah was the daughter of a Confederate veteran; Alfred Legate had served in the 4th Arkansas Infantry regiment during the war.

The couple's first child, Elsie Rose, was born in 1881. Their only son, Roy, was born in 1883 but died in the summer of 1885. Their final child, Gladys, was born in 1889. Vanhise was a farmer, but in October 1884, he was also appointed postmaster of the small town of Dixon, in Butler County, Kansas. It was a position he apparently held for about a year.

Vanhise spent his last years in Kansas farming near the town of Towanda, also in Butler County. He was a member of the Samuel Pike Post-305 of the GAR in Towanda, and their records show that in 1889, he was receiving a $6 monthly disability pension for contracting "lung fever" while in the service of his country. Lung fever is an obsolete term for a condition now known as pyrexia or pulmonary inflammation. Six dollars seems like a paltry sum but it would amount to $177.50 in current (2021) purchasing power.

Not long after the birth of their last child, Henry and Sarah made their final move, settling in Tustin around 1890. Like many of the veterans who came to the area, Vanhise raised citrus. For many years, the Vanhise home was located on the southeast corner of 17th Street and Prospect Avenue in Tustin. On their acreage, Henry grew oranges and walnuts.

Henry Vanhise died at home on August 21, 1924, at the age of seventy-seven. Henry was an active member of Sedgwick Post-17 of the GAR, and the members of the post provided the graveside services at his funeral when he was buried at Fairhaven Cemetery. At the time of his death, he and Sarah had been married for forty-seven years and had been living in Tustin for the past thirty-four years.

Three years later, on June 28, 1927, Sarah passed away at her home on 17th Street, just shy of her sixty-sixth birthday. After her funeral, she was buried beside Henry at Fairhaven Cemetery.

Henry and Sarah had four children. In addition to their son Roy, who died at two years of age, they must have lost another child in infancy, for the 1900 Federal census lists Sarah as having four children, two living. The two surviving children were:

- Elsie Rose Vanhise, born January 26, 1881, in Kansas. Elsie was about nine years old when she moved with her parents to Tustin. On January 9, 1907, she married a fellow Kansan, Guy I. Field, at her parents' home in Tustin. Guy was a citrus rancher, and for many years, they lived on East Chapman Avenue in Orange. They had one child, a son named Weldon. Guy died on November 2, 1941, at the age of sixty-three, and Elsie passed away on June 23, 1954, at the age of seventy-three.

- Gladys Vanhise, born October 31, 1889, in Kansas. She was just an infant when she came to Tustin with her parents. On New Year's Day, 1930, she married Lee B. Ward in Santa Ana. She was forty, and Lee, another fellow Kansan, was forty-nine. Lee was a World War I veteran who worked for many years for Consolidated Orange Growers in Orange. The couple lived on 17th Street and Prospect in Tustin, probably at the old Vanhise house. They had no children. Lee died February 3, 1956, at the age of seventy-five, and Gladys passed away November 18, 1957, at the age of sixty-eight.

William B. Wall

Major, Field & Staff

33rd Mississippi Infantry

William Wall grew up on a plantation in the South and earned a medical degree from a northern college. He was the chief surgeon of an infantry regiment that saw intense action throughout the course of the war. He was one of the earliest veterans to settle in Tustin and went on to become one of the most prominent and successful citizens of the area.

William Burgess Wall was born November 28, 1829, to Charles F. and Judith T. (Johns) Wall in Halifax County, in south central Virginia near the North Carolina border. The Walls must have been reasonably well off, as they owned a plantation, and by the time William was ten years old, the Wall household listed twenty-three people, including twelve enslaved people and two free people of color.

Charles Wall died sometime before 1840, when William was just a child, and his mother had moved the family to Panola County, Mississippi, by 1850. The family finances were still strong enough to provide William with a good education. He went north for medical school, graduating in 1853 from Jefferson Medical College of Thomas Jefferson University in Philadelphia.

With his medical degree in hand, Wall returned to Panola County and opened a practice. On May 14, 1856, Dr. Wall married Bethunia Perkins in Panola. Wall was twenty-four and his bride sixteen. The couple would have two daughters, Sarah and Mary.

On March 3, 1862, about a year after the Civil War began, Dr. Wall enlisted and was commissioned a First Lieutenant in the 33rd Mississippi Infantry regiment. He declined the position of assistant surgeon and, after being promoted to captain, commanded an infantry company for about three months. He was then appointed head surgeon of the regiment and promoted to major; he held that rank and position for the remainder of the war.

Surgery before the war was such a rarity that most Civil War surgeons had little experience and most had never cut into a living human body or treated gunshot wounds. Their roles as surgeons in the war were a "learn as you go" experience. It is estimated that about 30,000 amputations were done on Union soldiers during the war, with Confederate numbers about the same. The myth that these surgeries were performed without anesthesia is not true; ether, chloroform, or a combination of the two was usually used. However, Civil War doctors lacked knowledge of germ theory and infection, and lacked the drugs to combat them, even if they had known. Subsequently, soldiers would often survive the amputation only to die from a blood infection. This was the life that Dr. Wall lived for three years as a regimental surgeon.

The 33rd Mississippi had been organized in late 1861 and saw its first action at the Battle of Corinth in October 1862, and was involved in the various engagements of the Vicksburg Campaign in the summer of 1863. In 1864, as part of the Army of Tennessee, the 33rd took part in all the battles of the Atlanta Campaign, including New Hope Church, Peachtree Creek, Ezra Church, and Jonesboro.

Dr. Wall must have had his hands full after the Battle of Peachtree Creek, fought July 20, 1864, outside of Atlanta. His regiment held the exposed right flank of the Confederate line and suffered sixteen dead and eighty-three wounded; among the dead were three company commanders. A letter exists from a private in Company K, telling his wife about a comrade who had a leg amputated after a conference among the regiment's doctors, presumably including Dr. Wall.

The 33rd went on to take part in the battles of Franklin and Nashville, both resounding Confederate defeats. The regiment that had been 792 strong in the spring of 1862 was down to 85 officers and men fit for duty by December 1864. With the regiment so weakened, it was consolidated into the 22nd Mississippi Infantry regiment in April 1865 and surrendered along with the forces of General Joseph E. Johnston in North Carolina a month later. Major W.B. Wall was paroled with the rest of the Confederate forces in North Carolina on May 1, 1865.

After the war, Dr. Wall completed a post-graduate course in New Orleans and then returned to Panola to rebuild his medical practice. Bethunia Wall died two days after Christmas, 1871, at the age of thirty-one. Two years later, Dr. Wall remarried. His new wife was Mrs. Julia F. Norman, a widow from South Carolina with two daughters. William and Julia would have two children of their own, William and Pearl.

In 1875, Dr. Wall and a friend and fellow physician from Mississippi, Dr. John Paine, traveled together to California in search of suitable land for growing citrus. Dr. Wall purchased forty acres on Tustin Avenue in Tustin and then brought his wife and children west to join him.

It is not known why Dr. Wall, at the age of forty-five, decided to leave the South and move west, but he had two older brothers who had preceded him to California, albeit many years earlier. Isaac B. Wall and James A. Wall had come to California during the Gold Rush days and done well. In 1853, Isaac Wall became the fourth Speaker of the California Assembly, and in 1855, he was appointed collector of the Port of Monterey. Sadly, Isaac was murdered and robbed of his money belt while traveling by horseback from Monterey to San Luis Obispo on November 11, 1855. James Wall settled in Salinas, California, where he served as District Attorney before becoming a Superior Court judge.

The Wall property on the east side of Tustin Avenue ran north from Fruit Street, almost to 17th Street, and east to Yorba. He built a large, two-story white house back from the street, reached by a long winding driveway entered just north of Fruit Street. He also built a large barn, hog pens, and eventually a large citrus packing house, the first in the area.

Dr. Wall has been credited with planting the first large citrus orchard in Tustin, followed soon by Samuel Preble, Hiram Snow, Columbus Tustin, and P.T. Adams. Wall's orchards prospered, and the doctor was featured as a model orchardist in a promotional booklet published in 1887 to lure people to the area. A chart in the booklet showed that Dr. Wall's profit per acre had increased every year over a four-year period due to his efficient management.

For a number of years, Dr. Wall continued to practice medicine. In the 1880s, he shared an office on 4th Street in Santa Ana with his Tustin neighbor, Dr. Moses S. Jones, an eye, ear, nose, and throat specialist. But eventually, Dr. Wall gave up medicine to devote all his time to his horticultural interests.

In addition to his medical and farming endeavors, Dr. Wall found time for other civic-minded pursuits. He was active in the campaign to create Orange County, and when the new county became a reality in 1889, he was elected its first treasurer and re-elected to a second term. And although he eventually retired from medical practice, he was a founding member and the first president of the Orange County Medical Society. He also served for two years on the board of the Sycamore (Tustin) School District and was an active member of the First Baptist Church of Santa Ana for many years.

Dr. Wall was also very active in agricultural organizations. He helped found the Santa Ana Valley Irrigation Company, bringing water to the orchards of Tustin, and served on its board of directors. Dr. Wall was also credited with introducing chemical spraying to control red, purple, and black scale on citrus, and he was instrumental in developing a method of night fumigation in orchards to minimize damage to trees. In fact, Dr. Wall, with several Tustin orchardists, tried to patent their night fumigation, calling it the "Twilight Patent", but the courts annulled the patent on the grounds that darkness was not patentable.

Dr. Wall built the first packinghouse in the area on his Tustin Avenue property and, later, in partnership with another prominent Tustin businessman, Charles W. Wilcox, formed the Santiago Orange Growers Association and served as the president of the association for many years.

Dr. Wall was also a businessman with diversified interests. In addition to his agricultural organizations, he was, at the time of his death, president of the Santa Ana Oil Company, the Santa Ana Commercial Company, and the Pacific Coast Soda Company. The Santa Ana Commercial Company was a creamery that supplied butter and other dairy products to local markets.

The Pacific Coast Soda Company was not a beverage company but a mining operation extracting phosphates, sulphates, and salt in the Mojave Desert near Soda Lake. The company operated a large processing plant near the lake and another smaller factory about three miles southeast of Santa Ana along the Santa Fe Railroad line. Some of the most prominent men in the county were investors in the company, including James Irvine, John McFadden, A.D. Bishop, Daniel Halladay, and P.T. Adams.

Dr. Wall lost his second wife when Julia died on July 25, 1888, at the age of fifty-two. She and William had celebrated their fifteenth wedding anniversary just two weeks earlier. At the time of her death, her two children with William were still young; Will was fourteen and Pearl just ten.

It is not surprising that Dr. Wall, a Confederate veteran, did not belong to the party of Lincoln. Wall was a dedicated Democrat in a county largely dominated by the Republican Party. In 1892, Grover Cleveland was elected to the second of his two non-consecutive terms. Cleveland was the only Democrat elected to the presidency between 1856 and 1912.

Dr. Wall, on the far left, with employees at his packinghouse, 1892.

Dr. Wall attended a pre-inauguration banquet for the president-elect in Washington, D.C., where Cleveland made a rousing speech to his Democratic supporters. Hanging on the wall behind Cleveland was a poster of a crowing rooster. After the speech, Dr. Wall approached Cleveland, congratulated him on his victory, and mentioned that the rooster would make a great label for his citrus crates. Cleveland pulled the canvas poster off the wall, rolled it up, and handed it to the doctor.

Dr. Wall took out the copyright on the rooster label and used it on the citrus crates from his packinghouse until he closed it in 1900, when he merged with the Santiago Orange Growers Association. After Wall's death, his son sold the rights to all his citrus labels to the association for $50. From 1910 to 1967, the Rooster was the primary label used by the Santiago Orange Growers Association, and it is estimated that it adorned between 45,000 and 50,000 citrus crates.

The orange crate label inspired by President-elect Cleveland

Dr. Wall was at the Sunset Club, a men's club in Santa Ana, of which he was a member and on the board of directors, when he suddenly fell ill with stomach pains. Feeling too sick to return home, he stayed at the home of a friend, Dr. J.L. Dryer. He passed away in Dryer's home two days later, on April 21, 1909, at the age of seventy-nine.

The funeral service two days later at his Tustin home was one of the largest in local memory; hundreds of mourners crowded the house and overflowed onto the lawn. The funeral service was conducted by the Baptist pastor, J. Herndon Garnett. At Santa Ana Cemetery, a Mason ceremony was performed, and there were two sets of pallbearers that included a number of doctors and some of the most prominent citizens of the county, among them William H. Spurgeon, J.M. Lacy, John Cubbon, Hiram K. Snow, and Sherman Stevens. Dr. Wall's estate, valued at around $100,000, would be worth over $3 million in 2022 dollars.

Dr. William Burgess Wall was, without a doubt, one of the most well-liked, respected, and successful of the Civil War veterans to settle in Tustin.

The children of Dr. William B. Wall and his first wife, Bethunia Perkins, were:

- Sarah J. Wall was born around 1857 in Mississippi. In the 1870 Federal census, she was thirteen, but was no longer listed with the family in 1880; she would have been twenty-three and possibly married by then. Her father's obituary states he was survived by two daughters, Mary and Pearl, so it would seem that Sarah died sometime before 1909.

- Mary Perkins Wall was born November 2, 1859, in Mississippi and was about sixteen years old when she came with her family to Tustin. Mary, often known as Mamie, never married and, after her father's death, lived in Santa Ana, where she grew citrus and taught school. She passed away at her home on Birch Street in Santa Ana on October 3, 1942, at the age of eighty-two and is buried in the Wall plot at Santa Ana Cemetery.

The children of Dr. William B. Wall and his second wife Julia (Dillard) Norman were:

- William Dillard Wall was born April 18, 1874, in Mississippi, and was only an infant when his parents brought him to Tustin. William attended Tustin and Santa Ana schools and was a citrus grower, perhaps taking over his father's Tustin orchards. He later grew citrus in Ventura County and spent the last forty years of his life in Los Angeles. He never married and died on September 1, 1963, in Los Angeles, and is buried in the Wall plot at Santa Ana Cemetery.

- Pearl Wall was born September 16, 1877, in Tustin. She married a dentist, James Elton Lang, at her family home in Tustin on January 28, 1911, in a ceremony attended by over one hundred guests. By 1914, the couple was living on Crenshaw Boulevard in Los Angeles. They had no children and spent the rest of their lives in Los Angeles, where Elton had his dental practice. He died in 1948, and Pearl passed away on October 15, 1970, at the age of ninety-three and is buried at Santa Ana Cemetery.

Dr. Wall's stepdaughters were:

- Palmetto "Metto" Norman was born June 18, 1861, in South Carolina and was fourteen when the family moved to Tustin. She never married and was thirty-two years old when she died on December 31, 1893, in Ventura, California. She may have been living with her sister, Minnie, and her family at the time of her death. Metto is buried at Santa Ana Cemetery.

- Minnie R. Norman was born August 11, 1864, in Spartanburg, South Carolina, and was eleven years old when she moved with her family to Tustin. On February 22, 1887, she married Hiram K. Snow, Jr.

Hiram was a member of a prominent pioneer Tustin family. The couple had two sons, Norman R. Snow and Robert H. Snow. The family lived in Ventura County, where Hiram managed his father's citrus ranch. Minnie died of cancer on April 26, 1914, at the age of forty-nine. Hiram passed away in Los Angeles on February 3, 1929, at the age of sixty-three. They are both buried at Santa Ana Cemetery.

The Wall House on Tustin Avenue, shortly before it was razed

Joseph A. Wilkes

Private, Company K

6th California Volunteer Infantry

Joseph A. Wilkes was a young boy when he came west with his parents in the mid-1850s and was the only Tustin Civil War veteran who served in California during the war. After the war, Wilkes moved to southern California, living first in El Toro and then in Santa Ana, before arriving in Tustin in 1893.

Joseph Adcock Wilkes was born August 12, 1846, in Miller County, Missouri, to Albert G. Wilkes and Lucy Jane Adcock. Albert Wilkes had traveled to California in 1848 in pursuit of gold and returned to Missouri three years later. He had prospected for gold for a time but made his money in California by selling provisions to other miners. In 1856, he returned to California, this time with his family. The months-long, 2,000-mile journey across the plains was made by ox-drawn wagons, with the family, including 10-year-old Joseph, walking along beside. The family brought along many of their household possessions as well as their herd of cattle and a flock of sheep. The trip must have been

221

especially challenging for Lucy, who, besides driving one of the wagons, had to look after six children, three of whom were under ten years of age. Their wagons traveled through Donner Pass and arrived at Sutter's Fort after months on the trail.

Missouri was a slave state, and along with his six children, Albert brought a ten-year-old black girl, Susan, to California. Lucy had inherited two enslaved people from her mother: an older woman and a young girl, probably Susan. It is believed Albert opposed slavery and planned to emancipate Susan, and in any case, the California constitution prohibited slavery. Susan lived with the Wilkes family for several years, then moved away and married.

Albert Wilkes settled his family on a large ranch in the Tassajara Valley, east of the town of Danville. The family prospered, and Lucy gave birth to another child, her seventh, in 1859.

Sadly, Lucy Wilkes passed away in 1862 at the age of 47, leaving Albert a widower with six children still at home. Two years later, Albert married Jane Toomey, who became a loving stepmother to his children.

The year after his mother's death, Joseph Wilkes moved to the mining camp of St. Louis, in Sierra County, to try his hand at prospecting for gold. It was at St. Louis that 17-year-old Joseph enlisted as a private in Company K, 6th California Volunteer Infantry Regiment, on August 18, 1863. The 6th California was organized in February 1863 in San Francisco and served within the state until the end of the war. Without a transcontinental railroad or the Panama Canal, sending troops to fight in the East was impractical. Also, it was feared that if Union troops were sent away, it would embolden the many Southern sympathizers in the state.

In all, about 16,000 troops eventually served in California units during the war, and most were tasked with enforcing federal law and protecting government property. That is what Joseph

Wilkes did as a member of Company K, spending the majority of his enlistment at Benicia Barracks in the Bay Area. Wilkes was also part of the provost guard that patrolled San Francisco and performed guard duty at a powder mill in Santa Cruz. A month before Joseph enlisted, Private Peter Kleinkopf was executed for desertion and attempted murder at Benicia. He was the only soldier in California executed by firing squad during the war; the firing squad was made up of twelve men from Company K, 6th California Infantry.

California's most important contribution to the Union was financial. It is estimated that California gold financed one quarter of the Union war effort; $184 million, about $46 million a year, was shipped east between 1861 and 1864. Another assignment that took Private Wilkes away from Benicia was duty as a guard on steamships that ran along the California coast, transporting gold and silver from San Francisco to Panama. After just over two years of service, Joseph Wilkes was mustered out at Benicia Barracks on October 25, 1865. While Wilkes was serving the Union in California, he had relatives serving with the Confederate forces back east.

After the war, Joseph returned to work on the family ranch near Danville. In the early 1870s, he went south to Kern County, where he worked on the cattle ranch owned by his older brother, William. The two brothers married sisters; Joseph's bride was seventeen-year-old Caroline T. Reid, the daughter of Colonel John C. Reid, who had served in the 28th Alabama Infantry regiment during the war. In 1874, the year after their marriage, Caroline gave birth to a daughter, Maud. Maud was around four years old when her mother died and was buried at Oak Grove Cemetery in Kern County.

Now a widower, Joseph took Maud and moved to Stockton, where his father and stepmother lived. In 1880, shortly after the move, Albert Wilkes passed away, leaving a large estate to his sons. Joseph took his inheritance and moved back to Kern County, whcrc hc mct and married a local schoolteacher, Laura Beckett.

Laura Ellen Beckett was born in Lincoln County, Tennessee in 1856 and moved to California with her family in 1874. She was well educated, and upon arrival in Visalia, she became the first female instructor at a local co-educational academy, teaching Latin, Greek, and advanced mathematics; she would eventually be promoted to vice-principal of the institute.

Joseph Wilkes

Laura Ellen Beckett Wilkes

Laura was twenty-four and Joseph ten years older when they married on January 30, 1881. Later that same year, Joseph paid $2,000 for 1,200 acres of the Rancho Canada de Los Alisos, in what would later become Orange County. (The area where Joseph settled his family would later become the town of El Toro.)

The remains of the old Serrano family adobe were on the property, and Joseph had lumber hauled from Santa Ana to fix up the structure. He and Laura would live in the adobe for five years, and she would give birth to three children there: Jeanette in 1881 and twins Josephine and Lawrence in 1883. Joseph planted a 20-acre vineyard and built a dam on Aliso Creek to irrigate the grapes; the rest of the property was used to graze cattle, and he probably imported, from San Francisco, the first barbed wire used in the county.

In addition to raising three young children with the help of her stepdaughter, Maud, Laura taught El Toro's first school under a sycamore tree until the first schoolhouse was built with lumber brought in from McFadden's landing in Newport Beach. Laura was a true pioneer woman. One day, when Joseph was away, their dog treed a mountain lion near the adobe. Laura grabbed a rifle, shot the animal in the head, wrapped it in her apron, and dragged it home. When it was skinned, many believed it was the largest wildcat ever shot in the area.

Joseph himself was an avid outdoorsman who enjoyed hunting and fishing well into his later years. One account tells of Wilkes and a friend returning from a two-day hunting trip with six dozen quail, 140 rabbits, and two wildcats. Another article described how Wilkes, during a two-week hunting trip to Monterey County, had tracked a deer through the woods for three hours before shooting it; he was 74 years old at the time. Wilkes was once described as "a blond bean pole whose history was as long as his frame." And a grandson claimed his grandfather was "5'10', about 154 pounds, blond, with very blue eyes."

In 1884, Wilkes purchased additional acreage in remote upper Trabuco Canyon, intending to use it as more grazing land for his cattle. The property came with a small cabin and a large, established apiary, known as the Mountain Springs Bee Ranch. In the first year alone, the apiary produced over six tons of honey and brought in twice as much money as Wilkes paid for the property. All that honey attracted a large grizzly bear, known to the locals as Moccasin John because of a distinctive paw print. The bear had a habit of making nighttime raids on the apiary, and Wilkes tried several times to kill the intruder but was unsuccessful. He even tried setting out rifles and shotguns with tripwires attached to the triggers, but the elusive bear bypassed all his traps.

Around 1887, Joseph Wilkes sold his holdings in El Toro and Trabuco Canyon for $20,000 ($645,000 in 2024 dollars) and purchased property in Santa Ana. He had a house built at 1st and Oak Streets and moved the family into town. On September 29, 1888, Laura gave birth to another son, Alfred Lee "Fred" Wilkes.

In Santa Ana, Joseph had several enterprises; he owned a livery stable and ran a transfer (delivery) business. He once even transported a prisoner from Santa Ana to San Quentin Prison in the Bay Area. In 1888, he drove a stage for the Semi-Tropic Hotel on West 4th Street and also bought a trotter horse, which he raced at the Santa Ana track. Wilkes also acted as a poll judge at elections and at one point was considered a serious candidate for Postmaster of Santa Ana, but failed to get the appointment.

In 1893, the Wilkes family moved again, this time to Tustin. It was in Tustin that the couple welcomed their fifth and last child, Mary Bernice Wilkes, when Laura gave birth on November 27, 1894. For the next fourteen years, Joseph operated a dairy farm on Newport Road at the southern boundary of Tustin. In addition to the milk cows, he also raised and sold turkeys, and devoted another 64 acres to alfalfa. The Wilkes children, all of school age when they moved, attended Tustin Grammar School, and later went on to Santa Ana High School.

Around 1908, the family moved back to Santa Ana, first for a short stay on a walnut ranch on Grand Avenue and then to an orange ranch on north Bush Street. They lived at 2010 N. Bush Street until 1920 when they made their final move, back to Tustin.

Joseph and Laura lived their remaining years on an orange ranch at Santa Clara and Yorba Streets in Tustin, in a home they called "the Roost." By the time of this final move, Joseph was 74 and Laura 64. They lived off the income from the oranges and Joseph's military pension.

They were both members of the Orange County Historical Society, and Joseph was an active member of Sedgwick Post-17 of the GAR.

In 1937, Joseph's health began to fail, and he checked into the Soldiers Home hospital in Sawtelle, near Santa Monica. After several months in the hospital, it was believed his health was improving, but he took a turn for the worse and passed away at Sawtelle on December 4, 1937, at the age of 91. He was buried beside his son, Alfred, at Forest Lawn Memorial Park in Glendale. At the time of his passing, there were only two other Civil War veterans at the Soldiers Home, and he was Tustin's last Civil War veteran.

Laura survived her husband by almost five years, passing away in San Gabriel, at the home of her daughter Blanche, on July 6, 1942, at the age of 85. She was laid to rest beside her husband and son at Forest Lawn.

Sadly, three of Joseph Wilkes ' children preceded him in death. Maud, the daughter of his first wife Caroline, passed away in 1918 in Wasco, Kern County. She was just 44 and left a husband and two teenage children.

Lawrence, one of the twins, opted for a career in the US Navy. In 1922, he was a Chief Boatswain's Mate on a ship with the Asiatic Fleet in China. While on leave, he and a buddy were hiking in the local Chinese mountains when Lawrence suffered a fatal heart attack. He was just 39 and was buried at Fort Rosecrans National Cemetery in San Diego.

Dr. Alfred "Fred" Wilkes graduated from Santa Ana High School and USC Dental School and had a successful dentistry practice in Los Angeles. He purchased a yacht and died in a boating accident off Catalina Island in July 1935 at the age of 46.

The remaining daughters, Blanche, Josephine, and Mary, all married, raised families, and lived long lives.

Joseph Wilkes with one of his race horses.

In Closing

The Civil War veterans profiled in this booklet left their homes and farms and experienced the most profound event of their lives at a very young age. Nothing they would experience for the rest of their lives would match what they saw and did in those years they were away at war. They joined huge armies and fought in great battles. They saw men suffer, and they saw men killed. They were active participants in an unprecedented human slaughter.

These young men were exposed to a magnitude of destruction they could not have imagined before the war. They saw, and may have participated in, the burning of homes and barns, the destruction of crops, and the killing of livestock; acts that would have been repugnant to them as civilians. These experiences must have helped redefine their world views.

When the war ended, they returned to their homes and farms to pick up the pieces of their lives and make sense of what they had experienced. They married, raised families, and joined a great westward migration that would land them in Tustin, California.

Just as they had served their country in time of war, in peace they served their community, and that service had a profound impact on Tustin in its pioneering days. These veterans produced a state assemblyman, a county supervisor, a county treasurer, a city postmaster, a Justice of the Peace, and the town's first peace officer. They served on school boards, sat on church councils, and the boards of numerous agricultural organizations. When Joseph A. Wilkes died in 1937, the last of the Civil War veterans was gone from Tustin, but they had left a lasting legacy.

From Enemies to Neighbors

In the years immediately following the war, partisan feelings were still strong, and acts of violence were frequent, especially in the South, where freed slaves and Union sympathizers were often the targets of attacks from unreconstructed rebels. As the years passed, the animosity lessened, and by the 1890s, a spirit of reconciliation between the two factions had begun. In 1892, the Populist Party platform, in addition to advocating banking reform, a graduated income tax, and the eight-hour work day, also espoused reconciliation between the Blue and Gray. In fact, the top of their ticket was headed by a former Union general for president with a one-legged ex-Confederate as his running mate.

The reconciliation between the two factions was cemented by the advent of war with Spain in 1898. The Spanish-American War saw Americans from the North and South come together to fight a common enemy. Several of the generals of the American forces were even former Union and Confederate officers, now fighting on the same side. By the turn of the century, battlefield reunions were common with former enemies shaking hands and sharing stories at sites where forty years earlier they had been trying to kill each other.

Early Tustin had a fine example of that spirit of reconciliation in Dr. William B. Wall and Charles F. Bennett. The two men could not have had more opposite upbringings. Charles Bennett was a native New Englander raised on a family farm and, early on, influenced by the abolitionists around him and by his mother's Quaker principles. As a youth in Illinois, he even helped runaway slaves to freedom on the Underground Railroad. William Wall was born into a wealthy, slave holding family and raised on plantations in Virginia and Mississippi. Wall attended medical school and ran a medical practice in addition to farming. Bennett was a farmer and merchant.

When Bennett moved his family to Tustin in 1887, he purchased land south of and adjacent to Dr. Wall's property on Tustin Avenue, making them next-door neighbors. (Although their houses were probably separated by several acres of orchards.) It was not unusual for men on opposite sides in the war to end up as neighbors, but in this case, Bennett and Wall had not just been on opposing sides but had actually been on opposite sides of the same battlefield seven times!

Dr. Wall's 33rd Mississippi infantry and Bennett's 55th Illinois infantry first met at the battle of Corinth in October, 1862. They shared the same battlefield three more times in Mississippi: at Vicksburg, Jackson, and Champion Hill. Later, the regiments faced each other during the battle of Atlanta and at Ezra Church, both in Georgia. Each of these was a major battle with combined casualties on both sides numbering in the thousands.

The final confrontation between the units of Dr. Wall and Charles Bennett took place at the Battle of Bentonville in North Carolina. Although fought in March 1865, just a month before the war ended and when the outcome was all but a foregone conclusion, the battle was still hotly contested and produced over 1,500 Union casualties while the Confederates suffered over 2,500 killed, wounded, or missing.

No written record exists of the relationship between Dr. Wall and Bennett during the more than twenty years they spent as each other's closest neighbors. But they were two of the most prominent Democrats in the area, and it is not hard to imagine they attended some of the same conventions or served on some of the same committees. In fact, they both spoke at a meeting of the Tustin People's (Populist) Party Club in the summer of 1892. This was the election that sent Bennett to the state legislature.

They were also both successful citrus growers who belonged to some of the same agricultural organizations. Dr. Wall sat on the board of the Santa Ana Valley Irrigation Company, and Charles Bennett was an acknowledged expert on orchard irrigation.

If not actually friends, they certainly maintained a peaceful coexistence over their two decades as neighbors.

From 1862 to 1865, they may have caught a glimpse of each other across a smoke-filled battlefield and seen an enemy. In later years, they could look across neat orchards and well-tended lawns and catch a glimpse of a neighbor.

The GAR

The Grand Army of the Republic, or GAR, was a fraternal organization with membership open to veterans of the Union Army, Navy, and Marine Corps. It was founded in 1866, appropriately enough in Springfield, Illinois, the home of the veteran's martyred commander-in-chief, Abraham Lincoln. The first GAR post was actually established in Decatur, Illinois, and the first national commander of the organization was former Union General John A. Logan.

The GAR became a powerful lobbying organization, at first advocating for the rights of the newly freed slaves and later, after a membership drop, reemerging as a force assisting Union veterans in applying for and obtaining pensions. The GAR was also a staunch supporter of Republican political policies. At its peak in the early 1890s, the organization boasted a membership of over 400,000.

The GAR was organized into departments on the state level and posts on the local level. There were posts in every state and very few towns of any size did not have a GAR post, usually named after a prominent Union officer. These local posts were involved in planning Decoration Day (later called Memorial Day) ceremonies, marched in 4th of July parades, rendered military honors at the services of their deceased comrades, and generally kept the memory of the Civil War generation alive in their communities. There were also several auxiliaries to the GAR, probably the most prominent being the Women's Relief Corps, or WRC.

Almost all the Union veterans of Tustin belonged to Sedgwick Post 17 of the GAR. The post, headquartered in Santa Ana, was founded in February 1881 and was named in honor of Union Major General John Sedgwick, who was killed on May 9, 1864, at the Battle of Spotsylvania Court House in Virginia.

Over the years, the Sedgwick Post met at four different locations in Santa Ana. The first meeting place was Dibble Hall, located at the corner of Fourth and Main Street. From about 1904 until 1928, the veterans met at 310 1/2 E. Fourth Street. They next moved to the Knights of Pythias building at Broadway and Fifth Street before moving to their final location at 204 1/2 E. Fourth Street in 1935. The WRC would often use these same buildings, but on different days from the GAR meetings.

The GAR also held annual encampments, both local and national. The encampments allowed the old soldiers to get together and reminisce in a relaxed, vacation atmosphere. From September 9 to 14, 1912, Los Angeles hosted the national encampment attended by an estimated 20,000 veterans and their families from around the country. The six-day affair was filled with receptions, speeches, band concerts, and beach excursions.

At least two Tustin veterans, U.C. Holderman and W.L.G. Haskins, made trips to Los Angeles for the festivities, and it is probable that more men from Tustin were part of the Sedgwick Post contingent of one hundred that marched in the big parade in downtown Los Angeles on September 12, 1912. Fifty women of the Sedgwick WRC marched alongside the men in the parade.

Several Tustin veterans also held GAR leadership roles. H.W. Smith served as commander in 1923, and for the last eight years of his life, James H. Brown served also as commander of Sedgwick Post-17. Before moving to Tustin, Charles H. Bennett was commander of his GAR post in Nebraska, as was W.L.G. Haskins in West Boylston, Massachusetts. After leaving Tustin, Henry H. Higley served a term as commander of his post in Long Beach, and George W. Mason served a term as commander of the Gordon Granger Post in Orange.

The death of James Brown in 1935 left the Sedgwick Post with only five remaining veterans, a number drastically reduced from its peak membership of three hundred. In fact, Brown's graveside services were conducted by the Sons of the Union

Veterans of the Civil War due to the lack of able-bodied veterans to perform the task. The last surviving member of the Sedgwick Post died in June 1940. The memory of local Civil War veterans is now carried forward by the Sedgwick-Granger Camp 17 of the Sons of the Union Veterans of the Civil War.

Sons of the Union Veterans fire a military salute at the funeral of Sedgwick Post-17 Commander James H. Brown, November 12, 1935, in Santa Ana.

The Boys Brigade

The Boys Brigade was a Christian youth organization founded in Glasgow, Scotland, in 1883. Its goal was to instill "Christian manliness" in boys by combining military discipline, physical fitness, outdoor activities, and religious services. The Brigade's motto was "Be Sure and Steadfast." The organization quickly spread to the United Kingdom and the United States, and by 1910, there were 10,000 members worldwide.

In the early 1890s, Southern California was home to several Boys' Brigade companies, among them a very active one in Tustin. The Tustin Boys Brigade company was established in late 1891 and sponsored by the Tustin Presbyterian church. It was composed of boys aged 12 to 18 from some of the leading families in town.

The pastor of the church, Rev. James P. Stoops, acted as company Captain and the boys elected two lieutenants, four sergeants and four corporals from their ranks.

The boys were outfitted in Civil War era blue uniforms, and one of their first endeavors was a successful fundraising drive to equip the company with .32 rifles. The company was involved in patriotic and religious events in the community and marched with GAR members in local parades. The company even had its own orchestra and a vocal quartet. A number of the boys in the company were sons of Tustin Civil War veterans.

The highlight of the year for the Brigade was the week-long encampment each summer held on Santa Catalina Island. The 1893 encampment was attended by over five hundred boys from various Southland Brigade companies. The railroads and steamship companies offered special fares, and local National Guard units loaned tents to the boys for the week.

The encampment was run like a military post with a daily routine of reveille at 6 a.m., guard mount, company drill, dress parade, evening prayers, and taps at 9:30 p.m. But there was also a special time set aside for fun activities, including baseball, swimming, boating, fishing, hiking, mountain climbing, and ocean excursions. There were also fireworks, campfires, songs, and, just to keep the boys on the straight and narrow, there was plenty of preaching and religious services.

Tragedy struck the Tustin Company when sixteen-year-old Horace J. Snow fell ill and died in February 1893, just a month after being elected second sergeant. His funeral was conducted by Rev. Stoops. The Boys Brigade Company acted as an honor guard and as pallbearers and fired a twenty-one-gun salute at his graveside before taps were played.

The Tustin Company was considered one of the model units in the state, and it is unclear when or why it disbanded; perhaps it was in 1895 when Rev. Stoops left to assume the pastorate of a church in Monrovia, California. The organization is still active worldwide, with most of its companies now based in the United Kingdom.

The Tustin Boys Brigade company on Santa Catalina Island, 1892.

In the photo on this page, in the front row, extreme left to right: Capt. James Stoops, Charlie Ballard, <u>Ed Adams</u>, <u>Horace Snow</u>, Fred Bladgett, Homer Bowman, <u>Ray Alderman</u>, Ben McCharles, Herald Janes, Cliff Baker, Quin Davidson, Harvey Rice, Nathan Cartmel, <u>Will Jerome</u>, Will Mason, Willie Bowman, Dan Adams, John Gould, <u>George Haskins</u>, <u>Ben Jerome</u>, Lanier Bartlett, Van Alstyne, Bert Liehy, Harvey Baker, Will Keim, and Byron Crawford, From the back row left to right: Charlie Fairbanks, Merrill Rice, Edmund Snow, <u>Will Wall</u>.

The underlined names above indicate boys who were sons of Tustin Civil War veterans.

The Civil War Generation

The photograph above, from a 1928 newspaper article, shows three generations of the Stutsman family: Judge Abraham Stutsman, his son, Superior Court Judge Carl Stutsman, and Carl Jr. The photo was taken upon landing after a three-hour airplane flight. While it is a memorable photo for the Stutsman family album, it also reveals a great deal about the journey of the Civil War generation.

In 1861, twenty-year-old Abraham Stutsman rode off to war on horseback, and near the end of his life, he spent three hours aloft, soaring among the clouds, something he probably never dreamed of as a child growing up on a farm in Iowa. Those Civil War veterans who, like Stutsman, lived into the 1920s and 1930s witnessed remarkable changes in their lifetime.

The men of the Civil War generation were born into a predominantly agrarian country of small farms, where most of the labor was performed by man and beast. By the end of their lives, the Industrial Revolution had transformed the country into an urbanized industrial giant, with much of the farm labor now mechanized.

In their lifetime, these men had seen transportation evolve from horse and buggy to railroads and the automobile and finally to the miracle of manned flight. A trip to the West Coast had been reduced from months to days to hours.

They had lived through three wars and witnessed the assassinations of three presidents. They were born in a country where slavery, the owning, buying, and selling of human beings, was legal, and those who fought for the Union had helped put an end to that travesty. In fact, many of the social, economic, and political changes in the country were a direct result of the war they had fought. In all, it was a remarkable journey for Abraham Stutsman and the men of his generation. Their world had changed greatly over the course of their lives, and through their service, they had played a direct role in shaping those changes.

The Final Resting Place

The GAR monument at the entrance of Santa Ana Cemetery

Twenty-nine of Tustin's thirty-three Civil War veterans are buried in either Santa Ana Cemetery or the adjoining Fairhaven Memorial Park. The four exceptions are Abraham Stutsman (Inglewood). H.H. Higley (Long Beach), David Robinson, and Joseph A. Wilkes (Glendale).

Santa Ana Cemetery is located at 1919 E. Santa Clara Ave., Santa Ana, California, 92705. Fairhaven Memorial Park is located at 1702 Fairhaven Ave., Santa Ana, California, 92705, adjacent to the Santa Ana Cemetery.

The location of each veteran's grave, including GPS coordinates, can be found in Gordon Bricken's ***Pioneers in Blue and Gray*** or on the OCCGS Civil War Veterans Project website at **occgs.com/projects/civil_war/civil_war.html**.

Sources

Tustin

BOOKS

Ainsworth, Ed, *Journey with the Sun: The Story of Citrus in its Western Pilgrimage*, Sunkist Growers, Los Angeles.

Ball, Guy D., Images of America: Tustin, Arcadia Publishing, Mt. Pleasant, SC, 2011.

Dumke, Glenn, S., *The Boom of the Eighties in Southern California*, Huntington Library, San Marino, 1944.

Jordan, Carol, H., *Tustin: An Illustrated History*, Tustin Area Historical Society, Tustin, 2007.

Lovret, Juanita, *Tustin as It Once Was*, History Press, Charleston, 2011.

DIRECTORIES

Los Angeles City and County Directory 1886-87, A.A. Byron & Co. Publishers, 1886.

OTHER

Sanborn Fire Insurance Company Map, Tustin 1895.

The photograph of Columbus Tustin used with permission of the Tustin Area Historical Society.

P.T. Adams

BOOKS

Armor, Samuel, (ed.), *History of Orange County with Biographical Sketches*, Historical Record Company, Los Angeles, 1911, pages 421-424, 587-588.

Bricken, Gordon, *Pioneers in Blue and Gray, Civil War Veterans in Orange County*, Bricken Press, Santa Ana, 2009, page 87.

Huntley, Helen Gulick & William, (ed. Edna Phelps), *Tustin Scrapbook*, Tustin Area Historical Society, 1969, pages 61, 67, 69, 78, 91.

Jordan, Carol, H., *Tustin: An Illustrated History*, Tustin Area Historical Society, Tustin, 2002, page 21.

Sleeper, Jim, *Turn the Rascals Out! The Life and Times of Orange County's Fighting Editor, Dan Baker*, California Classic, Trabuco Canyon, 1973, page 203.

MILITARY RECORDS

OCCGS Civil War Veterans Project-Peter Taylor Adams

National Parks Service Soldiers & Sailors Database, Frontier Regiment (46th Texas Cavalry)

Texas State Historical Association Handbook of Texas Frontier Regiment by Robert Dunnam

WPA Texas Ranger Index, "Peter T. Adams"

GOVERNMENT RECORDS

Bexar County Deeds Book, 916, page 317: Peter Adams-Sarah Walton Family

1870 United States Federal Census: Ulvalde, Texas"

1880 United States Federal Census: Tustin, Los Angeles, California

1900 United States Federal Census: Santa Ana, Orange, California-Tustin Precinct

1910 United States Federal Census: Santa Ana, Orange, California-Tustin Precinct

1920 United States Federal Census: Tustin, Orange, California

Texas Marriage Index, 1824-2014: PT Adams-Elizabeth H. Downs

California Death Index, 1905-1939: Peter T. Adams

DIRECTORIES

US Find A Grave Index, 1600's-current: Elizabeth Henrietta Adams, Peter
Taylor Adams

NEWSPAPERS

"Death of Mrs. Adams", *Santa Ana Weekly Blade*, May 5, 1892, page 3.

"E.L. Adams", *Los Angeles Times*, July 25, 1902, page 16.

"M.V. Adams Dies Suddenly of Heart Failure", *Santa Ana Register*, March 28,
1908, page 3.

"Mrs. John Gowen Burned to Death as a Result of Gasoline Iron Explosion",
Santa Ana Register, January 13, 1911, page 1.

"Pays Tribute to Woman's Heroism", *Santa Ana Register*, January 16, 1911,
page 2.

"Pioneer Passes to the Beyond", *Santa Ana Register*, September 18, 1922, page
10.

"Early Pioneer Passes: He Came Here in 1877", *Santa Ana Register*, December
3, 1924, page 6.

"Aged Pioneer Called by Death", *Santa Ana Register*, December 6, 1924, p. 2.

"Couple Arrive Here Following Wedding in San Jose", *Santa Ana Register*,
December 27, 1934, page 10.

"Tustin Man is Reported Missing by Navy" undated newspaper clipping

"Adams", *Long Beach Press Telegram*, May 17, 1950, page 33.

"Early Tustin Home Yields to Growth", *Santa Ana Register*, March 1, 1964
page F6.

"Frances Plumb Services Held", *Tustin News*, November 8, 1979, page 1.

***The photograph of the Adams house and Adams family used with permission
of the Tustin Area Historical Society.***

Albert N. Alderman

BOOKS

Bricken, Gordon, *Pioneers in Blue and Gray, Civil War Veterans of Orange County*, Bricken Press, Santa Ana, 2009, page 57.

Friis, Leo, J., *David Hewes: More Than the Golden Spike*, Fries-Pioneer Press, Santa Ana, 1974, page 62.

Guinn, J.M., *Historical & Biographical Record of Southern California*, Chapman Publishing Company, Chicago, 1902, pages 686-687.

Jordan, Carol H., *Tustin: An Illustrated History*, Tustin Area Historical Society, 2007, page 31.

MAGAZINES

"Death by Dew Point: Extreme Heat Conditions Affected Battle Strategy and Killed Soldiers", by Jeffry J. Harding, *Civil War Times,* Autumn 2022, Vol. 61, No. 4, page 52.

MILITARY RECORDS

OCCGS Civil War Veterans Project: Albert N. Alderman

Civil War Soldier Records and Profiles, 1861-1865: Albert N. Alderman

Civil War Draft Registration Records, 1861-1865: Albert N. Alderman

Civil War Pension Index: General Index to Pension Files, 1861-1934: Albert N. Alderman

Roster of Ohio Troops-Company K, 29th Ohio Infantry

GOVERNMENT RECORDS

1850 United States Federal Census: Orwell, Ashtabula, Ohio

1860 United States Federal Census: Windsor, Ashtabula, Ohio

1870 United States Federal Census: Cedar, Callaway, Missouri

1870 United States Federal Census: Windsor, Ashtabula, Ohio

1880 United States Federal Census: Tustin, Los Angeles, California

1900 United States Federal Census: Santa Ana, Orange, California-Tustin
Precinct

California Death Index, 1905-1939: Albert N. Alderman, Heber B. Alderman

DIRECTORIES

US Find A Grave Index, 1600's to current: Elizabeth Alderman, Albert N.
Alderman

NEWSPAPERS

"Church Wedding at Tustin", *Los Angeles Herald*, September 18, 1884, page 6.

"His Death Accidental", *Los Angeles Times*, January 10, 1906, page 24.

"One of Orange County's Pioneers Passes Away", *Santa Ana Register*, August
21, 1908, page 5.

"Clarence Sheet, Pioneer Here Dies", *Santa Ana Register*, February 1, 1930,
page 11.

***Photographs of the headstones of Albert and Elizabeth Alderman were taken
at Santa Ana Cemetery by Paul Loya and Timothy Zierer.***

Edwin F. Ambrose

MAGAZINES

"The Dartmouth Cavalry, 1862", *Dartmouth Alumni Magazine*, January, 1919.

MILITARY RECORDS

OCCGS Civil War Veterans Project: Edwin Freeman Ambrose

Civil War Soldier Records and Profiles, 1861-1865: Edwin Freeman Ambrose,
Thomas L. Ambrose

Civil War Soldiers, 1861-1865: Chaplain Thomas L. Ambrose

Soldiers & Sailors of New Hampshire in the War of the Rebellion 1861-1865,
Adjutant General's Report, 1895.

12th New Hampshire Volunteer Infantry-Thomas L. Ambrose

"List of American Civil War units by state"-Wikipedia: 7th Rhode Island
Cavalry Squadron

GOVERNMENT RECORDS

1850 United States Federal Census: Ossipee, Carroll, New Hampshire

1860 United States Federal Census: New Hampton, Belknap, New Hampshire

1880 United States Federal Census: Malden, Middlesex, Massachusetts

1900 United States Federal Census: Los Angeles, Ward 9, Los Angeles,
California

1910 United States Federal Census: Los Angeles Assembly District 69, Los
Angeles, California

1920 United States Federal Census: Los Angeles Assembly District 63, Los
Angeles, California

1930 United States Federal Census: Los Angeles, Los Angeles, California

Maine Marriage Index, 1670-1921: Edwin F. Ambrose-Emily J. Goodwin

California Voter Registers, 1866-1898: Edwin F. Ambrose, Newport, Orange,
CA, 1892

California Death Index, 1940-1997: Thomas L. Ambrose

California Biographical Index Cards, 1781-1990: Thomas Lyford Ambrose

DIRECTORIES

US Find A Grave Index, 1600s-current: Nathaniel Ambrose, Chaplain Thomas
Lyford Ambrose, Emily J. Ambrose, Sarah Ambrose, Judge Thomas
Lyford Ambrose

NEWSPAPERS

"The Christian Alliance", *Los Angeles Herald*, December 12, 1892, page 14.

"Brevities-The Christian Alliance", *Los Angeles Herald*, December 17, 1892, page 6.

"E.F. Ambrose, age 57...", *Los Angeles Times*, February 24, 1894, page 11.

"Died-In Tustin", *Los Angeles Herald*, February 24, 1894, page 8.

"Marriage Licenses", *Los Angeles Herald*, October 7, 1905, page 8.

"Official Death List-Ambrose, Emily", *Los Angeles Times*, May 13, 1922, page 16.

"Sara Tuthill Ambrose, Wife of Judge Passes", *Los Angeles Times*, April 8, 1957, page 52.

"Service Set for Ex-Judge T.L. Ambrose", *Los Angeles Times*, April 13, 1965, page 45.

"Ambrose, Judge Thomas Lyford", *Los Angeles Times*, April 14, 1965, page 43.

"Memorial Services for Superior Court Judge', *Los Angeles Times*, April 18, 1965, page 192.

The photograph of the headstone of Edwin F. Ambrose was taken at Santa Ana Cemetery by Timothy Zierer.

Charles F. Bennett

BOOKS

Armor, Samuel, (ed.), History of Orange County with Biographical Sketches, Historical Record Company, Los Angeles, 1911, pages 395-398.

Bennett, Harvey, Francis, "A Sketch of the Lives of Harvey Franklin & Frances Lillian (McDonnell) Bennett of El Toro, Orange County, California, 1993, Tustin Historical Society Collection.

Bricken, Gordon, *Pioneers in Blue and Gray, Civil War Veterans of Orange County*, Bricken Press, Santa Ana, 2009, pages 59-60.

Guinn, J.M., *Historical & Biographical Record of Southern California*,
   Chapman Publishing Company, Chicago, 1902, pages 969-970.

Huntley, Helen Gulick & William, (ed. Edna Phelps), *Tustin Scrapbook*, Tustin
   Area Historical Society, 1969, page 63.

MILITARY RECORDS

OCCGS Civil War Veterans Project: Charles F. Bennett

Civil War Soldier Records and Profiles, 1861-1865: Charles F. Bennett

Adjutant General's Report-Muster Roll, Company G, 55th Illinois: 1st Sgt.
   Charles F. Bennett

"List of American Civil War Units by State"-Wikipedia: 55th Illinois Infantry

GOVERNMENT RECORDS

1850 United States Federal Census: Kent, Litchfield, Connecticut

1860 United States Federal Census: Deer Park, La Salle, Illinois

1870 United States Federal Census: Deer Park, La Salle, Illinois

1880 United States Federal Census: Medicine Creek, Furnas, Nebraska

1900 United States Federal Census: Santa Ana, Orange, California-Tustin
   Precinct

1910 United States Federal Census: Santa Ana, Orange, California-Tustin
   Precinct

1920 United States Federal Census: Tustin, Santa Ana, California

1940 United States Federal Census: Tustin, Orange, California

Illinois Marriage Index, 1860-1920: C.F. Bennett-Helen M. Beach

California Death Index, 1905-1939: CF Bennett

DIRECTORIES

US Find A Grave Index, 1600's-current: Mary Helen Beach

1899-1900 Orange County Directory, Belt Fine Publishers, Santa Ana, p. 191.

1908-1909 Santa Ana Directory, Register Publishing Co., Santa Ana, page 106.

NEWSPAPERS

"The Tustin People's Party Club", *Los Angeles Times*, July 26, 1892, page 7.

"Assemblyman C.F. Bennett", *Los Angeles Herald*, January 26, 1893, page 6.

"Description of Apricot Orchard Near El Toro", *Santa Ana Register*, November 2, 1909, page 2.

"Marriage Licenses", *Santa Ana Register*, October 30, 1913, page 8.

"Obituary-Charles F. Bennett", *Santa Ana Register*, January 11, 1921, page 7.

"Old Time Resident Dies in California", *Public Mirror* (Arapahoe, Nebraska), January 20, 1921, page 1.

"Harvey Bennett Services Held", *Tustin News*, July 1, 1971, page 1.

"Civil War Vets Found Tustin to Their Liking", by Juanita Lovret, *Tustin News*, May 5, 2008, page 8.

"Bennett Family Put Down Roots in 1880s", by Juanita Lovret, *Tustin News*, February 11, 2010, page 8.

The photograph of Charles Bennett and the photograph of the Bennett House are used with the permission of the Tustin Area Historical Society.

James H. Brown

BOOKS

Bricken, Gordon, *Pioneers in Blue and Gray, Civil War Veterans in Orange County*, Bricken Press, Santa Ana, 2009, page 61-62.

Harlowe, Jerry, *Monitors: The Men, Machines and Mystique*, Thomas Publications, Gettysburg, 2001.

Huntley, Helen Gulick & William, (ed. Edna Phelps), *Tustin Scrapbook*, Tustin Area Historical Society, 1969.

Pullen, John, J., *A Shower of Stars: The Medal of Honor and the 27th Maine*, Stackpole Books, Lanham, MD, 2017.

ORAL HISTORIES

William Martin Huntley interviews, Oral History Program at California State
Fullerton, Interviewed by Stephen Gould, May 21-22, 1968, page 29.

MILITARY RECORDS

OCCGs Civil War Veterans Project: James H. Brown

Civil War Soldier Records and Profiles, 1861-1865: James H. Brown

U.S. Naval Enlistment Rendezvous, 1855-1891: James Brown

GOVERNMENT RECORDS

1855 Massachusetts State Census: James Brown

1860 United States Federal Census: Alfred, York, Maine

1870 United States Federal Census: Bodega, Sonoma, California

1880 United States Federal Census: San Francisco, San Francisco, California

1900 United States Federal Census: Santa Ana, Orange, California-Tustin
Precinct

1910 United States Federal Census: Santa Ana, Orange, California-Tustin
Precinct

1920 United States Federal Census: Tustin, Orange, California

1930 United States Federal Census: Tustin, Orange, California

California County Birth, Marriage & Death Records, 1849-1980: James H.
Brown-Sarah M. Goodwin

California Voter Registers, 1866-1968: 1868 James Henry Brown, Lumberman,
Bodega, Sonoma, CA; 1886 James Henry Brown, Lumberman, Bodega,
Sonoma, CA; 1892 James H. Brown, Tustin, CA

DIRECTORIES

1899-1900 Orange County Directory. Belt Fine Publishers, Santa Ana, page
191.

1908-1909 Santa Ana Directory, Register Publishing Co., Santa Ana, page 106.

1916 Santa Ana, Tustin, Garden Grove Directory, Santa Ana Directory Co., LH Padgham Publisher, page 292.

NEWSPAPERS

"Marriage Announcement", *Los Angeles Evening Express*, March 7, 1895, p. 7.

"W.C.T.U Meeting", *Santa Ana Register*, October 9, 1914, page 13.

"Union Veteran Lodges Hold Meeting", *Santa Ana Register*, January 24, 1927, page 24.

"Sarah Brown is State Officer", *Santa Ana Register*, May 4, 1930, page 7.

"90th Birthday is Observed by G.A.R. Leader", *Santa Ana Register*, March 2, 1935, page 7.

"Commander of Sedgwick Post Answers Call", *Santa Ana Register,* November 8, 1935, page 1.

"Funeral Announcement James H. Brown", *Santa Ana Register*, November 8, 1935, page 3.

"Brown Funeral to be Held Tuesday", *Santa Ana Register*, November 9, 1935, page 3.

"Military Rite Marks Funeral for J.H. Brown", *Santa Ana Register*, November 13, 1935, page 9.

"A Medal of Honor Story", by Juanita Lovret, *Tustin News*, undated.

The photograph of James & Sarah Brown used with permission of the Tustin Area Historical Society.

Levi J. Colby

BOOKS

Huntley, Helen Gulick & William, (ed. Edna Phelps), *Tustin Scrapbook*, Tustin Area Historical Society, 1969.

MILITARY RECORDS

OCCGS Civil War Veterans Project-Levi Jackson Colby

Civil War Soldier Records and Profiles, 1861-1865 Levi J. Colby

List of American Civil War Units by State -Wikipedia- 24th Wisconsin Infantry

Roster of Wisconsin Volunteers, War of the Rebellion, 1861-1865, Vol. II, page 268, Wisconsin Historical Library, online version.

GOVERNMENT RECORDS

1850 United States Federal Census: Franklin, Milwaukee, Wisconsin

1870 United States Federal Census: Lake, Milwaukee, Wisconsin

1880 United States Federal Census: Tustin, Los Angeles, California

1900 United States Federal Census: Santa Ana, Orange, California

1884 Los Angeles County Voter Registration Record: Levi J. Colby

1892 Orange County Voter Registration Record: Levi J. Colby

NEWSPAPERS

"Passengers for San Francisco", *Los Angeles Daily Star*, Oct. 3, 1873, page 2.

"Hotel Arrivals", *Los Angeles Herald*, May 12, 1874, page4.

"C. Tustin et. al to L.J. Colby", *Los Angeles Herald*, Feb.17, 1875, page 4.

"The Republican Camp", *Los Angeles Daily Star*, July 29, 1877, page 4.

"Conveyances", *Los Angeles Evening Express*, December 4, 1877, page 3.

"Property Transfers", *Los Angeles Herald*, April 17, 1881, page 3.

"Property Transfers", *Los Angeles Herald*, January 24, 1882, page 3.

"Mr. L.J. Colby of Tustin sold his place...", *Los Angeles Times*, April 7, 1883, page 1.

"From Sedgwick Post 17", *Los Angeles Herald*, August 21, 1888, page 1.

"Death of Levi J. Colby", *San Francisco Chronicle*, July 15, 1903, page 3.

"The funeral of Levi J. Colby", *Los Angeles Times*, July 16, 1903, page 18.

"Santa Ana Current Events", *Los Angeles Times*, July 21, 1903, page 18.

"Death of Mrs. Colby of North Broadway", *Santa Ana Register*, Aug. 12, 1907, page 1.

"Administration Begun on A $100.000 Estate", *Santa Ana Register*, Aug.26, 1907, page 1.

Samuel L. Eddy

BOOKS

Huntley, Helen Gulick & William, (ed. Edna Phelps), *Tustin Scrapbook*, Tustin Area Historical Society,1969, pages 9,30,35,67.

Jordon, Carol, H., *Tustin: An Illustrated History*, Tustin Area Historical Society, Tustin, 2007, pages 31, 46, 116.

Lovret, Juanita, *Tustin as it Once Was*, History Press, Charleston, 2011, p. 22.

MILITARY RECORDS

OCCGS Civil War Veterans Project: Samuel Eddy

Civil War Soldiers Records and Profiles, 1861-1865: Samuel L. Eddy

"Minor Michigan Cavalry Units of the American Civil War"- *Wikipedia*: 1st Michigan Lancers

Civil War Pension Index to Pension Files, 1861-1934: Samuel L. Eddy-Sarah Eddy

GOVERNMENT RECORDS

1850 United States Federal Census:Palmyra, Wayne, New York

1860 United States Federal Census: Bay City, Bay, Michigan

1870 United States Federal Census: Bay City, Bay, Michigan

1880 United States Federal Census: Tustin, Los Angeles, California

1900 United States Federal Census: Santa Ana, Orange, California-Tustin
Precinct

1910 United States Federal Census: Santa Ana, Orange, California-Tustin
Precinct

Illinois Marriage Index, 1860-1920: Samuel L. Eddy-Sarah Ann Hutchinson

California Voter Registers, 1866-1898: 1871 Samuel Lafayette Eddy,
blacksmith, Elk Horn, San Joaquin

California Voter Registers, 1866-1898: 1879 Samuel Lafayette Eddy,
blacksmith, Tustin City

California Voter Registers, 1866-1898: 1884 Samuel Lafayette Eddy,
blacksmith, Tustin City

DIRECTORIES

1886-1887 Los Angeles City and County Directory, A.A. Byron & Co.,
Publishers, page 162.

US Find A Grave Index, 1600s to Current: Samuel L. Eddy. Sarah A. Eddy

NEWSPAPERS

Obituary-Samuel Eddy, *Santa Ana Herald*, September 22, 1888, page 2.

Obituary-Mrs. Sarah Eddy, *Santa Ana Register*, January 20, 1917, page 10.

"Travel Notes- Mrs. & Mrs. Ralph Eddy", *Santa Ana Register*, January 20,
1917, page 5.

Obituary-Mrs. Sarah Eddy, undated Riverside newspaper.

George W. Hale

BOOKS

Bricken, Gordon, *Pioneers in Blue and Gray, Civil War Veterans in Orange County*, Bricken Press, Santa Ana, 2009, page 68.

MILITARY RECORDS

OCCGS Civil War Veterans Project: George Washington Hale

"List of American Civil War Units by State"-Wikipedia: 27th Illinois Infantry, 129th Illinois Infantry

27th Illinois Infantry Regiment-FamilySearch: Company B Roster, Adjutant General's Report, George Hale

129th Illinois Infantry Regiment-FamilySearch" Company I Roster, Adjutant General's Report, George Hale

GOVERNMENT RECORDS

1850 United States Federal Census: Scott, Illinois

1860 United States Federal Census: Township 15, Range 13, Scott, Illinois

1900 United States Federal Census: Bluffs, Scott, Illinois

1910 United States Federal Census: Bluffs, Scott, Illinois

1920 United States Federal Census: Sefton, Fayette, Illinois

1930 United States Federal Census: Decatur, Macon, Illinois

1940 United States Federal Census: Tustin, Orange, California

Illinois Marriage Index, 1860-1920: George Hale-Rebecca L. Braham

Illinois Death & Stillborn Index, 1916-1947: Rebecca Braham Hale

California Death Index, 1905-1939: George Hale

DIRECTORIES

US Find A Grave Index, 1600s-Current: George Washington Hale

Santa Ana City Directories, 1949, 1954, 1956: Ira & Daisy Price

NEWSPAPERS

Obituary-George Hale, *Santa Ana Register*, March 3, 1933, page 8.

"George W. Hale, 87, Civil War Veteran Succumbs in West", *Decatur Herald*, (Decatur, Illinois), March 7, 1933, page 3.

"Ira Price, Former Resident Dies in California", *Clinton Daily Journal*, (Clinton, Illinois), April 25, 1958, page 6.

"Former Resident, Mrs. Daisy Price", *Tustin News*, January 14, 1960, page 1.

Orrin Hanlon

BOOKS

Bricken, Gordon, *Pioneers in Blue and Gray, Civil War Veterans in Orange County*, Bricken Press, Santa Ana, 2009, page 69.

MILITARY RECORDS

OCCGS Civil War Veterans Project: Orrin Hanlon

Civil War Soldier Records and Profiles, 1861-1865: Orrin Hanlon

Civil War Soldiers, 1861-1865, page 10: Orrin Hanlon

Civil War Soldier Database Index, 1861-1865: Orrin Hanlon

Civil War Pension Index to Pension Files, 1861-1934: Orrin Hanlon, 17 February 1892

Report of Adjutant General of State of Indiana, 1861-1865, Vol. 4, Indianapolis, 1866, (online version), page 602.

"List of Civil War Units by State"- Wikipedia: 26th Indiana Infantry

GOVERNMENT RECORDS

1850 United States Federal Census: District 7, Boone, Indiana

1860 United States Federal Census: Washington, Clinton, Indiana

1870 United States Federal Census: Lost Creek, Vigo, Indiana

1880 United States Federal Census: Terra Haute, Vigo, Indiana

1900 United States Federal Census: Symmes, Edgar, Illinois

1910 United States Federal Census: Symmes, Edgar, Illinois

1920 United States Federal Census: Tustin, Orange, California

Indiana Marriages, 1810-2001: Orrin Hanlon-Mary Haney

Illinois Marriage Index, 1860-1920: Orrin Hanlon-Nettie Kirby

California Voter Registrations, 1900-1968: Orrin Hanlon, Tustin, 1914; Mrs.
Nettie Hanlon, Tustin, 1918-1920

California Death Index, 1905-1939: Orbin H. Hanlon

California Death Index, 1940-1997: Nettie Hanlon, Mrs. Margaret Dodd, Millie
Williams, Emma Maynard, Thelma E. McCament

DIRECTORIES

US Find A Grave Index, 1600s-current: Orrin Hanlon, Nettie Hanlon, Millie
Williams, Emma Mae Maynard

NEWSPAPERS

"Pensions Granted", *The Inter-Ocean* (Chicago), September 24, 1892, page 14.

"First Prize…", *Santa Ana Register*, May 3, 1915, page 4.

"Lost-Roan Pony", *Santa Ana Register*, June 4, 1915, page 11.

"Orrin Hanlon and Vaughn Maynard", *Santa Ana Register*, April 2, 1919, page
14.

"Here's A List of Sedgwick Post Members", *Santa Ana Register*, May 30, 1922,
page 7.

"Hanlon-Mr. Orrin", *Santa Ana Register*, May 27, 1928, page 3.

"Solomon Dodd is Called by Death", *Santa Ana Register*, August 11, 1930,
page 2.

W.L.G. Haskins

BOOKS

Hedrick, Joan, D., *Harriet Beecher Stowe: A Life*, Oxford University Press, New
York, 1994, pages 104-109.

Huntley, Helen Gulick & William, (ed. Edna Phelps), *Tustin Scrapbook*, Tustin
Area Historical Society, 1969, page 29.

Jordan, Carol, H., *Tustin: An Illustrated History*, Tustin Area Historical Society,
2007, pages 52, 116.

Sleeper, Jim, *Turn the Rascals Out! The Life and Times of Orange County's
Fighting Editor Dan M. Baker*, California Classics, Trabuco Canyon, 1973,
page 378.

LETTERS

Boston Public Library, Anti-Slavery Collection, Letters/Correspondence, Letter
from David Lee Child, Wayland, MA, August 12, 1866.

ORAL HISTORIES

William Martin Huntley interviews, Oral History Program at Cal State Fullerton,
interviewed by Stephen Gould, May 22, 1968, page 44.

MILITARY RECORDS

OCCGS Civil War Veterans Project: William Lloyd G. Haskins

Civil War Records and Profiles,1861-1865: William G. Haskins

"List of American Civil War Units by State"-Wikipedia: 51st Massachusetts
Infantry, 4th Massachusetts Heavy Artillery

National Gallery of Art (website for government collections), 54th
    Massachusetts Colored Infantry Roster

GOVERNMENT RECORDS

1840 United States Federal Census: Putnam, Muskingum, Ohio

1850 United States Federal Census: West Boylston, Worcester, Massachusetts

1860 United States Federal Census: West Boylston, Worcester, Massachusetts

1865 Massachusetts State Census: West Boylston, Worcester

1870 United States Federal Census: Worcester, Ward 4, Worcester,
    Massachusetts

1880 United States Federal Census: West Boylston, Worcester, Massachusetts

1900 United States Federal Census: Santa Ana, Orange, California-Tustin
    Precinct

1910 United States Federal Census: Santa Ana, Orange, California-Tustin
    Precinct

Massachusetts Town and Vital Records, 1610-1980: William LG Haskins-Alice
    M. Ross

California County Birth, Marriage, & Death Records, 1849-1980: William LG
    Haskins-Dora Ironmonger

DIRECTORIES

US Find A Grave Index, 1600s-Current: William Lloyd G. Haskins, Alice Ross
    Haskins. Dora E. Haskins

Find A Grave Memorial-Nashville, Tennessee: Sgt. George P. Haskins

1899-1900 Orange County Directory, Belt Fine Publishers, Santa Ana, pages
    190, 193.

1908-1909 Santa Ana City Directory, Register Publishing Co., Santa Ana, pages
    23, 102, 107, 110.

1916 Santa Ana, Tustin, Garden Grove Directory, Santa Ana Directory Co.,
    L.H. Padgham, page 297.

"W.L.G. Haskins", *Los Angeles Times*, December 31, 1891, page 7.

"Home Guard", *Los Angeles Herald*, May 10, 1898, page 9.

"Santa Ana Brevities", *Los Angeles Times*, April 17, 1899, page 9.

"Court Town Notes", *Los Angeles Times*, July 11, 1905, page 18.

"Sudden Death of Mrs. Haskins", *Santa Ana Register*, March 4, 1909, page 5.

"Marriage Licenses", *Santa Ana Register*, March 8, 1910, page 10.

"Meeting of Sunday school Official Board", *Santa Ana Register*, March 15, 1910, page 5.

"Obituary-Dora Haskins", *Santa Ana Register*, July 12, 1915, page 8.

"W.L.G. Haskins of Tustin is Dead", *Santa Ana Register*, November 19, 1919, page 3.

"Obituary-George Haskins", *Santa Ana Register*, July 7, 1927, page 3.

"Obituary-Edith Field", *Santa Ana Register*, April 10, 1937, page 3.

"Obituary-David Dudley Field", *Santa Ana Register*, April 12, 1937, page 3.

"Florence Haskins Called by Death", *Santa Ana Register*, January 28, 1944, page 5.

Benjamin F. Hennacy

BOOKS

Merrill, James M., *The Rebel Shore: The Story of Union Sea Power in the Civil War*, Little, Brown and Company, Boston, 1957.

Mooney, James L., *Dictionary of American Naval Fighting Ships*, Naval Institute Press, (on-line version).

Ringle, Dennis J., *Life in Mr. Lincoln's Navy*, Naval Institute Press, Annapolis, 1998.

ARTICLES

"The Role of the Marine Corps during the Civil War", **wearethemighty.com**
website.

MILITARY RECORDS

U.S. Marine Corps Muster Rolls, 1798-1958
Pvt. Benjamin F. Hennacy, 3 Sep 1862, 1 April 1863, 27 Oct 1864

U.S. Civil War Pension Index, 1861-1934
Benjamin F. Hennacy, 12 January 1872, Approved

GOVERNMENT RECORDS

1870 United States Federal Census, Beaver Falls, Beaver, Pennsylvania

1880 United States Federal Census, Big Beaver, Beaver, Pennsylvania

1900 United States Federal Census Santa Ana, Orange, California-Tustin
Precinct

Iowa Select Marriage Index, 1758-1996 - B.F. Hennacy-Rachael A.
Stuckenbruck Graves

DIRECTORIES

1889 Lincoln, Nebraska City Directory

1891 Denver, Colorado City Directory

1896 Los Angeles, California City Directory

1910 Santa Ana, California City Directory.

U.S. Find A Grave Index, 1600s-current
Sarah L. Hennacy
Rachael A. Hennacy
Benjamin F. Hennacy
Cpl. Phil Sheridan Hennacy

NEWSPAPERS

"B.F. Hennacy and family left today…", *Los Angeles Herald*, February 4, 1898, page 7.

"The premises of B.F. Hennacy…", *Los Angeles Times*, December 2, 1900, p. 9.

"Alleged Boy Burglars Freed at Santa Ana", *Los Angeles Times*, June 2, 1901, page 10.

"B.F. Hennacy a West Fourth street…", *Los Angeles Evening Express*, Dec. 30, 1902, page 7.

"B.F. Hennacy has gone to Philadelphia…", *Los Angeles Herald*, Sep.13, 1905, page 5.

"Interesting W.R.C. Meeting", *Santa Ana Register*, Feb. 7, 1908, page 5.

"Sycamore Installs", *Santa Ana Register*, July 13, 1908, page 5.

"Stopped Fight at 1:30 Yesterday Morning", *Santa Ana Register*, Feb. 14, 1910, page 8.

"Many to Go to Grand Encampment", *Santa Ana Register*, April 16, 1910, p 8.

"Mrs. Hennacy Critically Ill", *Santa Ana Register*, April 14, 1913, page 5.

"Died: Hennacy in Santa Ana", *Santa Ana Register*, April 16, 1913, page 5.

"Mrs. Hennacy's Funeral Postponed…", *Santa Ana Register*, April 17, 1913, page 5.

"Card of Thanks", *Santa Ana Register*, April 22, 1913, page 8.

"Under Probation", *Santa Ana Register*, October 4, 1913, page 8.

"Didn't Last Long", *Santa Ana Register*, October 6, 1913, page 8.

"Personals: B.F. Hennacy is very miserable…", *Santa Ana Register*, Feb. 4, 1914, page 5.

"B.F. Hennacy went to Wilmington", *Santa Ana Register*, Jan. 24, 1917, page 5.

"Hennacy-In this city…", *Santa Ana Register*, March 25, 1918, page 5.

"B.F. Hennacy's Estate Left to His Stepson", *Santa Ana Register*, Mar. 27, 1918, page 3.

"Notice To Creditors", *Santa Ana Register*, August 31, 1918, page 13.

"Phil Hennacy Now in A.E.F. On Rhine", *Santa Ana Register*, May 5, 1919, page 2.

Henry H. Higley

BOOKS

Guinn, J.M., *Historical and Biographical Record of Southern California*, Chapman Publishing Co., Chicago, 1902, pages 659-661.

Huntley, Helen Gulick & William, (ed. Edna Phelps), *Tustin Scrapbook*, Tustin Area Historical Society, 1969, pages 69, 76.

Swanner, Charles, D., *The Story of Company L, "Santa Ana's Own"*, Fraser Press, Claremont, 1958, page 29.

Des Moines County History, 1890, (online version), pages 338, 371.

MILITARY RECORDS

"List of American Civil War Units by State"-Wikipedia: 15th Iowa Infantry Regiment

History of the Fifteenth Iowa Volunteer Infantry from October 1861 to August 1865, R G Ogden & Son, 1887 (online version), pages 61-67.

Roster and Records of Iowa Soldiers, War of the Rebellion, Historical Sketches of Volunteer Organizations, Vol. II, 15th Iowa Infantry, page 892.

US Veterans Administration Master Index, 1917-1940: Henry H. Higley

US Military Registers, 1858-1923: Henry H. Higley

Iowa Grand Army of the Republic Records, 1861-1949: Henry H. Higley

GOVERNMENT RECORDS

1856 Iowa State Census: Danville, Des Moines

1860 United States Federal Census: Danville, Des Moines, Iowa

1870 United States Federal Census: Danville, Des Moines, Iowa

1880 United States Federal Census: Danville, Des Moines, Iowa

1895 Iowa State Census: Danville, Des Moines

1900 United States Federal Census: Santa Ana, Orange, California-Tustin
Precinct

1910 United States Federal Census: Long Beach, Los Angeles, California

1920 United States Federal Census: Long Beach, Los Angeles, California

1930 United States Federal Census: Lynwood, Los Angeles, California

California Death Index, 1905-1935: Henry H. Higley, Henry Franklin Higley

DIRECTORIES

US Find A Grave Index, 1600s-Current: Henry H. Higley

1899-1900 Orange County Directory, Belt Fine Publishers, Santa Ana, p. 193.

NEWSPAPERS

"Santa Ana Doctor Cures Lockjaw", *Los Angeles Times*, January 9, 1902, p. 18.

"Tustin Notes and Gossip", *Los Angeles Express*, June 11, 1903, page 5.

"H.H. Higley and Wife Home from Visit to Iowa", *Long Beach Evening
Telegram*, October 31, 1905, page 1.

"The G.A.R. Post has elected officers", *Los Angeles Times*, December 12, 1910,
page 16.

"Obituary-Mrs. Mary E. Higley", *Long Beach Daily Telegram*, August 21, 1914,
page 5.

"Obituary-Mrs. Mary E. Higley", *Long Beach Press*, August 21, 1914, page 4.

"Obituary-Henry H. Higley", *Long Beach Press*, January 18, 1934, page 5.

"Obituary-Pearl Higley", *Long Beach Independent*, March 14, 1961, page 14.

"Obituary-Henry Higley, 82", *Long Beach Independent*, June 12, 1963, page 10.

Lewis Hillyard

BOOKS

Armor, Samuel, ed., *History of Orange County with Biographical Sketches*, Historic Record Company, Los Angeles, 1911, page 580-581.

Bricken, Gordon, *Pioneers in Blue and Gray: Civil War Veterans in Orange County*, The Bricken Press, Santa Ana, 2002, page 70.

MILITARY RECORDS

OCCGS Civil War Veterans Project-Lewis Hillyard

Civil War Soldier Records and Profiles, 1861-1865 Lewis Hillyard

Civil War Soldiers, 1861-1865 Lewis Hillyard

List of Union Regiments in the Civil War, Wikipedia, 25th Iowa Infantry

GOVERNMENT RECORDS

1850 United States Federal Census: Jefferson, Grant, Indiana

1860 United States Federal Census: Canaan, Henry, Iowa

1870 United States Federal Census: Canaan, Henry, Iowa

1880 United States Federal Census: Mt. Union, Henry, Iowa & Center, Boone, Indiana

1900 United States Federal Census: Canaan, Henry, Iowa & Long Island, Phillips, Kansas

1910 United States Federal Census: Santa Ana, Orange, California-Tustin precinct

1920 United States Federal Census: Santa Ana Ward 2, Orange, California

U.S Quaker Meeting Records, 1681-1935, Jacob Hillyard & Martha Hillyard

Iowa Select Marriage Index, 1758-1996

Lewis Hillyard & Sarah J. Kenyon, 19 January 1866, Henry County

Indiana Marriage Index, 1800-1941

    Lavina Pugh & John F. Franklin, 23 July 1877, Boone County

California County Birth, Marriage, and Death Records, 1849-1980

    Louise H. Franklin & Lewis Hillyard, 14 February 1901, Santa Ana

DIRECTORIES

U.S. Find A Grave Index, 1600s-current   Sarah Hillyard

NEWSPAPERS

"Deceased Iowa Soldiers", *Muscatine Weekly Journal* (Iowa), March 20, 1863, page 3.

"Gone To Rest", *Long Island New Leaf* (Kansas), March 12, 1891, page 8.

"Mr. Lewis Hillyard….", *Long Island New Leaf*, March 3, 1894, page 1.

"Mr. Lewis Hillyard of Iowa…", *Long Island New Leaf*, March 28, 1896, p. 1.

"L. Hillyard who purchased the Wiley Farm, *Long Island New Leaf*, Sep. 10, 1896, page 3.

"Lew Hillyard moved to the farm", *Long Island New Leaf*, Oct. 31, 1896, p. 1.

"H.H. Hillyard, Bakery & Lunch Room", *Long Island New Leaf*, Nov. 14, 1896, page 1.

"Mr. Lewis Hillyard and family…", *Long Island New Leaf*, Aug. 7, 1897, p. 1.

"Obituary-Lewis Robert Hillyard", *Long Island New Leaf*, March 5, 1898, p. 1.

"Obituary-Clara R. Barclay", *Long Island New Leaf*, January 7, 1899, page 1.

"Mr. Lewis Hillyard will hold a sale…", *Long Island New Leaf*, Jan. 14, 1899, page 1.

"Lewis Hillyard and Miss Louise Franklin…", Los Angeles Times, Feb. 15, 1901, page 17.

"Mrs. L.H. Hillyard of Tustin…", *Long Island New Leaf*, June 29, 1901, page 1.

"Lewis Hillyard of Tustin…", *Long Island New Leaf*, March 22, 1902, page 1.

"Church Happenings", *Santa Ana Register*, February 16, 1907, page 2.

"The teachers of the Sunday school ..", *Santa Ana Register*, March 2, 1907, p. 8.

"Surprised Tustin Friends", *Santa Ana Register*, March 2, 1907, page 5.

"W.C.T.U. Organize Department Work", *Santa Ana Register*, March 30, 1907, page 3.

"Met at Home of Louis Hillyard", *Santa Ana Register*, May 11, 1907, page 8.

"Party at Hillyard Ranch", *Santa Ana Register*, October 10, 1908, page 8.

"Iowa Man Buys Ranch", *Santa Ana Register*, April 24, 1909, page 3.

"Hillyard Purchases Property at Tustin", *Santa Ana Register*, July 21, 1909, page 6.

"A Valentine Luncheon", *Santa Ana Register*, February 15, 1910, page 5.

"Mr. Lewis Hillyard sold 10 acres ...", *Santa Ana Register*, June 11, 1910, p. 2.

"Garnetts Again in Town", *Santa Ana Register*, September 17, 1912, page 5.

"Returned From Utah", *Santa Ana Register*, October 26, 1916, page 10.

"Warren Hillyard is in Miners Regiment", *Santa Ana Register*, May 11, 1918, page 5.

"Obituary-Henry H. Hillard", *Santa Ana Register*, September 16, 1918, page 5.

"Warren K. Hillyard, County Surveyor", *Santa Ana Register*, March 11, 1924, page 9.

"Hillyard-Mr. Lewis Hillyard", *Santa Ana Register*, October 15, 1928, page 3.

"Hold Services for Local Man Wednesday", *Santa Ana Register*, October 16, 1928, page 11.

"Obituary-Stella Franklin Skelton", *Harlan County Journal* (Nebraska), Jan. 16, 1964, page 10.

"Warren "Cap" Hillyard", *Santa Ana Register*, January 13, 1965, page 56.

"The Greatest Prep Game", *Santa Ana Register*, January 14, 1965, page 32.

Upton C. Holderman

BOOKS

Armor, Samuel, (ed.), *History of Orange County with Biographical Sketches*, Historic Record Company, Los Angeles, 1911 & 1921 editions.

Bricken, Gordon, *Pioneers in Blue and Gray, Civil War Veterans in Orange County*, Bricken Press, Santa Ana, 2009.

Swanner, Charles, D., *The Story of Company L, "Santa Ana's Own"*, Fraser Press, Claremont, 1958.

MILITARY RECORDS

OCCGS Civil War Veterans Project: Upton C. Holderman

Civil War Soldier Records and Profiles, 1861-1865: Upton C. Holderman

"List of American Civil War Units by State"-Wikipedia: 22nd Iowa Infantry

The 22nd Iowa: A Brief History - **22iowa.com**

Civil War Pension Index, 1861-1934: Upton C. Holderman

GOVERNMENT RECORDS

1850 United States Federal Census: Newport, Johnson, Iowa

1860 United States Federal Census: Graham, Johnson, Iowa

1870 United States Federal Census: Graham, Johnson, Iowa

1880 United States Federal Census: Denver, Adams, Nebraska

1890 Veterans Schedules of US Federal Census: West Blue, Adams, Nebraska

1900 United States Federal Census: Santa Ana, Orange, California-Tustin Precinct

1910 United States Federal Census: Santa Ana, Orange, California-Tustin Precinct

1920 United States Federal Census: Orange, Orange, California

Iowa Select Marriage Index, 1758-1996: Upton C. Holderman-Almira E. Morse

California Birth, Marriage & Death Records, 1849-1980: Lyda Morse
    Holderman-W.W. Cooker

California Death Index, 1905-1939: UC Holderman, Alma M. Holderman

California Death Index, 1940-1997: Emma M. Lamb, Lyda Marsh, Upton Grant
    Holderman

DIRECTORIES

US Find A Grave Index, 1600s-current: Uppie Ethel Holderman, John Charles
    Lamb, Myron Charles Holderman, Nelson Miles Holderman, Mina Alice
    Holderman

1899-1900 Orange County Directory, Belt Fine Publishers, Santa Ana, p. 194.

1908-1909 Santa Ana City Directory, Register Publishing Co., Santa Ana,
    page 111.

1916 Santa Ana, Tustin, Garden Grove Directory, Santa Ana Directory Co.,
    L.H. Padgham, page 298.

NEWSPAPERS

"Cooker-Holderman", *Santa Ana Register*, May 16, 1908, page 5.

"U.C. Holderman is Dead", *Santa Ana Register*, June 13, 1913, page 5.

"U.C. Holderman Funeral", *Santa Ana Register*, June 16, 1913, page 5.

"Licensed to Wed", *Santa Ana Register*, August 28, 1914, page 5.

"To Welcome Bride and Groom", *Santa Ana Register*, January 11, 1919, page 5.

"Final Service on Monday for Mrs. Coate, 83", *Santa Ana Register*, April 21,
    1929, page 3.

"Obituary-Eugene Harold Marsh", *Santa Ana Register*, October 27, 1938, p. 3.

"Late Flash! Col. Holderman Dies", *St. Helen Star*, (St. Helena, CA), September
    3, 1953, page 1.

"Capt. Holderman, Hero of World War I, Dies", *San Bernardino County Sun*,
    September 4, 1953, page 38.

"Obituary-Mina Holderman", *Tustin News*, July 2, 1992, page 7.

George W. Hubbard

BOOKS

Armor, Samuel, (ed.), *History of Orange County with Biographical Sketches*, Historical Record Company, Los Angeles, 1911, pages 591-592.

Bricken, Gordon, *Pioneers in Blue and Gray, Civil War Veterans in Orange County,* Bricken Press, Santa Ana, 2009, page 71.

Faust, Drew, Gilpin, *This Republic of Suffering: Death and the American Civil War*, Vintage Books, New York, 2008.

Huntley, Helen Gulick & William, (ed. Edna Phelps), *Tustin Scrapbook*, Tustin Area Historical Society 1969, page 70.

Jordan, Carol, H., Tustin: *An Illustrated History*, Tustin Area Historical Society, Tustin, 2007, page 68.

Martin, Claude, B., *Martin's Memoirs*, private manuscript, 1978, page 22.

Phisterer, Frederick, *New York in the War of the Rebellion*, J.B. Lyon Company, Albany, 1912, (online version).

Westfall, Douglas, *Prisoners of War: The Story of Two Americans,* The Paragon Agency, Orange, 2001.

MILITARY RECORDS

OCCGS Civil War Veterans Project: George Washington Hubbard

Civil War Soldier Records and Profiles, 1861-1865: George W. Hubbard

Civil War Pension Index: General Index to Pension Files, 1861-1934: George W. Hubbard

New York Civil War Muster Roll Abstracts, 1861-1900: George W. Hubbard

"List of American Civil War Units by State"-Wikipedia: 16th New York Infantry, 121st New York Infantry

Annual Report of the Adjutant General of the State of New York, 1903, page 93, (online version).

"Libby Prison"-Wikipedia

"Salisbury National Cemetery"-Wikipedia

GOVERNMENT RECORDS

1850 United States Federal Census: Putney, Windham, Vermont

1860 United States Federal Census: Malone, Franklin, New York

1870 United States Federal Census: Malone, Franklin, New York

1880 United States Federal Census: Malone, Franklin, New York

1900 United States Federal Census: Santa Ana, Orange, California-Tustin
Precinct

1910 United States Federal Census: Santa Ana, Orange, California-Tustin
Precinct

1920 United States Federal Census: Tustin, Orange, California

1940 United States Federal Census: Tustin, Orange, California

California Voter Registers, 1866-1898: George W. Hubbard, Tustin, 1892

Michigan Death & Burial Index, 1867-1995: W.R. Day

DIRECTORIES

US Find A Grave Index, 1600s-Current: Emma L. Day, Marcia A. Hubbard,
Clinton Samuel Hubbard, Claribel Macomber

1899-1900 Orange County Directory: Belt Fine Publishers, Santa Ana, p. 194.

1916 Santa Ana, Tustin, Garden Grove Directory, Santa Ana Directory Co.,
L.H. Padgham, page 298.

City of Tustin Historical Survey-Hubbard House

NEWSPAPERS

"Marriage Licenses", *Los Angeles Herald*, January 9, 1889, page 2.

"Obituary-Emma L. Day", *Los Angeles Times*, January 31, 1894, page 9.

"Obituary-Emma L. Day", *Los Angeles Evening Express*, January 31, 1894,
page 5.

"Thank You Notice", The *Los Angeles Times*, February 2, 1894, page 9.

"Mr. Hubbard, the wealthy hop buyer", *Los Angeles Evening Express,* September 23, 1896, page 5.

"Dealers in Hops", *Statesman Journal* (Salem, Oregon), January 1, 1899, page 17.

"Obituary-Marcia Hubbard", undated Malone, New York newspaper.

"George W. Hubbard Called by Death", *Santa Ana Register*, July 22, 1922, page 2.

"Mrs. Alice Hubbard Passes in Tustin", *Santa Ana Register*, April 18, 1942, page 3.

William A. Jerome

BOOKS

Armor, Samuel, (ed.), *History of Orange County with Biographical Sketches*, Historic Record Co., Los Angeles, 1921, page 1657-1568.

Huntley, Helen Gulick & William, (ed. Edna Phelps), *Tustin Scrapbook*, Tustin Area Historical Society, 1969, page 71.

McDowell, Don, *The Beat of the Drum, The History, Events and People of Drum Barracks, Wilmington, California*, Graphic Publishers, Santa Ana, 1993.

Swanner, Charles, D., *Santa Ana: A Narrative of Yesterday, 1870-1910*, Saunder Press, Claremont, CA, 1953, page 151-152.

ORAL HISTORIES

William Martin Huntley interview, Oral History Program at California State Fullerton, interviewed by Stephen Gould, May 21-22, 1968, pages 12,70.

MAGAZINES

"Chiricahua Pass", *Wild West,* Autumn, 2022, page 12-13.

<h1 style="text-align:center">LETTERS</h1>

After-action report, Brig. Gen. Thomas C. Devlin, Commander Sub-District of Southern Arizona to Col. John P. Shelbourne, Asst. Adjutant General, Dept. of California, Oct. 30, 1869.

Medal of Honor Acknowledgment, E.D. Townsend, Adjutant General to Pvt. Charles H. Ward, January 14, 1870.

Adjutant General to Honorable Phil D. Swig, April 15, 1929.

Donation form, William Jerome to Tustin Area Museum, June 19, 1980.

Undated, unsigned letter with biographical information on William Jerome, presumably from a descendant.

<h2 style="text-align:center">MILITARY RECORDS</h2>

OCCGS Civil War Veterans Project: William Ambrose Jerome

U.S. Army Register of Enlistments, 1798-1914: William Jerome

Drum Barracks muster rolls, Charles H. Ward

List of American Civil War Units by State: 1st Pennsylvania Cavalry

<h2 style="text-align:center">GOVERNMENT RECORDS</h2>

1870 United States Federal Census: Apache Pass, Pima, Arizona Territory

1880 United States Federal Census: Orange, Los Angeles, California

1900 United States Federal Census: Santa Ana, Orange, California-Tustin Precinct

California County Birth, Marriage and Death Records, 1849-1980: Wm Jerome-Martha Ward

California County Marriages, 1850-1952: Wm. Jerome-Martha Ward

Naturalization Record Indexes, 1791-1992: William Jerome, June 28, 1877, Los Angeles

California Voter Registers, 1866-1898: William Jerome, Los Angeles, 1879

California Voter Registers, 1866-1898: William Jerome, Tustin, 1892

279

California Biographical Index Cards, 1781-1990: William Centennial Jerome

California Death Index, 1905-1939: Martha Jerome

DIRECTORIES

US Find A Grave Index, 1600-Current: William Jerome, Martha Jerome, William C. Jerome, Benjamin W. Jerome

1899-1900 Orange County Directory, Belt Fine Publishers, Santa Ana, page 194.

NEWSPAPERS

"Police Regulations", *Los Angeles Evening Express*, June 9, 1876, page 3.

"Last evening….", *Los Angeles Daily Star*, November 15, 1876, page 4.

"About 11 o'clock….", *Los Angeles Herald*, January 9, 1878, page 3.

"Officer Jerome", *Los Angeles Evening Express*, January 16, 1878, page 3.

"About half-past 7 o'clock", *Los Angeles Daily Star*, January 25, 1878, page 3.

"Chief Harris", *Los Angeles Herald*, February 6, 1878, page 5.

"Night before last….", *Los Angeles Herald*, February 17, 1878, page 3.

"William Jerome sworn", *Los Angeles Herald*, April 11, 1878, page 3.

"Hunt For Stolen Gold", *Los Angeles Daily Star*, May 21, 1878, page 3.

"Chief Harris", *Los Angeles Herald*, June 5, 1878, page 3.

"Yesterday afternoon…", *Los Angeles Herald*, August 13, 1878, page 3.

"Attempted Suicide", *Los Angeles Herald*, October 1, 1878, page 3.

"The New County", *Los Angeles Times*, July 14, 1889, page 3.

"Santa Ana", *San Francisco Call*, August 24, 1892, page 1.

"Sudden Death", *Los Angeles Times*, August 22, 1900, page 15.

"Tustin Items", *Santa Ana Weekly Blade*, August 24, 1900, page 2.

'Sudden Death", *Santa Ana Weekly Blade*, August 24, 1900, page 4.

"William Jerome", San Francisco Call, August 22, 1900, page 7.

"William C. Jerome", *Santa Ana Register*, May 9, 1914, page 4.

"Death Summons Loved Pioneer of Valley", *Santa Ana Register*, January 29, 1921, page 2.

"Long Local Line Behind Jerome Girl", *Santa Ana Register*, July, 8, 1936, page 11.

"W.C. Jerome, Santa Ana Civic Leader, Dies", *Los Angeles Times,* December 5, 1954, page 72.

"Funeral Arranged", *Los Angeles Times*, December 7, 1954, page 41.

The photograph of the Thacker Packing House employees was used with permission of the Tustin Area Historical Society.

Lorenzo Kiser

BOOKS

Jordan, Carol, *Tustin: An Illustrated History,* Tustin Area Historical Society, Tustin, 2007.

Westfall, Douglas, *Prisoners of the Civil War, The Story of Two Americans,* The Paragon Agency, Orange, 2001.

MILITARY RECORDS

OCCGS Civil War Veterans Project: Lorenzo Brown Kiser

US Army Register of Enlistments, 1798-1914, Lorenzo B. Kiser

Civil War Soldiers, 1861-1865, Lorenzo B. Kiser

Civil War Soldier Records and Profiles, 1861-1865, Lorenzo B. Kiser

Historical Sketches of Staff and Line with Portraits of Generals-in-Chief, Seventeenth Regiment of Infantry

US Veterans Administration Master Index, 1917-1940: Ira F. Kiser

Civil War Pension Index: General Index to Pension Files, 1861-1934: Lucy
Kiser-widow

GOVERNMENT RECORDS

1850 United States Federal Census: Somerset, Somerset, Pennsylvania

1860 United States Federal Census: Dixon, Lee, Illinois, Somerset, Somerset,
Pennsylvania

1870 United States Federal Census: South Dixon, Lee, Illinois, Jefferson,
Somerset, Pennsylvania

1880 United States Federal Census: Precinct 1, Seward, Nebraska

1900 United States Federal Census: Middle Creek, Lancaster, Nebraska

1910 United States Federal Census: Santa Ana, Orange, California-Tustin
Precinct, Alila, Tulare, California, Emerson, Harlan, Nebraska, Havelock,
Lancaster, Nebraska

1920 United States Federal Census: Tustin, Orange, California, Los Flores, San
Diego, California, Emerson, Harlan, Nebraska

1930 United States Federal Census: Tustin, Orange, California, Santa Ana,
Orange, California, Oceanside, San Diego, California

1940 United States Federal Census: Tustin, Orange, California, Santa Ana,
Orange, California

1950 United States Federal Census: Garden Grove, Orange, California

Nebraska Select County Marriage Records, 1855-1908: Olive May Kesei (Kiser)
- Theodore W. Bose, March 5, 1901, Lucy B. Kiser - Ira F. Kiser, June 4,
1903, Edmond Kiser -Rosetta Copies, March 30, 1905

California County Birth, Marriage and Death Records, 1849-1980: Lucy Kiser-
Charles Pilgrim, May 25, 1907, John R. Kiser-Jessie E. DeBaun, October
22, 1912, Harry T. Kiser-Florence Virginia Brookbank, December 20,
1912, Dudley C. Kiser-Alice Ruth Matthews, May 5, 1914

California Death Index, 1940-1997: Dudley Camron Kiser, October 18, 1959,
Harry T. Kiser, July 18, 1960, Florence V. Kiser, September 8, 1965, John
R. Kiser, August 7, 1966

DIRECTORIES

US Find A Grave Index, 1600s-current: Lorenzo B. Kiser, Lucy B. Pilgrim, Olive M. Bose, Edmond Lee Kiser, Harry T. Kiser, Dudley Cameron Kiser, Theodore W. Bose, Rosetta Kiser, Alice Ruth Kiser, Rev. Henry Berkey

1923 Santa Ana City Directory

1940 Anaheim City & County Directory

NEWSPAPERS

"Ira Kiser", *Lincoln Star*, February 6, 1905, page 5.

"A Week-End Wedding", *Santa Ana Register*, May 27, 1907, page 5.

"A Family Party", *Santa Ana Register*, February 1, 1908, page 8.

"Mr. and Mrs. Ed Kiser", *Santa Ana Register*, June 27, 1908, page 6.

"Mr. and Mrs. L.B. Kiser", *Santa Ana Register*, November 5, 1910, page 2.

"Mr. Ed Kiser and family", *Santa Ana Register*, November 4, 1911, page 6.

"Mr. Ed Kiser and family", *Santa Ana Register*, November 18, 1911, page 6.

"Marriage Licenses", *Santa Ana Register*, October 22, 1912, page 8.

"Mr. and Mrs. John Kiser", *Santa Ana Register*, November 15, 1912, page 7.

"Marriage Licenses", *Santa Ana Register*, December 19, 1912, page 6.

"John Kiser has purchased…", *Santa Ana Register*, November 28, 1913, page 3.

"Surprise Party", *Santa Ana Register*, January 30, 1914, page 3.

"Kiser-Matthews", *Santa Ana Register*, May 8, 1914, page 6.

"Birthday Surprise", *Santa Ana Register*, November 21, 1914, page 2.

"Mr. and Mrs. L.B. Kiser have just returned", *Santa Ana Register*, February 6, 1915, page 2.

"Another new home being built…", *Santa Ana Register*, March 6, 1915.

"L.B. Kiser of Tustin leaves.…", *Santa Ana Register*, September 17, 1917, p. 5.

"Mr. and Mrs. L.B. Kiser", *Santa Ana Register*, September 21, 1917, page 7.

"19-Year Resident of Tustin Called", *Santa Ana Register*, August 5, 1924, p. 2.

"Fire District At Tustin To Be Requested", *Santa Ana Register*, January 24, 1925, page 18.

"Funeral Notice", *Santa Ana Register*, January 27, 1925, page 3.

"Obituary-Lorenzo B. Kiser", *Santa Ana Register*, January 30, 1925, page 20.

"17 Members of Sedgwick G.A.R. Post Summoned Since Last Memorial Day", *Santa Ana Register*, May 27, 1925, page 7.

"Pilgrim Funeral Rites Held Today", *Santa Ana Register*, June 23, 1942, page 9.

"Tustinite of 60 Years Dies", *Tustin News*, August 11, 1966, page 1.

"Services Held for Mrs. Kiser", *Tustin News*, March 13, 1969, page 1.

Henry Kissel

BOOKS

Huntley, Helen Gulick & William, (ed. Edna Phelps), *Tustin Scrapbook*, Tustin Area Historical Society, 1969, page 32.

MILITARY RECORDS

OCCGS Civil War Veterans Project: Henry Kissel

Civil War Soldiers Records and Profiles, 1861-1865: Henry Kissel

Civil War Draft Registration Records, 1863-1865: Henry Kissel

American Civil War Regiments, 1861-1865: 192nd Pennsylvania Infantry

Civil War Pension Index, General Index to Pension Files, 1861-1934: Henry Kissel, July 29, 1892, California

GOVERNMENT RECORDS

1860 United States Federal Census: Lower Swatara, Dauphin, Pennsylvania

1870 United States Federal Census: Blue Springs, Gage, Nebraska

1880 United States Federal Census: Wellington, Sumner, Kansas

1900 United States Federal Census: Santa Ana, Orange, California-Tustin
    Precinct

1910 United States Federal Census: Ballona, Los Angeles, California

1920 United States Federal Census: Los Angeles Assembly Dist. 71, Los
    Angeles, California

California County Birth, Marriage, Death Records, 1849-1980: Annie J. Kissel-
    Thomas L. Cummins

California Voter Registers, 1866-1898: Henry Kissel, Tustin, 1892

Idaho Marriage Records, 1863-1969: Margaret R. Rawlings-Charles E. Utt

DIRECTORIES

1899-1900 Orange County Directory, Belt Fine Publishers, Santa Ana, p. 194.

NEWSPAPERS

"Died-Kissel", *Santa Ana Weekly Blade*, May 16, 1902, page 3.

"Catherine Kissel estate...", *Los Angeles Times*, June 7, 1902, page 16.

"Deaths-Kissel", *Santa Ana Register*, March 24, 1920, page 3.

"Henry Kissel", *Long Beach Press-Telegram*, March 24, 1920, page 16.

"Henry Kissel", *Long Beach Daily Telegram*, March 24, 1920, page 7.

"Mrs. Cummins Dies", *Bakersfield Morning Echo*, December 31, 1926, page 2.

"Cummins", *Santa Ana Register*, December 30, 1926, page 3.

**The photographs of the headstones of Henry and Catherine Kissel were taken
    at Santa Ana Cemetery by Paul Loya.**

Henry Leck

BOOKS

Kaufmann, Wilhelm, The Germans in the American Civil War, John Kallman
Publishers, Carlisle, PA, 1999.

Logan, Guy E. (Ed.), Roster and Records of Iowa Soldiers, War of the
Rebellion–Historical Sketches of Volunteer Organizations, Vol. 6, Iowa
General Assembly, 1911.3.

MILITARY RECORDS

OCCGS Civil War Veterans Project: Henry Leck

Civil War Draft Registration Records, 1863-1865, Henry Leck, Glenwood,
Mills, Iowa

GOVERNMENT RECORDS

1850 United States Federal Census: Plumcreek, Armstrong, Pennsylvania

1860 United States Federal Census: Indian Creek, Story, Iowa

1870 United States Federal Census: Lafayette, Nemaha, Nebraska

1880 United States Federal Census: Lafayette, Nemaha, Nebraska

1885 Nebraska State Census: Lafayette, Nemaha, Nebraska

1900 United States Federal Census: Santa Ana, Orange, CA-Tustin precinct

1910 United States Federal Census: Santa Ana Ward 3, Orange, California

1920 United States Federal Census: Santa Ana Ward 3, Orange, California

1930 United States Federal Census: Laguna Beach, Orange, California

1940 United States Federal Census: Laguna Beach, Orange, California

Pennsylvania Arriving Passenger and Crew Lists, 1798-1962

Henry Leck, 12 August 1841, Philadelphia

California Voter Registers, 1866-1898

    Henry Leck, 1892, Tustin

Mississippi Compiled Marriage Index, 1776-1935

    Francis A. Burr-Bolivar Muzzy, 26 March 1872

DIRECTORIES

US Find A Grave Index, 1600s-current
    Mariah Leck, Henry Leck

NEWSPAPERS

"Public Sale", *Nemaha Herald* (Nebraska), September 6, 1889, page 5.

"Obituary-Mrs. Leck", unattributed clipping, June 1904.

"Notice of Final Settlement", *The Western Call*, (Beloit, Kansas), July 19, 1907, page 2.

"Jasper Leck of Tustin…", *Santa Ana Register*, July 20, 1910, page 6.

"Democratic Candidates for County Officers", *Santa Ana Register*, Nov. 1, 1910, page 4.

"Leck Has Leased San Juan Springs", *Santa Ana Register*, May 30, 1911, p. 3.

"Notice to Public", *Santa Ana Register*, November 16, 1911, page 8.

"Leck Sells San Juan Hot Springs", *Santa Ana Register*, February 19, 1913, page 3.

"At Leck Home", *Santa Ana Register*, December 30, 1915, page 5.

"Forster-Leck", *Santa Ana Register*, February 3, 1917, page 3.

"Leck is Defeated", *Santa Ana Register*, August 28, 1918, page 1.

"Thanks for Support", *Santa Ana Register*, August 30, 1918, page 5.

"John O. Leck", *The Long Beach Sun*, August 25, 1937, page 7.

"Arley Leck Ill", *Coastline Dispatch* (San Juan Capistrano), Jan. 26, 1956.

"Arley H. Leck", *Santa Ana Register*, August 11, 1956.

Harvey B. Lewis

BOOKS

Dawson, Elmer, Ray, *A History of Tustin*, Master Degree Thesis, University of Southern California, 1938, page 68.

Huntley, Helen Gulick & William, (ed. Edna Phelps), *Tustin Scrapbook*, Tustin Area Historical Society, 1969, page 74.

Jordan, Carol, H., *Tustin: An Illustrated History*, Tustin Area Historical Society, Tustin, 2007.

Josephy, Alvin, M., *The Civil War in the American West,* Alfred A. Knopf, New York, 1991.

Pleasants, J.E., *History of Orange County, Vol. III*, J.R. Finnell & Sons, Los Angeles, 1931, pages 34-42.

Tolzman, Don Heinrich, *German Pioneer Accounts of the Great Sioux Uprising of 1862,* Little Miami Publishing, Milford, OH, 2002.

MILITARY

OCCGS Civil War Veterans Project: Harvey B. Lewis

Civil War Soldier Records and Profiles, 1861-1865: Harvey B. Lewis

"List of American Civil Units by State"-Wikipedia: 30th Wisconsin Infantry

Roster of Wisconsin Volunteers, War of the Rebellion, 1861-1865, Wisconsin Adjutant General's Office, Vol. III, 1886 (online version): 30th Wisconsin Infantry Regiment

Civil War Pension Index: General Index to Pension Files, 1861-1934: Harvey B. Lewis

GOVERNMENT RECORDS

1850 United States Federal Census: Fowler, St. Lawrence, New York

1860 United States Federal Census: Greenbush, Sheboygan, Wisconsin

1870 United States Federal Census: Kenyon, Goodhue, Minnesota

1875 Minnesota, US Territorial & State Census: Kenyon, Goodhue, Minnesota

1880 United States Federal Census: Tustin, Los Angeles, California

California Voter Registers, 1866-1898: Harvey B. Lewis, Tustin, 1879

DIRECTORIES

1892 Los Angeles City Directory & Gazetteer, Maxwell Publishing, Los Angeles, 1892, page 923.

US Find A Grave Index, 1600s-Current: Harvey B. Lewis, Theresa H. Lewis, Percy B. Lewis, Perry Eben Lewis, Minnie C. Lewis

NEWSPAPERS

"Some sickness if reported…", *The Los Angeles Mirror*, October 24, 1885, p. 7.

"Notice of Special Election", *Orange Tribune*, June 1, 1889.

"H.B. Lewis of Tustin Dead", *Los Angeles Times*, June 20, 1898, page 9.

"Woman Pioneer Dies in Tustin", *Santa Ana Register*, March 18, 1925, page 8.

"Lewis", *Santa Ana Register*, March 18, 1925, page 3.

"Mrs. Minnie Lewis Passes in Tustin", *Santa Ana Register*, December 23, 1942, page 9.

"Funeral Services for Pioneer Rancher", *Tustin News*, June 11, 1954, page 1.

"A Short History of the Tustin Post Office", by Thomas M. Pulley, *County Courier*, September, 2006, pages 3-4.

"A Forgotten Massacre on the Frontier", by Scott Martelle, *Los Angeles Times*, December 9, 2012.

The photograph of the Columbus Tustin Building and the Tustin Post Office and the photograph of the Lewis House used with permission of Tustin Area Historical Society.

Noah S. Long

MILITARY RECORDS

OCCGS Civil War Veterans Project: Noah S. Long

Civil War Soldier Records and Profiles, 1861-1865 Noah S. Long

National Parks Service, Civil War Battle Units- 44th Indiana Infantry regiment

44th Indiana Civil War Historical Association-Company C recruits Noah S. Long

The Iron Men of Indiana's 44th Regiment, Par 1, Biographical and Regimental Statistics by Margaret Hobson.

1890 Veterans Schedules of the U.S. Federal Census-Noah S. Long

Indiana Civil War Soldier Data Base Index, 1861-1865- Noah S. Long

GOVERNMENT RECORDS

1850 United States Federal Census: Whitley, Indiana

1860 United States Federal Census: Smith, Whitley, Indiana

1870 United States Federal Census: Lancaster, Nebraska

1880 United States Federal Census: Alexandria, Thayer, Nebraska

1900 United States Federal Census: Fairbury, Jefferson, Nebraska

1910 United States Federal Census: Santa Ana, Orange, CA-Tustin precinct

1920 United States Federal Census: Tustin, Orange, California

1930 United States Federal Census: Beverly Hills, Los Angeles, California

1950 United States Federal Census: Los Angeles, Los Angeles, California

Indiana Select Marriage Index, 1748-1993

    Jesse W. Long-Ann Mariah Ruch, 12 August 1847

Nebraska Select Marriage Records, 1855-1908

    Noah S. Long-Lois Palmer, 30 July 1872

1921 City Directory, 208 A Street, Tustin

1922 California Voter Registration Noah Long, 1702 E. 5th St, Santa Ana

DIRECTORIES

US Find A Grave Index, 1600s-current,
    Noah Salathiel Long, Frank Palmer Long, Louise Long

NEWSPAPERS

"N.S. Long was at his farm…", *The Fairbury Gazette* (Nebraska), July 18, 1891,
    page 5.

"N.S. Long has bought …", *Jefferson County Journal* (Nebraska), Dec. 17,
    1892, page 5.

"N.S. Long is laying a substantial brick...", *The Fairbury Gazette*, Oct. 28, 1893,
    page 5.

"N.S. Long has received….", *The Fairbury Gazette*, November 11, 1893, page
    5.

"Died at the home of N.S. Long", *The Fairbury Gazette*, April 3, 1897, page 5.

"N.S. Long has returned…", *The Fairbury Gazette*, October 6, 1900, page 5.

"Brother N.S. Long has recovered...", *The Fairbury Gazette*, March 7, 1903,
    page 5.

"Roster of Sedgwick Post", *Santa Ana Register*, May 31, 1916, page 9.

"Mr. and Mrs. Noah S. Long of Tustin", *Santa Ana Register*, March 23, 1917,
    page 5.

"Ran Away Together to War in '63", *Santa Ana Register*, February 14, 1919,
    page 3.

"Last Rites Held for Tustin Man", *Santa Ana Register*, May 10, 1921, page 6.

"Noah S. Long, Former S.A. Resident Dies", *Santa Ana Register*, Oct. 19, 1928,
    page 3.

"Death of N.S. Long", *The Fairbury-Journal News*, October 25, 1928, page 1.

"N.S. Long Dead", *The Fairbury Daily News*, October 25, 1928, page 1.

"Former Tustin Lady Dies", *Santa Ana Register*, June 16, 1930, page 1.

"Long-At 709 Canyon Drive", *Santa Ana Register*, June 16, 1930, page 3.

"Max F. Long", *The Honolulu Advertiser*, May 22, 1930, page 5.

"Licenses-Max F. Long-Louise Long", *Ventura Free Press*, August 6, 1931, page 2.

"Louise L. Long", *Times-Advocate* (Escondido, CA), July 15, 1966, page 6.

"Max F. Long", *Times-Advocate* (Escondido, CA), September 26, 1971, page 6.

George W. Mason

BOOKS

Passero, Loraine, Clara Mason Fox, *Pioneer, Painter, and Poet of Orange County*, California, Mill City Press, Minneapolis, 2013.

MILITARY RECORDS

OCCGS Civil War Veterans Project: George Winchester Mason

Civil War Soldier Records and Profiles, 1861-1865 George W. Mason

National Home for Disabled Volunteers Soldiers, 1866-1938 George W. Mason

Official Roster of Soldiers of State of Ohio in the War of the Rebellion, 1861-1866, Vol. V, 63rd Ohio Infantry Regiment, pages 381- 408.Cavalry

GOVERNMENT RECORDS

1850 United States Federal Census: Adams, Washington, Ohio

1860 United States Federal Census: Adams, Washington, Ohio

1870 United States Federal Census: Jackson, Noble, Ohio

1880 United States Federal Census: Lamard, Wayne, Ohio

1900 United States Federal Census: Union, Riverside, California

Orange, Orange, California

> Riverside, Riverside, California

> Los Angeles, Los Angeles, California

1910 United States Federal Census: Santa Ana, Orange, California-Tustin precinct

> Santa Ana Ward 2, Orange, California

> Santa Ana Ward 3, Orange, California

California Select Marriages, 1850-1945

> George W. Mason-C. Rosa Martin, 10 Dec. 1892 San Bernardino

> George W. Mason-Marien Taylor, 16 Jan. 1904 Riverside

California Voter Register, 1866-1898

> George Winchester Mason, 1892, Moreno, San Bernardino County

DIRECTORIES

US Find A Grave Index, 1600s-current
> Nellie McTaggert
> Nancy L. Mason
> Lourena Cecelia Green
> Clara Mason Fox

NEWSPAPERS

"G.W. Mason has just finished….", *The Facts* (Redlands, CA), November 1, 1892, page 4.

"Marriage Licenses", *Los Angeles Evening Express*, June 2, 1905, page 11.

"Mrs. E. Crabb of this city….", *Santa Ana Register*, September 20, 1913, page 2.

"Veteran of Civil War Dies at West Orange Hospital", *The Orange Post*, April 8, 1915.

"Funeral Services", *Santa Ana Register*, April 5, 1915, page 5.

"Mason-At Laguna Beach", *Santa Ana Register*, January 21, 1918, page 4.

“Mrs. Mason Passes Away”, *Lindsay (CA) Gazette*, November 8, 1946, page 6.

“Canyon Native Pens History of El Toro”, *Santa Ana Register*, November 15,
2013.

James McCloud

BOOKS

Dawson, Ray, Elmer, *A History of Tustin*, Masters Degree Thesis, University of
Southern California,1938, page 80.

Guinn, J.M., *Historical & Biographical Record of Southern California*,
Chapman Publishing Company, Los Angeles, 1902, pages 495-496.

ORAL HISTORIES

William Martin Huntley interviews, Oral History Program at California State
Fullerton, Interviewed by Stephen Gould, May 21- 22, 1968, page 55.

MILITARY RECORDS

OCCGS Civil War Veterans Project: James R. McCloud

Database of Illinois Veterans, 1775-1995: James McCloud

“List of American Civil War Units by State”-Wikipedia: 3rd Illinois Cavalry

GOVERNMENT RECORDS

1850 United States Federal Census: Franklin, Kendall, Illinois

1860 United States Federal Census: Odell, Livingston, Illinois

1870 United States Federal Census: Saunemin, Livingston, Illinois

1880 United States Federal Census: Santa Ana, Los Angeles, California

1900 United States Federal Census: Santa Ana, Orange, California-Tustin
Precinct

1910 United States Federal Census: Los Angeles Assembly Dist. 69, Los Angeles, California

California Birth, Marriage and Death Records, 1849-1980: James R. McCloud-Mary A. Weekley. Addie M. McCloud-Edw Tharp

DIRECTORIES

Rootsweb Marriage Record Index: JB McCloud-Ettie C. Weekley

US Find A Grave Index, 1600s-Current: James R. McCloud

NEWSPAPERS

"Horses entered in Fair…", *Santa Ana Weekly Blade*, October 9, 1890, page 2.

"Tustin Rancher Hurt", *Santa Ana Weekly Blade*, January 31, 1902, page 1.

"Kick Proved Fatal", *Los Angeles Times*, January 31, 1902, page 16.

"Died of Injuries", *Oakland Tribune*, January 31, 1902, page 7.

"Attacks Wife with Revolver", *Los Angeles Express*, November 9, 1906, page 9.

"Draws Gun on Officer", *Los Angeles Herald*, November 10, 1906, page 7.

"Says Not Guilty of Contempt", *Los Angles Record*, November 19, 1906, p. 1.

"Towed Girl He Tried to Kill", *Los Angeles Express*, November 24, 1906, p. 2.

"Edward Tharp", *Los Angeles Times*, November 25, 1906, page 20.

"United States Casualty List", *Santa Ana Register*, July 30, 1918, page 1.

"Service Flag Will Bear a Gold Star for Maj. McCloud", *Santa Ana Register*, August 2, 1918, page 10.

"John Anderson of Los Angeles…", *Santa Ana Register*, August 2, 1918, p. 12.

"Colorful Life of S.A. Hero Recalled", *Santa Ana Register*, April 28, 1930, p. 4.

Photograph of the McCloud headstone taken at Santa Ana Cemetery by Timothy Zierer.

Joseph Pollock

BOOKS

Armor, Samuel, (Ed.), *History of Orange County with Biographical Sketches*, Historical Record Company, Los Angeles, 1921.

Hoehling, A.A*., Thunder at Hampton Roads: The USS Monitor-It's Battle with The Merrimack and Its Recent Discovery*, Prentice-Hall, Englewood, New Jersey, 1976.

Ringle, Dennis J., *Life in Mr. Lincoln's Navy*, Naval Institute Press, Annapolis, 1998.

MILITARY RECORDS

OCCGS Civil War Veterans Project-Joseph Pollock

Civil War Pension Index; General Index to Pension Files, 1861-1934

New York Registers of Officers and Enlisted Men Mustered into Federal Service, 1861-1865

Register of Civil, Military, and Naval Service, 1863-1959

GOVERNMENT RECORDS

1850 United States Federal Census: Argyle, Washington, New York

1860 United States Federal Census: Argyle, Washington, New York

1865 New York State Census: Argyle, Washington, New York

1870 United States Federal Census: Squaw Grove, DeKalb, Illinois

1875 New York State Census: Argyle, Washington, New York

1880 United States Federal Census: Austin, Mower, Minnesota

1900 United States Federal Census: Moscow, Freeborn, Minnesota

1905 Minnesota State Census: Moscow, Freeborn, Minnesota

1910 United States Federal Census: Westminster, Orange, California

1920 United States Federal Census: Tustin, Orange, California

                           Anaheim, Orange, California

1930 United States Federal Census: Tustin, Orange, California

Illinois Marriage Index, 1860-1920 Joseph Pollock-Amanda R. Strever, 30 Nov 1876

Minnesota Birth and Christening Index, 1840-1980-Rheuamy Pollock, 6 Dec 1880

Minnesota Marriage from 1850-2019 Roy N. Pollock-Carrie E. White, 8 April 1909

World War I Draft Registrations Cards, 1917-1918 Roy Nelson Pollock

DIRECTORIES

US Find A Grave Index, 1600s-Current: Joseph Pollock, Carrie Pollock

NEWSPAPERS

"Real Estate Transfers", *Mower County Transcript*, April 2, 1884, page 3.

"Lines on the death of Rheuamy Pollock", *Mower County Transcript*, June 9, 1884, page 3.

"Seven years ago, Joseph Pollock", *Mower County Transcript*, January 21, 1891, page 5.

"Solace From Sam", *The Austin Daily Herald*, April 4, 1892, page 4.

"Joe Pollock's new house…", *The Austin Daily Herald*, June 20, 1893, page 3.

"Mrs. Fred Fenton drove out…", *The Austin Daily Herald*, January 21, 1893, page 4.

"F.E. Laken rented the new house of Joseph Pollock", *The Austin Daily Herald*, Aug 17, 1893, page 3.

"Cut On Reaper", *The Austin Daily Herald*, July 3, 1903, page 3.

"Mr. and Mrs. Joseph Pollock...", *The Austin Daily Herald*, August 27, 1903, page 3.

"Anniversary Surprise", *The Austin Daily Herald*, December 16, 1903, page 2.

"Joseph Pollock of Moscow", *Mower County Transcript*, Nov. 1, 1905, page 1.

"Joseph Pollock is another...", *The Austin Daily Herald*, Nov. 9, 1905, page 3.

"Jo Pollock Surprised", *The Austin Daily Herald*, Nov. 17, 1905, page 2.

"Jo Pollock left today...", *The Austin Daily Herald*, Dec. 5, 1905, page 3.

"We received a postal card...", *The Austin Daily Herald*, March 5, 1906, page 3.

"Joseph Pollock has located at Orange, Cal.", *Mower County Transcript*, Mar 21, 1906, page 3.

"Joe Pollock has his sale of stock...", *Mower County Transcript*, Mar 28, 1906, page 7.

"Mrs. Joe Pollock and son...", *Mower County Transcript*, May 2, 1906, page 7.

"Six-Acre Ranch Is Sold to Pollock", *Santa Ana Register*, June 5, 1908, page 3.

"Lizzie J. Finster to Roy N Pollock", *Santa Ana Register*, October 11, 1911, page 6.

"Old Soldiers of Orange Are for Roosevelt", *Santa Ana Register*, Mar 21, 1912, page 3.

"Buys Barton Ranch", *Santa Ana Register*, December 28, 1912, page 3.

"Pollock-At his residence...", *Santa Ana Register*, January 6, 1926, page 3.

"Amanda R. Pollock Called by Death", *Santa Ana Register*, Mar 6, 1934, page 14.

"Native Son of County Succumbs", *Santa Ana Register*, Feb 25, 1935, page 3.

'Roy N. Pollock", *Santa Ana Register*, December 3, 1953, page 47.

James W. Northcross

BOOKS

Armor, Samuel, (ed.), *History of Orange County with Biographical Sketches*, Historical Record Company, Los Angeles, 1921, page 561.

Bricken, Gordon, *Pioneers in Blue and Gray, Civil War Veterans in Orange County*, Bricken Press, Santa Ana, 2009, page 97.

Brigandi, Phil, (ed.), *The Plaza: A Local Drama in 5 Acts*, Wrangler Press, Orange, 1982, page 9.

MILITARY RECORDS

OCCGS Civil War Veterans Project-James Wolf Northcross

Civil War Soldiers, 1861-1865: James W. Northcross

Confederate Soldiers Compiles Service Records, 1861-1865: James W. Northcross, Pvt. Duckworth's Cavalry

Civil War Prisoner of War Records, 1861-1865: Jas. W. Northcross

National Park Service Soldiers & Sailors Database: James W. Northcross, 7th Tennessee Cavalry

"7th Tennessee Cavalry (Duckworth's)"-Wikipedia

Tennesseans in the Civil War, Vol. I, (online version): 7th Tennessee Cavalry

Confederate Hospitals in Richmond, by Robert Waite, Jr., 1964, (online version)

Headstone Applications for Military Veterans, 1925-1970, William L. Northcross, 2nd Tennessee Infantry, Spanish-American War

GOVERNMENT RECORDS

1850 United States Federal Census: Hardeman, Tennessee

1860 United States Federal Census: District 7, Gibson, Tennessee; Trenton, Gibson, Tennessee; District 10, Hardeman, Tennessee

1870 United States Federal Census: Gibson, Tennessee

1880 United States Federal Census: Hickory Grove, Gibson, Tennessee; Trenton, Gibson, Tennessee

1900 United States Federal Census: Orange, Orange, California

Tennessee Marriage Records, 1780-2002: JW Northcross-Leanorah Irwin, 1865

US Freedmen's Bureau Records, 1865-1878: N.N. Northcross-Wiley Northcross, (sharecropping contract)

Tennessee Wills & Probate Records, 1779-2008: N.N. Northcross, February 1882

California County Birth, Marriage and Death Records, 1849-1980: Ruth Northcross-William Harper, 1903, Dorothy Northcross-Irvin H. Cammack, 1904

California Voter Registers, 1866-1898: James W. Northcross, 1888, Orange; James W. Northcross, 1892, Tustin; Jas. W. Northcross, 1896, Tustin; James W. Northcross, 1900, El Modena

DIRECTORIES

1889-1900 Orange County Directory, Belt Fine Publishers, Santa Ana, page 210.

NEWSPAPERS

"Notice to Creditors", *Los Angeles Daily Herald*, June 9, 1882, page 3.

"Sixteenth District", *Milan* (Tennessee) *Exchange*, June 10, 1882, page 1.

"Margery A. Northcross", *Los Angeles Daily Herald*, January 22, 1887, page 7.

"James W. Northcross to William Sharples", *Los Angeles Times*, August 30, 1888, page 7.

"List of Delinquent Taxes", *Orange Tribune*, December 15, 1888,

"Orange County Alliance", *Orange News*, January 7, 1890.

"Miss Sallie Northcross is quite ill", *Orange News*, December 31, 1890.

"JW Northcross (fumigation ad)", *Orange News*, March 18, 1891.

"St. James Vicinity", *Orange News*, August 26, 1891.

"Marriage Licenses", *Los Angeles Herald*, February 27, 1897, page 10.

"Mrs. G.W. Northcross", *Los Angeles Times*, May 26, 1897, page 11.

"Mr and Mrs. James Northcross", *Los Angeles Times*, March 24, 1902, page 10.

"J.W. Northcross, 64, died", *Los Angeles Times*, April 15, 1902, page 16.

"Died, Northcross, Margery", *Santa Ana Weekly Blade*, May 1902.

"Marriage Announcement", *Los Angeles Times*, June 5, 1904, page 15.

"Carl Northcross", *Santa Ana Register*, April 28, 1908, page 3.

"Boys Condition Considered More Hopeful", *Santa Ana Register*, April 30, 1908, page 3.

"Mrs. Northcross Honored", *Santa Ana Register*, July 12, 1940, page 18.

"Mrs. Lenora Northcross, Pioneer to Observe 100th Birthday", *Orange Daily News*, July 18, 1940, page 4.

"Orange Woman 100 Years Old Today", *Santa Ana Register*, July 19, 1940, page 8.

"Miss Kathrene Northcross", *Orange Daily News*, March 23, 1943, page 8.

"Fifth War in Lifespan Interests Lagunan, 103", *Los Angeles Times*, July 19, 1943, page 32.

"Death Beckons Lenora Northcross", *Orange Daily News*, November 11, 1944, page 1.

"Miss Kathrene Northcross Passes Away", *Orange Daily News*, March 19, 1946, page 8.

"W.L. Northcross Dies in Laguna", *Orange Daily News*, March 14, 1950, p. 7.

"Rites Held for W.L. Northcross", *Orange Daily News*, March 17, 1950, page 3.

"Miss Nelms Northcross", *Orange Daily News*, October 31, 1956, page 3.

"Nelms Northcross Services Conducted", *Los Angeles Times*, November 2, 1956, page 28.

The headstone photographs for James and Nora Northcross were taken at Santa Ana Cemetery by Timothy Zierer.

The photograph of Camp Chase Confederate Cemetery in Columbus, Ohio was taken in October 2021 by Timothy Zierer.

David N. Robinson

MILITARY RECORDS

Report of Adjutant General of State of Indiana,

Adjutant General's Office, 1865, page 126.

8th Indiana Infantry, 3-year enlistments

David N. Robinson

Soldier's & Sailors Data Base-National Park Service

Robinson, David N.

8th Indiana Infantry

Private, Company I

Film# M540 Roll 65

List of American Civil War Units by State-Wikipedia

U.S. Army Register of Enlistments, 1798-1914

David N. Robinson

Civil War Pension Index: General Index to Pension Files, 1861-1934

David N. Robinson, 8th Indiana Infantry, 11th, 24th US Infantry

GOVERNMENT RECORDS

1850 United States Federal Census: Liberty, Wabash, Indiana

1860 United States Federal Census: Liberty, Wabash, Indiana

1861 Census of Canada: Williamsburg, Dundas, Canada West

1900 United States Federal Census: Santa Ana, Orange, CA-Tustin Precinct

1910 United States Federal Census: Los Angeles Assembly Dist. 71, Los Angeles, CA

1920 United States Federal Census: Burbank, Los Angeles, CA

Michigan County Marriage Records, 1822-1940

David N. Robinson-Abigail C. Tyrrell, 25 Nov.1884

DIRECTORIES

Find A Grave Index, 1600-Current,

David N. Robinson, Abigail C. Robinson

1908-1909 Tustin City Directory

NEWSPAPERS

"Robinson-Crawford", *Santa Ana Register*, September 15, 1913, page 5.

"Robinson, Edwin S.", undated newspaper obituary.

Henry W. Smith

BOOKS

Armor, Samuel, (ed.), *History of Orange County with Biographical Sketches*, Historic Record Co., Los Angeles, 1911, pages 558-559.

Bricken, Gordon, *Pioneers in Blue and Gray, Civil War Veterans in Orange County*, Bricken Press, Santa Ana, 2009, page 80.

Lovret, Juanita, *Tustin as It Once Was*, History Press, Charleston, 2011, p. 26.

Rischard, Maureen McClintock, *The Centennial History of the Tustin Presbyterian Church*, Tustin Instant Press, Tustin, 1984.

MILITARY RECORDS

OCCGS Civil War Veterans Project: Henry William Smith

Civil War Soldier Records and Profiles, 1861-1865: Henry W. Smith

"List of American Civil War Units by State"-Wikipedia. 13th Michigan Infantry

Roster of 13th Michigan Infantry Regiment-Company A,
    michiganinthewar.org

GOVERNMENT RECORDS

1850 United States Federal Census: East Bloomfield, Ontario, New York

1860 United States Federal Census: Charleston, Kalamazoo, Michigan

1870 United States Federal Census: Free Soil, Mason, Michigan

1880 United States Federal Census: Free Soil, Mason, Michigan

1900 United States Federal Census: Blendon, Davison, South Dakota

1901 Census of Canada: Turtle Mountain, Lisger, Manitoba

1910 United States Federal Census: Santa Ana, Orange, California-Tustin
Precinct

1920 United States Federal Census: Tustin, Orange, California

Michigan County Marriage Records, 1822-1940: Henry W. Smith-Louis
Weatherby

Michigan Marriage Records, 1867-1952: Henry W. Smith-Emily R. Daken

DIRECTORIES

1908-1909 Santa Ana Directory, Register Publishing Co., Santa Ana, page 115.

1916 Santa Ana-Tustin-Garden Grove Directory, Santa Ana Directory Co., LH
Padgham, page 305.

US Find A Grave Index, 1600s-Current: Henry W. Smith, Emily Rebecca Smith

NEWSPAPERS

"Smith-Blackmore", *Santa Ana Register*, March 20, 1907, page 4.

"Marriage Licenses", *Santa Ana Register*, April 6, 1911, page 8.

"Deaths-Smith", *Santa Ana Register*, May 14, 1919, page 5.

"Attention W.R.C.", *Santa Ana Register*, May 14, 1919, page 5.

"Mrs. H.W. Smith Buried at Tustin", *Santa Ana Register*, May 16, 1919, page 5.

"Civil War Veteran Claims Bride Here", *Pomona Progress*, September 15,
1919, page 5.

"Personals", *Santa Ana Register*, January 24, 1921, page 5.

"G.A.R.", *Santa Ana Register*, December 16, 1922, page 5.

"Smith", *Santa Ana Register*, January 23, 1926, page 3.

"Mrs. Belle Smith", *Pomona Progress*, June 19, 1935, page 15.

"Tustin Man Dies of Heart Attack", *Santa Ana Register*, August 21, 1941, p. 4.

"Last Rites Held for C.E. Smith, County Pioneer", *Tustin News*, December 7, 1967, page 16.

"Lena Smith Dies", *Daily Republic*, (Mitchell, South Dakota), December 26, 1969, page 2.

Thomas H. Smith

BOOKS

Bricken, Gordon, *Pioneers in Blue and Gray, Civil War Veterans in Orange County,* Bricken Press, Santa Ana, 2009, page 81.

Guinn, J.M., *Historical & Biographical Record of Southern California*, Chapman Publishing Co., Chicago, 1902, pages 662-665.

White, William Lee, *Let Us Die Like Men: The Battle of Franklin, November 30, 1864*, Savas Beatie, El Dorado Hills, CA, 2019.

MAGAZINES

"Englishmen Who Fought in the American Civil War", by Daniel Clarke, *History Today*, Vol. 63, April 2013.

"Immigrants in the Union Army", by Ryan Keating, (online article).

MILITARY RECORDS

OCCGS Civil War Veterans Project-Thomas H. Smith

Civil War Soldier Records and Profiles, 1861-1865: Thomas H. Smith

"List of American Civil War Units by State"-Wikipedia: Battery G, 1st Ohio Light Artillery

Civil War Pension Index: General Index to Pension files, 1861-1934: Thomas H. Smith, California, November 4, 1891

Glossary of Civil War Artillery Terms online glossary

GOVERNMENT RECORDS

1851 England Census: Norton, Herdfordshire, England

1860 United States Federal Census: Cleveland Ward 2, Cuyahoga, Ohio

1870 United States Federal Census: Clay, Washington, Iowa

1880 United States Federal Census: Harlan, Shelby, Iowa

1880 United States Federal Census: Gold Hill, Storey, Nevada

1900 United States Federal Census: Santa Ana, Orange, California-Tustin Precinct

1910 United States Federal Census: Santa Ana, Orange, California-Tustin Precinct

1920 United States Federal Census: Tustin, Orange, California

Ohio, U.S., County Naturalization Records, 1800-1977: Thomas H. Smith, Cuyahoga, Ohio, 1865

California Death Index, 1905-1939: Sarah Smith

World War I Draft Registration Cards, 1917-1918: Harry Roy Smith

DIRECTORIES

1908-1909 Santa Ana City Directory, Register Publishing Co., Santa Ana, page 116.

1916 Santa Ana, Tustin, Garden Grove Directory, Santa Ana Directory Co., L.H. Padgham, page 305.

US Find A Grave Index, 1660s-Current: Thomas H. Smith, Sarah Smith, H. Roy Smith, Flora J. Smith

NEWSPAPERS

"Marriage Announcement", *Los Angeles Times*, May 12, 1896, page 13.

"Here Are Officers", *Santa Ana Register*, May 30, 1922, page 7.

"Smith, Sarah", *Santa Ana Register*, December 26, 1922, page 3.

"Tustin Pioneer Passes After Brief Illness", *Santa Ana Register*, May 17, 1926, page 5.

"Pioneer Rancher Dies in Tustin", *Los Angeles Times*, May 18, 1926, page 12.

"H. Roy Smith Dies Suddenly at His Home", *Santa Ana Register*, October 20, 1932, page 2.

The photographs of the Soldiers & Sailors Monument in Cleveland were taken by Timothy Zierer.

Horace Snow

BOOKS

Glatthaar, Joseph, H., *Forged in Battle: The Civil War Alliance of Black Soldiers and White Officers*, The Free Press, New York, 1990.

Huntley, Helen Gulick & William, (ed. Edna Phelps), *Tustin Scrapbook*, Tustin Area Historical Society, 1969, page 84.

Jordan, Carol, H., *Tustin: An Illustrated History*, Tustin Area Historical Society, Tustin, 2007.

Meyer, Howard, N., *Colonel of the Black Regiment: The Life of Thomas Wentworth Higginson*, W.W Norton & Co., New York, 1967.

Neavin, Muriel, (ed.), *"Dear Charlie" Letters, Recording the everyday life of a young 1854 gold miner as set forth by Your Friend, Horace Snow*, Mariposa County Historical Society, 1979.

MILITARY RECORDS

OCCGS Civil War Veterans Project-Horace C. Snow

Civil War Soldier Records and Profiles, 1861-1865: Horace C. Snow

Civil War Soldiers, 1861-1865: Horace C. Snow

National Parks Service Soldiers & Sailors Data Base, 13th US Infantry regiment, 45th Colored Infantry regiment

"13th US Infantry Regiment"-Wikipedia

American Civil War Regiments, 1861-1865, 45th US Colored Troops

Returns for Military Posts, 1806-1916: Horace C. Snow, Camp William Penn, Sep. 1864

Muster Rolls, Company D, 45th US Colored Troops: 1st. Lt. Horace C. Snow

GOVERNMENT RECORDS

1856 Iowa State Census: Osage, Mitchell, Iowa

1860 United States Federal Census: Osage, Mitchell, Iowa

1870 United States Federal Census: Fairfield, Solano, California

1880 United States Federal Census: Eureka, Humboldt, California

Pennsylvania-New Jersey Church Records, 1669-2013: Horace C. Snow-Margaret F. Butcher

California County Birth, Marriage & Death Records: 1849-1980: Margaret Snow-Benjamin Frees, Martha C. Snow-S. Stevens, Blance A. Bullock-William B. Snow

California Voter Registers, 1866-1898: Horace C. Snow, Tustin, 1892

California Death Index, 1905-1939: Clarence H. Stevens

DIRECTORIES

Los Angeles City and County Directory, 1886-87, A.A. Byron & Co., Los Angeles, page 163.

US Find A Grave Index, 1600s-present: Horace C. Snow, Margaret Fox Snow, Carrie Bessie Snow, Horace J. Snow, William Butcher Snow, Blanch Amanda Snow, Margaret Grace Frees, Benjamin Franklin Frees, Martha C. Stevens, Sherman Stevens

NEWSPAPERS

"Obituary-Jonathan Frees", *Humboldt Times*, October 15, 1875,

"Last Tribute", *Humboldt Times*, October 17, 1875.

"Marriage Licenses", *Los Angeles Herald*, July 16, 1887, page 3.

"A Sudden Death", *Santa Ana Weekly Blade*, December 1, 1888, page 3.

"Military Funeral at Tustin", *Los Angeles Evening Express*, February 18, 1893, page 6.

"Tustin", *Los Angeles Times*, February 18, 1893, page 7.

"The Angel of Death", *Los Angeles Times*, August 26, 1895, page 9.

"News from Santa Ana", *Los Angeles Herald*, August 26, 1895, page 2.

"Angel of Death", *Los Angeles Times*, November 8, 1896, page 27.

"H.C. Snow", *Los Angeles Herald*, November 8, 1896, page 5.

"Horace C. Snow of Tustin", *Los Angeles Evening Express*, November 9, 1896, page 9.

"Honoring America's Black Freedom Fighters", *Los Angeles Times*, October 27, 2021, page A11.

The photographs of Horace Snow and the Snow brothers used with permission of the Tustin Area Historical Society.

Abraham H. Stutsman

BOOKS

Bricken, Gordon, *Pioneers in Blue and Gray, Civil War Veterans in Orange*, Bricken Press, Santa Ana, 2009, page 82.

Huntley, Helen Gulick & William, (ed. Edna Phelps), *Tustin Scrapbook*, Tustin Area Historical Society, 1969, page 86-87.

Sleeper, Jim, *Turn the Rascals Out! The Life and Times of Orange County's Fighting Editor Dan M. Baker*, California Classics, Trabuco Canyon, 1973, page 372.

Watkins, Hamilton, *Burlington Iowa: A Souvenir*, The Journal Company, 1896.

MILITARY RECORDS

Civil War Soldier Records and Profiles, 1861-1865 Abraham H. Stutsman

Rosters and Records of Iowa Soldiers, War of the Rebellion, Vol. 4, Company
    C, 1st Iowa Cavalry

"List of American Civil War Units by State"-Wikipedia: 1st Iowa Cavalry

GOVERNMENT RECORDS

1840 United States Federal Census: Morgan, Indiana

1856 Iowa State Census: Franklin, Lee, Iowa

1860 United States Federal Census: Yellow Creek, Chariton, Missouri

1870 United States Federal Census: Chariton, Lucas, Iowa

1880 United States Federal Census: Burlington, Des Moines, Iowa

1900 United States Federal Census: Santa Ana, Orange, California-Tustin
    Precinct

1910 United States Federal Census: Santa Ana, Orange, California-Tustin
    Precinct

1920 United States Federal Census: Tustin, Orange, California

1930 United States Federal Census: Tustin, Orange, California

Iowa Marriage Records, 1880-1851: Abraham H. Stutsman-Frances Allen

NEWSPAPERS

"Mrs. A.H. Stutsman…", *Los Angeles Times*, June 28, 1892, page 7.

"Mrs. A.H. Stutsman…", *Los Angeles Times*, July 26, 1892, page 7.

 "Judge A.H. Stutsman…", *Los Angeles Evening Express*, October 12, 1892,
    page 6.

"Mrs. Judge Stutsman…", *Los Angeles Times*, April 23, 1894, page 7.

"Burlington Excursions", *Los Angeles Herald*, June 26, 1896, page 3.

"Engagement Announcement", *Santa Ana Register*, March 23, 1908, page 1.

"In Memoriam-Mrs. Walter A. Stutsman", *Santa Ana Register*, November 28,
    1908, page 6.

"That Iowa Picnic", *Santa Ana Register*, August 21, 1913, page 5.

"Tustin Literature Section", *Santa Ana Register*, October 9, 1914, page 13.

"A.H. Stutsman, Jr. Dead at Age of 35", *Santa Ana Register*, September 28, 1920, page 3.

"Three Generations of Jurists in Flight", *Los Angeles Times*, May 12, 1928, page 29.

"Stutsman, Miss Carrie", *Los Angeles Times*, July 14, 1928, page 16.

"Corn State Takes Over Bixby Park", *Long Beach Sun*, August 9, 1931, page 1.

"Funeral of Tustin Pioneer Tomorrow", *Santa Ana Register*, August 10, 1931, page 3.

"Judge Stutsman and Miss Stephenson Wed", *Los Angeles Evening Express*, August 26, 1931, page 18.

"Death Claims A.H. Stutsman, Civil War Vet", *Santa Ana Register*, March 17, 1934, page 3.

"Judge Stutsman's Father Passes Away at Ranch Home", *San Pedro-News Pilot*, March 17, 1934, page 1.

"Walter Stutsman Called By Death", *Santa Ana Register*, June 16, 1936, page 6.

"Judge Stutsman Dies in Hospital", *Los Angeles Daily News*, July 15, 1950, page 28.

"Judge Stutsman Services Pending", *Hollywood Citizen-News*, July 15, 1950, page 3.

Henry Vanhise

MILITARY RECORDS

OCCGS Civil War Veterans Project-Henry Vanhise

Civil War Soldiers, 1861-1865: Henry L. Vanhise

Soldiers & Sailors Data Base-National Parks Service: Vanhise, Henry, L., 2nd New Jersey Cavalry

"List of American Civil War Units by State"-Wikipedia

Kansas Enrollments of Civil War Veterans, 1889, Henry L. Vanhise, Towanda

GOVERNMENT RECORDS

1850 United States Federal Census: West Windsor, Mercer, New Jersey

1860 United States Federal Census: Jackson, Ocean, New Jersey

1870 United States Federal Census: Denver, Richland, Illinois

1875 Kansas State Census: Doyle, Marion, Kansas

1880 United States Federal Census: Towanda, Butler, Kansas

1885 Kansas State Census: Lincoln, Butler, Kansas

1900 United States Federal Census: Santa Ana, Orange, California-Tustin Precinct

1910 United States Federal Census: Santa Ana, Orange, California-Tustin Precinct

1920 United States Federal Census: Tustin, Orange, California

Appointments of U.S. Postmasters, 1832-1971: Dixon, Butler, Kansas-October 10, 1884

California Voter Registers, 1866-1898: Henry L. Vanhise, Tustin 1896

California Birth, Marriage, Death Records, 1849-1980: Gladys Vanhise-Lee B. Ward

California Death Index, 1940-1997: Elsie Rose Field, Gladys Ward, Lee B. Ward

World War I Draft Registration Card: Lee B. Ward

DIRECTORIES

US Find A Grave,1600's-Current: Henry Vanhise, Sarah Vanhise

1899-1900 Orange County Directory, Belt Fine Publishers, Santa Ana, page 197.

1908-1909 Santa Ana City Directory, Register Publishing Co. Santa Ana, page 116.

"Were Married Beneath the Wedding Bell', *Santa Ana Register*, January 12, 1907, page 8.

"Two Civil War Veterans Are Summoned", *Santa Ana Register*, August 2, 1924, page 10.

"Vanhise", *Santa Ana Register*, June 28, 1927, page 3.

"Marriage Licenses Issued", *Santa Ana Register*, December 29, 1929, page 3.

"Newlyweds Will Live in Orange", *Santa Ana Register*, December 20, 1939, page 16.

"Guy Field, County Rancher Passes", *Santa Ana Register*, November 3, 1941, page 9.

"Services Held for Lee B. Ward", *Tustin News*, February 9, 1956, page 6.

William B. Wall

BOOKS

Armor, Samuel, (ed.), *History of Orange County with Biographical Sketches*, Historic Record Company, Los Angeles, 1911, pages 184 186.

Boardman, Patricia, *A Walk to Remember: Mini-biographies of pioneers buried in Santa Ana Cemetery*, 2009, pages 27-28.

Bricken, Gordon, *Pioneers in Blue and Gray, Civil War Veterans in Orange County*, Bricken Press, Santa Ana, 2009, page 100.

Dawson, Elmer, Ray, *A History of Tustin*, Masters Degree Thesis, University of Southern California, 1938.

Huntley, Helen Gulick & William, (ed. Edna Phelps), *Tustin Scrapbook*, Tustin Area Historical Society, 1969, page 90.

Seacrist, William, B., *California Feuds, Vengeance, Vendettas & Violence on the Old West Coast*, Word Dancer Press, Sanger, CA, 2005, pages 15-20.

Uncredited, A History of Santa City and Valley, It's Past, Flourishing Present and *Bright Future*, The Paragon Press, Orange, 1999, (re-print of 1887 edition), pages 11-13.

MAGAZINES

"The Truth About Civil War Surgery", by Alfred J. Bollet, *Civil War Times*, October, 2004.

"Letters From Atlanta Trenches", Matthew A. Dunn, 33rd Mississippi, *Journal of Mississippi History*, Vol. I, pages 110-127.

"The Rooster Brand", by Ed Salter, *Orange Countiana: A Journal of Local History, Vol. II, 1980*, page 20.

MILITARY RECORDS

OCCGS Civil War Veterans Project-Dr. William B. Wall

Confederate Soldiers Compiled Service Records, 1861-1865: William B. Wall

33rd Mississippi Infantry Regiment-Family Search

GOVERNMENT RECORDS

1820 United States Federal Census: Mary, Halifax, Virginia

1830 United States Federal Census: Halifax, Virginia

1840 United States Federal Census: South District, Halifax, Virginia

1850 United States Federal Census: District 13, Panola, Mississippi

1860 United States Federal Census: Panola, Mississippi

1870 United States Federal Census: District 4, Panola, Mississippi

1880 United States Federal Census: Santa Ana, Los Angeles, California

1900 United States Federal Census: Santa Ana, Orange, California-Tustin Precinct

California Death Index, 1905-1939: WB Wall

California Death Index, 1940-1987: James Elton Lang

California Birth, Marriage and Death Records, 1849-1980: Minnie R. Norman-Hiram K. Snow

DIRECTORIES

Directory of Deceased American Physicians, 1804-1929: William Burgess Wall

US Find A Grave Index, 1600s-Current: William Burgess Wall, Julia F. Wall, Mary Perkins Wall, William Dillard Wall, Pearl Lang, Palmetto E. Norman

Los Angeles City and County Directory, 1886-87, A.A. Byron & Co. Publishers, LA, page 134.

1908-1909 Santa Ana City Directory, Register Publishing, Santa Ana, pages H, 82, 118.

NEWSPAPERS

"Dr. W.B. Wall", *Californian*, (Salinas, California), February 1, 1890, page 3.

"Died-Miss Metto Wall", *Los Angeles Herald*, January 2, 1894, page 3.

"News from Tustin and Vicinity", *Santa Ana Register*, August 10, 1907, page 2.

"Party Goes to Soda Lake", *Santa Ana Register*, May 18, 1908, page 14.

"Saw Many Tons Lying in Sulfate Vats", *Santa Ana Register*, May 21, 1908, page 6.

"Dr. Wall is Seriously Ill", *Santa Ana Register*, April 20, 1909, page 8.

"Dr. WB Wall Died at 2:13", *Santa Ana Register*, April 21, 1909, page 8.

"Funeral Services for Dr. W.B. Wall", *Santa Ana Register*, April 24, 1909, p. 5.

"Dr. Walls Will Up for Probate", *Santa Ana Register*, May 14, 1909, page 8.

"Notice to Creditors", *Santa Ana Register*, June 5, 1909, page 3.

"Partial Distribution", *Santa Ana Register*, November 2, 1909, page 5.

"Brilliant Wedding Scene", *Santa Ana Register*, June 29, 1911, page 5.

"Mrs. H.K. Snow, Jr. Died in Los Angeles", *Santa Ana Register*, April 27, 1914, page 5.

"Snow", *Santa Ana Register*, April 17, 1914, page 5.

"In the Long Ago", *Santa Ana Register*, March 20, 1923, page 16.

"Hiram K. Snow, 63, Passes in L.A. Hospital", *Santa Ana Register*, February 14, 1929, page 9.

"Mary P. Wall, 82, Passes in Home, *Santa Ana Register*, October 3, 1942, p. 3.

"Fairhaven Burial for Ex-Citrus Man", *Tustin News*, September 5, 1963, page 6.

The photograph of the Wall packinghouse and the Wall home used with permission of the Tustin Area Historical Society.

The close-up photo of Dr. Wall is from the collection in the Orange County Archives.

Joseph A. Wilkes

BOOKS

Hurley, Richard, *California and the Civil War*, The History Press, Charleston, S.C., 2017.

Lessenger, James, E., *The Execution of Kleinkopf, The True Story of the Execution by Firing Squad of a Desperado and Deserter,* The Benicia Historical Museum, Benicia, 2009.

Osterman, Joe, *50 Years in Old El Toro: A Family, A Time, A Place,* Sultana Press, Fullerton, 1982

Sleeper, Jim, *A Boys Book of Bear Stories (not for Boys), A Grizzly Introduction to the Santa Ana Mountains,* California Classics, Trabuco Canyon, 1976.

MISCELLANEOUS

San Ramon Valley Genealogical Society Newsletter, Vol. XXVIII, No.2, July 2011 "Joseph Adcock Wilkes, Danville's Own Civil War Soldier" by Dan Stephenson

The Museum of the San Ramon Valley-Wilkes Family Collection

Memorial and Biographical History of the Counties of Fresno, Tulare and Kern, 1892.

Journal of the West, Vol. IV, No. 1-4, Library Edition, 1965. *"California, the Civil War and the Indian Problem",* by Leo P. Kirby

MILITARY RECORDS

Civil War Soldiers, 1861-1865 Joseph A. Wilkes, Co. K, 6th CA Infantry

Civil War Soldier Records and Profiles, 1861-1865, Joseph A. Wilkes

6th California Infantry Regiment-Wikipedia

GOVERNMENT RECORDS

1850 United States Federal Census: Placerville, El Dorado, CA

    United States Federal Census: District 13, Miller, Missouri

1860 United States Federal Census: Township 2, Contra Costa, CA

1870 United States Federal Census: Township 2, Contra Costa, CA

1900 United States Federal Census: Santa Ana, Orange, CA-Tustin Precinct

1910 United States Federal Census: Santa Ana Ward 2, Orange, CA

1920 United States Federal Census: Santa Ana Ward 2, Orange, CA

1930 United States Federal Census: Tustin, Orange, CA

California Voter Register for Joseph A. Wilkes

    1871 Kern County

    1878 Kern County

    1884 San Juan, Los Angeles County

    1888 Santa Ana, Los Angeles County

    1892 Santa Ana, Orange County

    1896 Santa Ana, Orange County-Tustin Precinct

    1901 Santa Ana, Orange County-Tustin Precinct

DIRECTORIES

US Find A Grave Index, 1600s-current

    Caroline T. Wilkes, Albert Gallatin Wilkes, Joseph Adcock Wilkes

City Directories:

    1895-1896 Wilkes, J.A., (Mrs. L.E). Tustin

    1903 Wilkes, J.A. (Mrs. J.A.), Dairyman, Newport Rd., Tustin

    1908 Wilkes, Joseph A., (Mrs. Laura E), Walnut grower, Grand Ave, Santa Ana

NEWSPAPERS

"Joseph A. Wilkes to Laura E. Wilkes…", *The Los Angeles Times*, Dec. 18, 1884, page 3.

"William A. Firebaugh to J A Wilkes...", *Los Angeles Herald*, January 19, 1887, page 7.

"Laura Wilkes and J A Wilkes…", *The Los Angeles Times*, July 26, 1888, page 7.

"J.A. Wilkes and Bill English returned...", *Los Angeles Evening Express*, Sep. 24, 1890, page 3.

"Santa Ana Collision", *Los Angeles Evening Express*, January 28, 1892, page 1.

"Figuring on Political Plums", *Los Angeles Herald*, November 17, 1892, page 6.

"Born to the wife of J.A. Wilkes", *The Los Angeles Times*, Dec. 1, 1894, p. 11.

"Peabody-Wilkes", *The Los Angeles Times*, December 27, 1904, page 18.

"Turkeys That Weigh and Bring a Big Price", *Santa Ana Register*, Nov. 24, 1906, page 3.

"For Sale-Span Mares", *Santa Ana Register*, April 15, 1907, page 3.

"North Side Club", *Santa Ana Register*, December 8, 1909, page 5.

"Orange Store Burglar…", *Santa Ana Register*, December 27, 1910, page 1.

"Interesting Wedding", *Santa Ana Register*, July 18, 1912, page 5.

"Roster of Sedgwick Post…", *Santa Ana Register*, May 31, 1916, page 9.

"Deaths-Grundt", *Santa Ana Register*, June 6, 1918, page 5.

"Married in Los Angeles", *Santa Ana Register*, June 24, 1918, page 5.

"Chief Boatswain's Mate L.B. Wilkes", *Santa Ana Register*, Nov. 7, 1918, p. 3.

"Joseph Wilkes Tells How He Used To...", *Santa Ana Register*, Aug. 23, 1919, page 9.

"Twenty-Five Acres Set To Walnuts...", *Santa Ana Register*, January 22, 1920, page 9.

"Married in Los Angeles", *Santa Ana Register*, April 17, 1920, page 5.

"Veteran S.A. Hunter...", *Santa Ana Register*, August 10, 1920, page 7.

"Mr. and Mrs. Joseph Wilkes....", *Santa Ana Register*, December 21, 1920, page 5.

"S.A. Man at Funeral....", *Santa Ana Register*, March 12, 1921, page 2.

"W.P. Wilkes, Pioneer is Called", *Santa Ana Register*, March 3, 1922, page 13.

"Santa Ana Man Passes Away in Chinese Port", *Santa Ana Register*, Aug. 31, 1922, page 4.

"Navy Man Dies Near Chef...", *Oakland Tribune*, October 7, 1922.

"Beckett, Mrs. C.E.", *Santa Ana Register*, October 18, 1926, page 3.

"Goes To Visit Home He Left In 1856", *Santa Ana Register*, June 16, 1927, page 7.

"Wilkes-Marleau Nuptials", *Eagle Rock Sentinel* (Los Angeles), Nov. 29, 1929, page 1.

"Golden Wedding Anniversary...", *Santa Ana Register*, February 4, 1931, p. 13.

"Yachtsman Loses Life", *The Los Angeles Times*, July 28, 1935, page 1.

"Wilkes Rites To Be Held Today", *Santa Ana Register*, July 29, 1935, page 2.

"Veteran Improved", *Santa Ana Daily Evening Register*, January 7, 1937, p. 10.

"Ninety-First Birthday", *Santa Ana Register*, August 14, 1937, page 18.

"Invalid Improving", *Santa Ana Register*, December 4, 1937, page 10

"S.A. Pioneer is Called By Death", *Santa Ana Register*, December 4, 1937, p. 1.

"Laura Ellen Wilkes", *The Los Angeles Times*, July 9, 1942, page 16.

"Arrange Funeral of S.A. Pioneer", *Santa Ana Register*, July 9, 1942.

"Distribution of Estate Ordered", *Santa Ana Register*, April 9, 1946, page 7.

"A California Pioneer", *Placerville Mountain Democrat*, Nov. 30, 1979.

"Days Gone By…", *East Bay Times*, April 7, 2010.

All photographs of James and Ellen Wilkes used with the permission of the Museum of the San Ramon Valley.

The GAR

BOOKS

Bricken, Gordon, *The Civil War Legacy in Santa Ana,* Santa Ana Historical Preservation Society, Santa Ana, 2002.

Bricken, Gordon, *Pioneers in Blue and Gray, Civil War Veterans in Orange County,* Bricken Press, Santa Ana, 2009.

WEBSITES

GAR Records project: **www.suvc.org/garrecords**

"Grand Army of the Republic" - Wikipedia

DIRECTORIES

Los Angeles City and County Directory, 1886-87, A.A. Byron & Co., page 117.

1908-1909 Santa Ana City Directory, Register Publishing Co., Santa Ana, p. 12.

NEWSPAPERS

"Local Post to Be in Line", *Santa Ana Register*, September 7, 1912, page 8.

"Thousands G.A.R. Veterans in Los Angeles", *Pomona Daily Review*, September 9, 1912, page 1.

"The Program for Today in Los Angeles", *Venice Daily Democrat*, September 9, 1912, page 8.

"Personals", *Santa Ana Register*, September 10, 1912, page 5.

"Santa Ana G.A.R. in Parade", *Santa Ana Register*, September 12, 1912, page 5.

"Here's List of Sedgwick Post Membership", *Santa Ana Register*, May 20, 1922, page 7.

"G.A.R.", *Santa Ana Register*, December 16, 1922, page 5.

"17 Members of Sedgwick G.A.R. Post Summoned Since Last Memorial Day", *Santa Ana Register*, May 27, 1925, page 7.

The Tustin Boys Brigade

BOOKS

Rischard, Maureen McClintock, *The Centennial History of the Tustin Presbyterian Church*, Tustin Instant Press, Tustin, 1984.

WEBSITES

"The Boys Brigade"-Wikipedia

Our History-The Boys Brigade: **boys-brigade.org.uk-history**

NEWPAPERS

"The Tustin Boys Brigade", *Los Angeles Times*, January 10, 1892, page 7.

"Tustin", *Los Angeles Times*, February 14, 1892, page 7.

"The First Tustin Company of the Boys Brigade", *Los Angeles Times*, June 28, 1892, page 7.

"The Tustin Boys Brigade", *Los Angeles Times*, August 1, 1892, page 7.

"Tustin", *Los Angeles Times*, January 7, 1893, page 7.

"Orange is organizing a Boys Brigade", *Los Angeles Herald*, January 26, 1893, page 6.

"Military Funeral in Tustin", *Los Angeles Evening Express*, February 18, 1893, page 6.

"The Boys Brigade Camp", *Los Angeles Herald*, June 25, 1893, page 16.

The photograph of the Tustin Boys Brigade on Santa Catalina Island used with permission of the Tustin Area Museum.